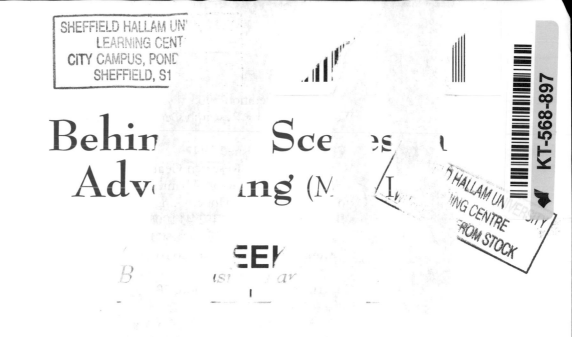

Behind the Scenes in Advertising (Mark III)

Jeremy Bullmore

Revised third edition

WARC

**World Advertising
Research Center**

Third edition 2003
World Advertising Research Center

First published 1991
World Advertising Research Center
Farm Road, Henley-on-Thames
Oxfordshire RG9 1EJ, United Kingdom
Telephone: +44 (0) 1491 411000
Facsimile: +44 (0) 1491 418600
E-mail: enquiries@warc.com

A CIP catalogue record for this book is
available from the British Library

ISBN 1 84116 132 2

Typeset in 11/14pt Plantin Light by Marie Doherty
Printed and bound in Great Britain by
Cromwell Press, Trowbridge

Cover by The Partners Design Consultants Ltd, Albion Courtyard,
Greenhill Rents, London EC1M 6PQ

Contents

Chapters marked with an asterisk are new for this edition.

Preface to the third edition

The first edition of this book, published in 1991, contained bits and pieces I'd written between 1970 and 1988. The second edition, published in 1998, dropped six pieces and added 25 new ones. This third edition has dropped seven and added another 41 (marked with a * on the contents page).

It seems that I've written about three times as much in the fifteen years since I stopped working in an advertising agency as I did during the thirty-something years when I was. There are two possible explanations for this. Either I've simply had more time (which is certainly true), or I've discovered that confident theorising becomes a great deal easier when you no longer have to translate that theory into daily practice.

I owe thanks to many people and I list them below, carefully alphabetised. For his contribution to this edition, however, I must single out David Tiltman of WARC: editor, structuralist, sense-maker and patient nag. He has been faultlessly helpful.

Without each of the others, it is a fact known only to me that this book would have been less good. In a hundred ways they have encouraged, commissioned, contributed and enabled. I am hugely grateful to you all: Conor Dignam, Judie Lannon, Simon Marquis, Feona McEwan, John Noble, Craig Smith, Martin Sorrell and David Stuart.

My debt to those acknowledged in the introduction to the first edition (page vii) remains as great as ever.

Introduction to the first edition: Nobody taught me nothing

I joined the London office of J. Walter Thompson Company Limited in October 1954 and retired from it at the end of December 1987. It was both the first proper job I ever had and the last proper job I ever had.

On my first morning as a trainee copywriter I was given something called a requisition by someone called a controller. The requisition turned out to be a written request for some words for an advertisement for Pan-American World Airways, and the controller was the traffic man who tried to make sure things happened on time. The requisition stipulated that the space to be filled was a six-inch double and the copy was required for that day. I didn't know what a six-inch double was, I knew nothing at all about Pan-American World Airways, and my boss was away ill.

Learning on the job is what you do in advertising agencies. It is true that some good agencies, and J. Walter Thompson was and is one of them, take training extremely seriously. Courses and seminars are run and people are taught how to work in teams, how to approach problems, how to make media decisions, how to plan strategies. But learning on the job is still what matters most.

You learn from everyone. You learn from your boss, from your friends, from your enemies, from people in other departments, from your clients and from your competitors. You work a lot of it out for yourself – in fact this book might have been called *Picking It Up As You Go Along*. Long before you think you're ready, you will find yourself responsible for other people. I think I learnt more from subordinates than I ever did from superiors: you have to think harder when talking to them; you have to find words and principles to explain your instinctive reactions to their ideas.

Rather rumly, there aren't many helpful books to read. Of the few that there are, most make sense only after you've been doing the job for a year or two. The best that I know are by Claude Hopkins, David Ogilvy, Rosser Reeves and James Webb Young. Even more surprisingly, there are virtually no worthwhile videotapes.

It is perfectly possible for you to have a brilliant advertising idea on your first morning before lunch. (I didn't.) What is not possible at all is for you to know why it's a good idea. That's the skill that takes time to develop – and that's the bit that makes it difficult, and why it all continues to be both baffling and rewarding. Advertising people who fail to develop a curiosity about advertising – why it exists, how it works, what it does – invariably get bored and stale and, sooner or later, fired. It is often said of them that they've burnt themselves out, but the truth is that they never looked beneath the surface; and the surface of advertising can get very boring quite quickly.

All the pieces in this book were written for specific reasons over the last twenty years or so. Some were articles for the trade press; some for internal use; some were speeches or presentations. They all, in different ways, poke about a bit beneath the surface.

So you won't find anything much about *advertisements*, for example: how to write them, how to use music, how big the picture ought to be or whether cartoons are a Good Idea. And you won't find anything at all about the money side of advertising: how much you need to spend and where to spend it.

What I hope you will find are insights; some helpful thoughts and speculations about the nature of *advertising*: what it is, what it does, how it works, how it impinges on real life and how to make it happen. As dividers between these sections, I've included some other insights of a rather different kind, principally there to convey the flavour of working in an advertising agency, because it can be, and often is, a heady combination of pressure and bathos, achievement and absurdity. In 33 years, I never found it boring.

About the only disadvantage of staying with one agency all your working life is that you never work with your competitors. I am never certain if I like so many of them so much because they are intrinsically so likeable, or because I've never had to work with them.

One great and recent treat, through membership of the WPP Group board, has been the chance to get to know David Ogilvy. It has not been a disappointment. Not only has he written a most generous Foreword (on the inside cover of the third edition), but he has also provided a title for this book. ('It suggests skulduggery and sex,' he wrote. If so, there will be disappointment.)

While it is true that nobody taught me nothing, some people taught me a lot more than others. Alphabetically these are Bernard Gutteridge, Stephen King, Denis Lanigan, Tom Sutton, Chris Thomas and John Treasure, all at J. Walter Thompson.

It was Ann Page, as my secretary, who started to keep the things I wrote. Without her thoughtfully invisible discipline, there would have been no book.

The thought of the book itself, together with many helpful suggestions, came from Harry Clark, and the time he has generously spent collecting material is greatly appreciated.

I am also much indebted to Terry Hamaton, who designed and drew the delightful illustrations for 'The consumer has a mind as well as a stomach' (page 139).

My principal debt of gratitude must be to the corporate J. Walter Thompson: a remarkable advertising agency around the world. It gave me interest and income for 33 years; and even, as I left, the means by which the words of this introduction have been processed.

My tragic past

Written in 1977 as one of a series for Campaign *on 'How I Got Into Advertising'. It covers some of the same ground as 'The case of the missing policeman' (page 258) but is a good deal more reliable factually. Edited slightly to avoid repetition.*

My father, who was a copywriter at Greenly's, started his own breakaway agency in the mid-1920s. It was called Bullmores Ltd. and was a founder member of the reconstituted Institute of Practitioners in Advertising in 1927. Soon afterwards his business went into liquidation. Disillusioned, he joined MI6 for whom he worked, off and on, until his death in mysterious circumstances in Calcutta in 1947.

My family was deeply scarred by this experience, and, although I was not born until 1929, I was brought up to believe that it was the advertising business that had brought ruin upon my father. As I grew older, I grew ever more determined to succeed where he had failed; to vindicate his reputation; to conquer the trade that had conquered him. And so it was, on leaving university in the early 1950s, that my only thought was to join an advertising agency and work my way up.

At this point I think I should reveal that, while the first paragraph above is factually true, the second paragraph (with the exception of my date of birth) is not.

I was dimly aware that my father had been in something called advertising, but since I never met him from the time I was five, and since my mother never spoke about him at all, advertising as a career seemed no more attractive to me, on the infrequent occasions when I thought about a career, than, say, agricultural engineering.

The only thing I was any good at at school was writing. I still experience a shiver of shame and triumph when I remember that I achieved a Distinction in the Higher School Certificate (A-levels to non-wrinklies) on the strength of a paper I wrote about six set books, none of which I'd read.

Because I was good at writing, I chose to read English when I arrived at Oxford. No one had told me that the English curriculum at Oxford was one-third Latin, one-third Anglo-Saxon and one-third the inhuman dissection of English literature.

My tutor was J.I.M. Stewart, who still writes detective stories under the name of Michael Innes. On the top of my third essay he neatly pencilled the following encouraging comment: 'You can write; but remember, this can be something of a disadvantage in the study of the English language.'

So I stopped reading English at Oxford, although I didn't think to mention it to anyone, and I wrote a piece of verse for Isis. *This featured three men then writing film reviews for the magazine. They were called Colin Curley, Derek Knight and Terence Twigg, and I was young enough to find their names funny. It wasn't very good, but everything that has happened to me since can be traced directly back to that one piece of verse.*

I was asked to write more, and did. I was asked to write the annual revue for the Experimental Theatre Club, and did. I spent most of one vacation writing it instead of revising Books IV and VI of the Aeneid *(if that's how it's spelt). The revue was staged in the summer term in a marquee pitched in the grounds of Merton College. I can't remember why.*

The revue was a success but my third attempt at passing my Latin Preliminary Examination was not.

I telephoned Jim Stewart. 'I wonder,' I said, 'if you could tell me what my position is.'

'Well, Jeremy,' he said, then paused for several seconds, 'I don't think you've got one.'

So I went home to Norfolk, bred some ducks and studied Punch *so that I could learn how to write the kind of humorous piece it might accept. I had just about mastered its preferred style when Malcolm Muggeridge took over as editor and the style changed. At about the same time, meat came off ration and nobody wanted to buy ducks. In the course of a few weeks, I'd learned two important lessons about marketing and communications.*

But I did go on writing songs and sketches for the ETC, then under the leadership of Ned Sherrin, and would return furtively to Oxford to see them performed. In 1953, Ned took a company to Edinburgh, and this led to a shortened revue appearing on BBC television.

Not many people can have seen this but George Butler did. George was then head of the art department at J. Walter Thompson and knew that something called commercial television was due to start in 1955. He wrote a letter to the BBC who passed it on to us. We'd never heard of J. Walter

Thompson but Ned and I both needed jobs. I put on my blue suit and went off to be interviewed.

It very quickly became clear that George Butler had forgotten that he had ever written the letter. He pointed out that he ran the art department and that I couldn't draw. In 1954, art directors were required to draw.

As I stood up to go, relieved that this bizarre encounter was to be mercifully short-lived, George remembered that there was also something called the editorial department. That's what the copy department was called in 1954.

'Perhaps you should take the copy test,' he said, with more charity than conviction.

So I did. I was interviewed by Norman Bassett, head of the copy department, who told me about the Great Margarine War; and by a psychologist, who asked me what I thought about a series of obscene ink-blots.

Months passed. By this time, another version of the revue, unhappily titled Oxford Accents, *was appearing at a very small underground theatre called the Watergate, off the Strand. That was all Watergate meant in 1954.*

Kenneth Tynan panned it. I was paid £12 for the six-week run, and I still needed a job. Eventually I was summoned from a gliding course in Dunstable and offered £10 a week to start as a trainee copywriter. It was pointed out that the offer would have been more generous had I been a graduate.

Gratefully I accepted, amazed that anyone should pay me to do anything. When I discovered that what I was required to do was totally absorbing and infinite in its variety, my amazement increased. It's still with me.

Part One
What advertising is

Advertising: what is it?

Most discussion about advertising's social and economic effect is conducted as though all advertising is designed, almost conspiratorially, to have a uni-directional influence. I first tried to point out the distinction between *advertising* and *advertisements* in a J. Walter Thompson London publication in 1975. I tried again when asked to write this introduction to the *Advertising Association Handbook* in 1983. (I am credited with having helped edit it; in fact, Mike Waterson did it all.) Whenever an occasion arose – and often when it didn't – I went on trying to make the distinction but have yet, to my knowledge, to convince anyone of its validity. Either I'm wrong or the continued confusion suits lazy-minded pundits. The piece contains a definition of advertising which has found its way, not always without challenge, into several standard advertising books. Winston Fletcher, probably rightly, thinks he's got a better one.

Almost as many claims have been made about advertising as advertising makes about products. A small selection might include:

- Advertising is evil
- Advertising exploits human inadequacy
- Advertising is wasteful
- Advertising is the mainspring of the economy
- Advertising prevents small, enterprising companies from breaking into established markets
- Advertising is a force for change.

A moment's reflection is enough to make one realise that each of these statements, favourable and unfavourable alike, is a generalisation direct-ly equivalent to a statement such as 'Television makes children violent.' Some television *programmes* may make children violent; some may help them learn to read. Some *advertisements* may be wasteful; some may act as a force for change, but as I hope to show, not all advertisements can possibly have identical effects.

Advertising is simply one of many available channels of communication. It is available, at a price, to everyone – and allows people to make contact with one or more other people for an almost infinite number of different ends. *Advertisements* are the messages that advertising carries, in an attempt to achieve those ends.

The almost infinite number of different users, uses, aims, purposes, motives, audiences, media and methods makes the question 'What is advertising?' peculiarly difficult to answer. The sign outside a church naming next Sunday's preacher is an advertisement. So are these:

- Locally Grown Strawberries
- We Need 175 Mountain Commandos
- Rights Issue
- Chairman's Statement
- Lost Budgerigar
- Labour Isn't Working
- Confessions Of A Pop Performer (X)
- Britain Will Win With Labour
- Broad-minded Midlands-based Male Seeks Mature Relationship
- Could You Manage An Off-Licence?
- Save It!
- Cats Will Die Unless We Continue To Help Them.

These are all advertisements and they are all part of advertising.

The nearest I can get to a definition that encompasses all these possible differences is: 'Any paid-for communication intended to inform and/or influence one or more people.'

First: 'paid-for'. An advertisement that is not paid for is not an advertisement, though its cost may be minimal and the payment may not be to a media owner.

Second: 'communication'. Every advertisement is attempting to bridge a gap between a sender and one or more potential receivers. That bridge is a form of communication. To buy a 16-sheet poster site and leave it absolutely blank is not to advertise. There must, in other words, be content as well as medium.

Third: 'intended'. Not all advertisements 'work', in the sense of achieving their desired objectives, but they are nonetheless part of advertising.

Fourth: 'inform and/or influence'. The purely informative advertisement may be rare, and the distinction between information and persuasion may be difficult to draw (what about 'Gratuities Not Included' on a British Rail breakfast bill, for example?), but an advertisement does not have to set out to influence either attitude or behaviour in order to qualify.

And finally: 'one or more people'. All advertisements are addressed to people: sometimes one ('Gypsy. Am back. Call soon. Lollipop') and sometimes millions ('Don't Waste Water').

Some years ago, a lady in Dulwich decided that she no longer needed her second-hand electric riding camel so she bought a space in *The Times*. This space was filled with an advertisement which was in turn read by one or more other people, previously unknown to the lady from Dulwich, who happened to want a second-hand electric riding camel and were well prepared to pay £400 o.n.o. to get one. The lucky applicant was happy; the lady from Dulwich was happy; *The Times* was happy; *The Times*' readers were happy (since the insertion cost helped to pay for their newspaper); and the second-hand electric riding camel found itself once more both wanted and useful.

Exactly the same simple principle applies to the Department of Energy, when it wants us to conserve energy; to the Prudential, when it wants to recruit personnel for its pensions and administration departments; to the Home Office, when it wants us to keep matches away from children; to a foreign government that feels itself to be misunderstood and wants to put its case; and to Heinz, when it wants to make clear the virtues of its baby foods to millions of parents it's never met.

All these advertisers have just this in common: they wanted to achieve something and chose advertising as one means of achieving it. How they used that advertising, the advertisements themselves, varied enormously in style, intent, format, price, size and medium. Whether or not they were as satisfied with the results of their expenditure as the lady from Dulwich, only they will know. So to attempt to identify some shared and general purpose or effect in all those advertisements is manifestly absurd.

'Is advertising wasteful?' is a non-question since 'are advertisements wasteful?' can be answered only by the person who paid for each one and sometimes not even then. Was the Dulwich lady's advertisement wasteful? Demonstrably not. (Alas, the cost-effectiveness of other advertisements is much less easy to demonstrate.) But it would have been wasteful had her electric riding camel rotted away in its Dulwich attic, unknown to all those who were longing to acquire it. In other words, it would have been wasteful *not* to advertise.

By substituting 'advertisements' for 'advertising', equivalent points can be made about all the statements at the beginning of this chapter, and many more besides.

Do advertisements prevent small, enterprising companies from breaking into established markets? Ask Polaroid or Bernard Matthews.

Are advertisements a force for change? Ask the manufacturers of those brand leaders that have continued to lead their markets for 30, 40 years or more.

Advertising, as such, can do absolutely nothing. It is simply there, waiting to be used. Advertisements, in theory, can do practically everything: introduce the new, confirm the old, congratulate existing buyers/users/consumers/employees, or attempt to convert them. Advertisements can, and do, encourage consumption and encourage thrift, and advocate a vote for any number of competing brands, companies or political parties.

Television, as we have seen, suffers from the same semantic confusion. Like advertising, it is simply an available channel of communication: there are cameras, transmitters and receivers. How can these inoffensive and inanimate pieces of hardware, of themselves, encourage violence? (Except, of course, by failing to function.)

It is both legitimate and healthy to question the effect of television programmes, just as it is to question the effect of certain advertisements, but to suggest that advertising does this or television does that is nonsense.

In fact, one of the few commercially available channels of communication not to suffer from this confusion between the container and the thing contained is the telephone system. Some subscribers use the telephone to sell insurance policies; some to call the plumber; some to say 'How are you?'; some to get in touch with the Samaritans; and some, no doubt, to arrange for the collection of a new consignment of hard drugs. Some unhappy subscribers use the telephone for breathing down heavily and saying 'knickers'. Again, the same channel of communication is being used for an infinite number of different purposes, including, sadly, some undeniable abuses.

However, because no one ever confuses the telephone system with telephone conversations, we have, so far at least, been spared the suggestion that radical reforms and controls are required in order to prevent one man in a raincoat from saying 'knickers', however understandably distressed the receiver of that message might be.

The distinction between advertising and advertisements is clear, and it's been made many times before by many people. Yet somehow it always seems to get forgotten in the heat of commercial, social and political thundering.

This handbook seeks, among other things, to spell out in some detail the diversity of the industry so often thought of as one homogeneous whole, as witnessed by phrases of the 'advertising is…' sort. It seeks to show the great diversity of the media and the great diversity of types of advertiser. It attempts to spell out the role of the advertising agency in producing effective advertising. It touches on the role of advertising in the economy, on some sensitive issues in advertising, on advertising controls, and on public attitudes to advertising.

As co-editor, my one great hope for this book is that having looked at even part of it, the reader will never again feel inclined to say 'advertising is…'.

Competitive persuasion

In the 1950s and 1960s, at least among the chattering classes as they were to become known, both 'competition' and 'persuasion' were pretty dirty words. Vance Packard's *The Hidden Persuaders* was published in 1957; and though most people neglected to read the book, the title alone entitled them to agree with it. I first came across the phrase 'competitive persuasion' in a paper written by John Brunner when he was on the *Observer*. It was, I believe, part of that paper's submission to the Shawcross Commission on the Press, which would date it to 1961. The piece below was first written for *JWT in Britain* in 1978 and was reprinted in *Campaign* later that year.

We come to most of our decisions in this country as a result of what has been called 'the principle of competitive persuasion'.

As voters, we are offered the choice of more than one candidate, more than one political party. All parties, all candidates, have not only the right but the responsibility to put their cases to us as convincingly, as competitively and as persuasively as they can. We listen, we note, we compare and when it's time to vote, we make a choice.

The reasons for that choice are almost certain to be complex. Indeed, in the strict sense of the word, they may not be 'reasons' at all. Our choice may be influenced by habit, inertia, background, self-interest, political or social principle, misconception, prejudice, distaste for the alternatives – or a marvellously muddled combination of them all. But that's our privilege. It's our vote, and we can spend it as we wish.

As readers we are offered the choice of more than one newspaper, each in turn trying to persuade us not only of its own merits but of the merits of different ways of life and alternative governments. And again, we read, absorb, reject, modify – and make up our own minds.

As jurors we are offered the two alternative and often irreconcilable views of prosecution and defence. Again, we listen, discuss – and come to a conclusion.

The priceless value of this principle of competitive persuasion can be fully recognised only when we examine attempts to improve on it. If we try to eliminate 'wasteful' competition, or to save people from 'illogical' choices, we move rapidly towards authoritarianism and then on to totalitarianism.

Our television companies are required, by Charter and by Acts of Parliament, to observe what is called 'balance'. Well-intentioned though it undoubtedly was, the impracticality of this requirement becomes daily more apparent. Television programmes, like newspapers, are made by people – which is to say, subjective, passionate, differing, opinionated, fallible individuals. And it is inconceivable that the producers of programmes on property development or social benefits should, as individuals, remain genuinely neutral however hard they might try. Yet that seems to be what is expected of them because they are regarded not as individuals but as representatives of their companies.

Any serious programme, despite earnest and often comically contrived attempts to preserve 'balance', is likely to excite cries of outrage from at least one interested party because the reception of any communication is inevitably subjective: so much so that it is quite possible for all political parties, simultaneously, to believe that the BBC is joined in a conspiracy against them.

Not only does 'balance' not work, it's also potentially dangerous. If we are led to believe that because television programmes are balanced they express the truth, our critical faculties will be less alert. We may be tempted to think: 'It must be true, it was on television.'

It has long been fashionable to mock party political broadcasts – and it's certainly true that as pieces of communication, as examples of advocacy, they are frequently inept and occasionally, one would suspect, downright counterproductive. But at least, as viewers, we are left in no doubt as to their stance and their purpose. They are clearly labelled, unashamedly biased, with no pretensions to 'balance'. Balance is achieved not within broadcasts but, by strict allocation of time, between broadcasts. And it is up to each party to use its allocation of time as skilfully and persuasively as possible.

The same is true of conventional, paid-for advertising. Each advertisement is clearly seen to be an advertisement – or should be. This is why advertisements that do their best to look like editorial are quite properly prohibited by the codes of advertising practice. As receivers of advertisements, we know that the advertiser is trying to put his own case as effectively as possible. But almost without exception, every advertiser, whether he's the manufacturer of branded goods or the Royal Air Force advertising for recruits, is in competition with other advertisers. So we can listen, compare, absorb, modify, reject, accept – and reach our own conclusions. The principle of competitive persuasion is at work again.

There are, however, some people and some bodies who seem to want to introduce into advertising the equivalent of 'balance' in broadcasting. Just as well intentioned, they want to protect us from our own instincts, our own freedom to spend our money as we spend our vote. They want to apply their own standards to everyone; to add more and more controls to what an advertiser says and how he says it; to aim for greater 'truth' in advertising.

This trend, as with attempts at 'balance', is at best foolish, at worst dangerous.

Certainly, no man should be allowed to advertise a non-existent cottage in Cornwall, keep the deposits and disappear – but there's more than enough legislation to cope with him already. Other advertisers, whether rogues teetering on the brink of the law or those who make a mistake, are dealt with through a vigorous system of self-regulation. But some of the more extreme consumerists want to go beyond that. They believe that the principle of competitive persuasion leads to a cynical, sceptical society and that advertising that is more 'truthful' (in their terms) would be in everyone's interest.

I believe the opposite to be the case. I believe that competitive persuasion leads to a discriminating, alert, intelligent society in which each member can arrive at his or her own decisions – whether or not they seem rational, sensible and correct to any self-appointed protector.

Further, I believe that – while we should make every effort to check our facts and ensure that our advertisements are honest – we should be pleased rather than worried that people question the 'truthfulness' of advertising. They are acute enough to recognise that the essence of competitive persuasion lies in promise, hyperbole, emotion and all the other time-honoured techniques of rhetoric. Should the time ever come – which it won't – when everybody believes implicitly in every party political broadcast and every commercial advertisement, I for one would want to leave not only the business but the country.

The truth of the matter is that people enjoy being persuaded, being courted, been wooed, being wanted.

We may, as individuals, find certain advertisements irrelevant, boring, offensive, silly, extravagant and antisocial. Indeed, it's inevitable.

If a large number of people share that view, and they also happen to be the very people to whom the advertisement is addressed, then it's clearly a bad advertisement. But any damage that is done, is done not to the consumer but to the advertiser.

Every client we have is in competition with other advertisers. Every client we have is trying to improve his product or service, to tailor it more accurately to the needs of its ultimate users, and to promote it honestly and persuasively.

Win or lose, competition and competitive persuasion are in the interests of everyone in the country; and it remains a delight to be part of that process.

Whatever happened to the Hidden Persuaders?

The most famous book about advertising is not about advertising. Vance Packard published *The Hidden Persuaders* in 1957 and his death last month at the age of 82 prompted me to read it again.

At the time he wrote it, a great economic change was taking place in America. Noted by theologians as well as economists, the new age of abundance was turning the long-standing relationship of production and consumption upside-down. Until then, it had been the accepted responsibility of production to satisfy demand. Now, quite suddenly it seemed, it had become the responsibility of demand to absorb production.

This reversal of roles created a need for marketing men. Packard calls them merchandisers. Their job was to create competitive demand for increasingly similar competitive products – and to do that, they needed to acquire a deeper, richer understanding of the relationship that existed between products and consumers. And in order to do *that*, they needed help: which came from a bunch of entrepreneurial psychologists and social scientists who called themselves motivational researchers.

These are the hidden persuaders of the title. Most of them were not only doctors or professors but also had sinister foreign names: Ernest Dichter, PhD, was their high priest. What they did was *depth* research: they raided the privacy of people's minds so that they could, allegedly, more easily (and subconsciously) be persuaded to buy more of what they didn't need. Traditional researchers could tell you what people *said* they thought. Motivational researchers told you what people *really* thought (even if they didn't know it themselves).

In his three-paragraph introduction to the British Pelican edition, Packard uses the word 'manipulate' or a derivative four times. The publisher's note warns: 'the frightening processes evolved and applied by American super-advertising scientists are having an increasing effect upon the potential victims in Britain'.

This scary-science card is used to great effect. Dr Dichter ran the Institute for Motivational Research. One chapter talks of the psychoseduction of children. Spooky references are made to Minnesota multiphasic personality inventories, Rorschach and Thematic Apperception Tests, hypnosis, and Cassirer's epistemology of symbolic forms. Oddly, subliminal advertising (the rumours of which did so much for Packard's sales, and which many people believe the book to be about) is not mentioned; there's just a single, dismissive reference to something called 'subthreshold effects'.

In fact, without knowing it, the book describes the first fumbling attempts to distinguish brands from products. (Gardner and Levy were themselves motivational researchers; their 'The product and the brand' had been published in the *Harvard Business Review* in 1955.) Reading the book again, it seems clear that Packard himself was not greatly alarmed by his own revelations: he found the merchandising process fascinating and largely innocent. The language, and above all the title, were there to persuade us (subconsciously, of course) to buy the book.

And we did. Few, I suspect, read it. But with a title like that, you think you don't have to.

The hair restorer that didn't

In 1974, the Advertising Association held one of its most memorable
conferences. Hostility to advertising was running high, at least in political
circles, and the conference was addressed by both Shirley Williams as
Consumer Affairs Minister and the first Director General of Fair Trading, John
Methven. Both made clear their doubts about the efficacy of current voluntary
advertising controls. Ronnie Kirkwood enlisted my help in a presentation he
had been invited to make at the same conference (see also 'The case of the
missing policeman', page 258) and we chose, perhaps riskily, to adopt a
satirical approach. The following is a short excerpt from the speech. It recounts
an entirely fictional future event – but the argument is much the same as that
contained in 'Competitive persuasion' (page 12).

In 1999 [*a distant 25 years in the future at the time of the conference*], a manufacturer called Rebozo Laboratories ran an advertisement for a hair
product called Pom. The illustration was of a markedly balding man and
the text read: '*GOING BALD? New Pom can help arrest hair loss.*'

Although this claim was fairly muted and qualified, it was still demonstrably a lie. Under controlled clinical conditions, with a volunteer panel
of 1,000 balding men, it was found that the 500 using Pom lost no less
hair than the 500 using massage alone. Furthermore, although the product was described as 'new', it was established that there had been no significant change in formulation for 13 years.

It was a blatant example of a manufacturer playing on the concerns
and neuroses of a particular group of people and deliberately attempting
to mislead them into believing his product could do something he knew
perfectly well it could not. The advertisement was withdrawn and
Rebozo Laboratories were very properly fined a great deal of money.

And there the matter might have rested had it not attracted the attention of Alexander Morrison, then Professor of Communications at
Redruth University. Professor Morrison was a leading authority on

communications theory and had been watching the development of advertising controls with keen professional interest.

His own view, unfashionable at the time, was that consumer protectionists, with whose aims he greatly sympathised, were nevertheless extremely naive in their view of how communications actually worked – and he decided to use the case of the hair restorer in an experiment of his own.

The first thing he did was to prepare a new version of the irresponsible advertisement. He kept the illustration of the balding man exactly as it was and he kept the headline exactly as it was – but he took out the offending copy altogether so the advertisement simply read: *'GOING BALD?'* No copy, no claim – just a picture of the product. And he tested this version for communication and persuasion using the original advertisement – the one that had explicitly claimed to arrest hair loss – as a control.

What he found in no way surprised him. The original advertisement still misled: a substantial number of men was led to expect that Pom might prevent their loss of hair continuing. But his new version, the one that claimed absolutely nothing, was significantly *more* misleading. Indeed, a large number of men interpreted it as promising not just a reduction in the rate of hair *loss* but actual *restoration*. Encouraged by this finding, Professor Morrison went one stage further and produced yet another version of the ad.

Again the same illustration of the balding man was used, but this time the copy read: *'GOING BALD? New enriched Pom guarantees you a completely new head of hair in just five minutes!'*

Again he tested this for communication and persuasion against the original, and again his findings failed to surprise him. The original continued to mislead as before – *but his third version misled absolutely nobody.* It was instantly and totally repudiated by his panel, not one of whom said he would ever be tempted to try it.

Professor Morrison published the results of his experiment in an article in *Communications Today*. He conceded that the third version had been deliberately extreme and therefore to some extent unrealistic. But he pointed out the apparent paradox that an advertisement that said absolutely nothing, and that was therefore legal, could mislead the consumer not only more than the original but a great deal more than the third version, which contained blatant lies and unsubstantiable claims, and was therefore totally illegal. As he put it himself: 'Here is a proven instance where the consumer is in fact far better protected by a demonstrable lie than by an unclaimed truth.'

Being a man who enjoyed encouraging controversy and challenging accepted wisdom, he went on to suggest that to require all advertising to be decent, legal and truthful was in fact acting against the interests of the consumer. In a memorable last paragraph he wrote: 'Indeed, there is a growing body of evidence to suggest that the consumer would most actively be protected by insisting that all advertising be *untruthful* at least in certain demonstrable respects, and that fact should be widely known and understood by the public at large.'

If you know that the ad is misleading, how can you be misled?

One of the most misleading words in the advertising lexicon is the word misleading.

Here it is in familiar context: 'I strongly disapprove of this advertisement for *Professor Mirrakle's Elysian Anti-Wrink*. Though containing no lies, it is clearly misleading – by which I mean that others, less intelligent than I, might well be misled.'

There is something wonderfully surreal about the phrase 'clearly misleading'. An advertisement may, of course, be judged to be misleading in intention; but if it is clearly misleading, it is difficult to see how it can in fact mislead. Linguistic philosophers would enjoy the debate.

At the heart of the problem of misleading advertising is the uncomfortable truth that no factually accurate ad can safely be described as misleading until there is clear evidence that one or more people have actually been misled by it. A further uncomfortable truth is that every advertisement will be decoded and interpreted on an individual basis by each of those receiving it. The reception and interpretation of advertising messages – as with every message of every kind – is a highly subjective process. If you are crippled by debt, you may decode honest offers of consolidated, low-interest loans with unfounded optimism. If you are crippled by shyness, you may need only to know of the existence of that correspondence course for you to be convinced of its potential to change your life. If you are crippled by neither, you will respond to those very same messages with complete indifference.

As the ITC scratches its head and wonders whether psychiatrists, religious groups, hair clinics and escort agencies should be allowed to advertise on television, others remain concerned to protect the vulnerable. 'Who decides whether an ad for a miracle cure was misleading?' asks Jocelyn Hay, indefatigable chair of *Voice of the Listener and Viewer.*

There are adequate laws to deal with the miracle bit, but the answer to her question remains as it has always been: irrespective, it seems to me, of product category. Banning legitimate categories from television confers on them an undeserved implication of seediness: like the turf accountant behind a blacked-out window.

It is impossible to make any justifiable distinction between legal businesses trading legally – and is in any case unnecessary. Are people really more likely to be gulled by a commercial for hair therapy than by one for hairspray?

The urge to protect the vulnerable is understandable and well meant. Anyone found guilty of deliberately exploiting the desperate should be banned from selling anything to anybody for all time.

But all attempts to ensure that nobody, ever, can read more into an advertisement than the product delivers are founded on a total misconception about the nature of communication – and will remain as doomed to failure as they have always been.

Illustrated by a line drawing of a great many elegant people at a cocktail party, a famous advertisement once boasted: 'Everybody's Talking About Shepherd Brand Mini-Casters'. This was a lie – and demonstrably so.

It was so clearly misleading that it misled absolutely no one.

The 60-ft peacock in Times Square: a role model for the networks

Any time now, the Nissin Food Products Company Ltd of Tokyo will unveil a new advertisement for Nissin Cup Noodles.

Dominating the north face of Number One Times Square, it will be 60 ft high, employ prodigious quantities of red neon, live steam and animated noodle, and will cost $1 million to install and another $130,000 a month to expose.

Those who believe that modern, accountable media planning should deliver a measurable audience composed exclusively of solus users will disapprove. How can a single poster site, reaching an unknown audience, not one of whom may be a cup noodle groupie, conceivably deliver a pay-back on $2.5 million?

For years, I've been haughtily disparaging about the terms 'classified' and 'display'. A far more useful way to think of advertising, I've argued, is to distinguish between advertising that people consciously go out and look for; and advertising that consciously goes out and looks for people.

All classified advertising, of course, belongs to the first category – and so, it seems, will much of the new media advertising: www.advertising doesn't come looking for you; you choose to go looking for it.

But the kind of advertising that is most valuable to brands is the kind of advertising that is least likely to be sought after by people.

Brand advertising has to draw attention to itself. If it's skilfully done, it will be at worst tolerated and at best warmly received; but it is never an invited guest. People don't go out for a nice drive of a Sunday afternoon to catch up on the new posters. They don't say: 'You know, Cheryl, I rather fancy we've fallen behind on our Ariel ad intake recently. Let's stay at home this evening and take some in.' Brand advertising has to go out looking for people; that's why it attracts all the criticism and that's why it's difficult to do well.

All of which has belatedly made me wonder if the origin of the word 'display' may not be typographical after all, but zoological: 'Display – a pattern of behaviour by which the animal attracts attention while courting.' Even if it isn't, it should be. What better inspiration for your creative team than a peacock of unbounded vanity, spreading and parading its multi-coloured magnificence in the face of some indifferent peahen – with the prospect of a right good consummation as the reward for success?

The Nissin Cup Noodle sign will be *on display* in Times Square. Twenty million people a year will take photographs of it. Millions of postcards will celebrate it. Documentaries and feature films will give it, for nothing, further glamour and distribution. Nissin cup noodles will become a famous global brand on the strength of a single poster.

Fame, by its very nature, is indiscriminate – so only mass media can deliver it. The real competition for traditional mass media will come not from the internet but from other magnificent forms of indiscriminate display: stunts, sponsorship, round-the-world balloon trips and 60-ft peacocks in Times Square.

2003 note: The internet, of course, carries both kinds of advertising. Much of it people actively choose to look for, but banner advertising attempts to ambush the browser in much the same way as the giant peacock. As a private medium, however, it still lacks the ability to create indiscriminate fame. See 'Never underestimate the value of bathwater' (page 166).

Two hot tips: beware Barnum, remember Ratner

It was probably Phineas T. Barnum who said that all publicity is good publicity. For showmen it may be good advice. And as long as you don't think about it too carefully, it's not bad advice generally. These days, modern marketing directors and their sophisticated advertising agencies tend to under-rate the solid commercial value of crude fame. They're so busy calibrating some miniscule shift in brand-positioning on their Boston Grids that the good old-fashioned benefits of familiarity and brand celebrity get lost in the detail. Most publicity, more often than not, is mostly good. But that is not what Barnum said.

As always, what every hypothesis demands is challenge. So if someone presents you with the Barnum hypothesis, I suggest you look them straight in the face and say 'Ratner!' Poor old Gerald generated so much free publicity for himself and his shops that they took away his job and had to change the company's trading name. I do not think Gerald Ratner would agree with Phineas T. Barnum.

It's been said that Peter Mandelson deliberately raised his public profile during the summer in the belief that the massive publicity would carry him shoulder-high on to the NEC. Even more recently, Tony Banks has become far better known than he's ever been, with terminal implications for his political career.

Watergate, Lockerbie, Hoover, Brent Spar: some publicity is bad publicity.

With the inevitable and continuing trend away from traditional freestanding brands towards corporate brands and service brands, all this becomes a lot more important. Parent brands, master brands, company brands will need lots of simple salience, lots of familiarity, lots of well-knownness. But when a corporate reputation takes a nasty knock, the effects are impossible to contain completely; they can sweep like a virus through the entire enterprise. If you stick to your policy of free-standing brands, damage limitation is relatively easy. Tylenol can be kept in an isolation ward while the rest of Johnson & Johnson carries on trading. Corporate branding makes that impossible.

So at a time when the value of simple publicity is due for rediscovery, when event marketing and sponsorship and joint ventures are attracting increasing interest and investment, and when corporate reputations are being asked to extend their authority over an ever greater diversity of goods and services, the word Ratner should be in pokerwork above every chief executive's desk: not as a deterrent but as a reminder.

Publicity is not just a cheaper form of advertising: it is different in kind. You should not assume you can control it. It's not that difficult to get a flame started but you can never be sure of being able to douse it. Unlike advertising, publicity can kill.

To act as though all publicity was good publicity is to be one of those who, also according to Phineas T. Barnum, are born every minute.

Why soft-sell is hard to sell: it isn't selling

Here's a bit of a puzzle, then. Everybody agrees that hard-sell and soft-sell are pretty meaningless phrases, yet everybody goes on using them.

They seem to be most favoured by those believing that the only true paradigm for advertising is the hi-performance brain-invader, by which something called a consumer proposition is rifled repetitively into consumers' heads until they can play it back flawlessly to day-after recallers. This, approvingly, is called hard-sell. Anything else, disapprovingly, is called soft-sell. (These are the same people who complain that a commercial is insufficiently branded, when what they really mean is that the product name has only featured five times.)

If that was all there was to it – hard, good; soft, bad – the deadly phrases would have expired long ago.

But there's another distinction they're sometimes used to make which is a good deal more useful: and it's mainly to do with different kinds of immediacy. If you want your audience to do something soon – cut a coupon, send a fax, pick up a phone, go to a sale – then you'll probably want to be sharp and urgent. These qualities are not sympathetic. They can be strident. They may not add long-term value to your brand. And you may not care.

But if the purpose of your advertising is to charge your brand's batteries, to add to its warmth and desirability, to remind existing users of its presence and its purpose, then you'll be looking for another kind of immediacy: of connection rather than action. Urgency, with its attendant stridency, will be unwanted and unwise. You'll need to be well mannered.

Depending on whether it's a real one or not, there are two good ways to sell a Rolex. The first is from a dodgy barrow on Oxford Street with the punters passing at walking speed. You have 15 seconds to get them before you lose them. The price is low enough to tempt them and high enough to make them hesitate. You do not pause to calculate possible damage to long-term brand values and corporate reputation. You will never see these punters again. You will hit them hard.

And the other way to sell a Rolex is the way they sell real ones in real life: politely and assuredly, with a style and grace to match the merchandise; conscious, as always, that every advertisement should be making a small investment in the brand's eternal worth.

The first approach is hard, the second soft. The second is far more difficult to do. But in meeting their own quite different objectives, they are comparably effective. Marketing needs both.

In fact, of course, the villain word is neither hard nor soft but sell. Sell implies that you're after an immediate, directly linked transaction; yet a great deal of advertising is not. A great deal of advertising is maintaining brand relevance and brand value. So 'sell' favours hard but not soft. Hard-sell sounds muscular and commercial; and soft-sell sounds weedy and a contradiction in terms. But I bet we all go on using them.

Big prize in worst-ever ad competition!

Today I announce a Christmas competition. It is open to all copywriters, the only judge is me and I am confident of winning.

The prize will go to the worst advertisement ever written. Entries are invited from everywhere but by the time I have revealed my own submission, you will know yourself beaten.

One of the first bits of business I worked on was a toothbrush account. For many successful years the advertising had featured the bend in the handle, which aided reach, torque and therefore hygiene. I found this boring.

In my second week I went proudly to my copy supervisor. I had not only written the words but drawn the picture.

A toothbrush was shown lying on its back, bristles upwards. It was supported along its length by the following words, vertically arranged in the form of columns:

HYGIENIC. COLOURFUL. ECONOMICAL. MODERN. LONG-LASTING. REAL NYLON. UNIQUE HANDLE.

And the headline, as by now you will have guessed, read: The Seven Pillars of Wisdom.

My supervisor, I could tell, was stunned and humbled by this virgin brilliance. The pause was a long one.

Eventually he said, 'It is to your credit that you have thought of both words and pictures at the same time. And it is encouraging that you have found room for the name of the product in the headline.' There was another pause. 'Everything else is appalling.' And he went on to tell me why. It was by far the longest conversation I had ever had with him.

He asked me if I had given a moment's thought to my audience: did I know who bought toothbrushes – men or women – and why? Did I know what they read? Why should I assume that they were among the 5 per cent of the population who had heard of T.E. Lawrence? And why would it help if they had? He talked to me about irrelevant puns, and their powers of distraction. He talked to me about brands – and asked what sort of brand I thought Wisdom was. And he talked to me at even greater length about the need for single-mindedness and how the more copy points you emphasised, the more diffuse the message became. And he talked to me about showing-off.

'I very much doubt,' he said in summation, 'if there has ever been an advertisement that showed less understanding of product, purpose, audience or even the most primitive principles of persuasion. This could well be the worst advertisement ever written.'

I like to think, in my competitive way, that he was right. And I also like to think that, even in the intervening 40 years or so, no other advertisement has come close to challenging it.

Feel free to try, however. Simple ineptness stands no chance. Evident contempt for established principle is essential. Send them to me. There's a new toothbrush, in the colour of your choice, for the lucky winner.

Part Two

Advertising and marketing

Polishing the apples – the value of marketing communications

It's always a good question to put to a new client: we all know what you make – but are you as certain what your customers are buying?

Simple as it sounds, it's a constructively difficult question to answer.

You make expensive pens; but that's not what people are buying. What people are buying will be prestige, or personal pleasure, or the hope of gratitude from a recipient.

You make multi-coloured chocolate buttons; but that's not what people are buying. What people are buying is a moment's welcome peace from demanding children.

You make laptop PCs; but that's not what people are buying. What people are buying will be self-sufficiency, self-esteem, efficiency and mobility.

As Theodore Levitt pointed out many years ago: people don't want a quarter-inch drill; they want a quarter-inch hole. And for every product or service, there's an equivalent distinction to be made   though seldom so easily or so elegantly.

So it was time, it seemed to me, to ask exactly the same question of ourselves – of those of us in marketing services. We know what we make, all right: what we produce. But what is it exactly that our clients are buying?

Here are some of the more familiar 'products' of the marketing services industry: advertisements, pack designs, tracking studies, market analysis, strategic counsel, retail interiors, corporate videos, annual reports, corporate identities and liveries, sales promotions, media, database

A very slightly edited version of an essay from the WPP Group plc Annual Report and Accounts published in 1998.

marketing, employee communications, public relations and public affairs advice.

Worldwide expenditure on all marketing services in 1997 was estimated at almost $1 trillion and there continues to be a more-or-less steady growth in such expenditure. That figure represents the aggregate of millions of different decisions voluntarily made by millions of individuals in millions of different competitive enterprises – so it can presumably be assumed that marketing companies, with attitudes ranging from cheerful confidence to resigned reluctance, believe their marketing expenditures to be necessary.

But, as with Ted Levitt's drill, nobody wants to buy advertisements or research reports for their own sakes, to be kept proudly behind glass in the corporate lobby. As with Ted Levitt's drill, all these products are bought in the hope that they will do something: to provide the equivalent of Ted Levitt's hole. Precisely what that something is, and how it differs from service to service, is a great deal harder to identify and articulate. To say that they are bought by companies to make themselves more successful is both true and unhelpful. It tells us what these services are expected to achieve but not how.

Each service, each discipline, has a different function, often complementary; most have many more than one; and the functions may change for each client company or each brand over time.

What this essay sets out to do is to probe just a little beneath the surface, and try to isolate some of the underlying needs that marketing services meet, for most client companies, most of the time.

So let us practise what we preach, and start with the consumer. And in the case of marketing services, of course, our immediate consumers are our clients.

All clients are different. They have perhaps just one thing in common: *They all need to put a competitive case; and they all want to do it cost-effectively.*

The need 'to put a case' means the need to communicate, by whatever means, with a wider group. And this holds true for repeat purchase consumer goods, for capital goods, for charities, for financial services, for personnel recruitment, for business to business, for media. Within their own sectors, they are all in open competition and they are all seeking to enhance their competitive positions.

It is kindergarten stuff to say that if a company sets out to improve its profitability, it has only two distinct areas of action open to it: not as alternatives, but as different approaches. It can minimise costs and it can maximise value.

But one way to clarify the contribution of marketing services is to ask: which are the disciplines that help client companies minimise costs; which are the ones that help client companies maximise value; and which, if any, can do both?

The first function of market knowledge, for example, is to minimise subsequent marketing waste. Before you can begin to put a competitive case, you need to know your market, what your prospective consumers think of you, what they think of your competitors, what their misconceptions are, what they know and what they think they know. Without such knowledge, you'll be transmitting blind. You'll be reaching the wrong people with the wrong appeals: that's a waste of time and a waste of money. Worse, you'll almost certainly be making the wrong product.

In the same way, money spent on the monitoring of your communications as you go along does not of itself add value to those communications, but it's the only way to identify error and so make subsequent expenditure more efficient.

The product that's sold is called *research*.

The product that's bought is more like a global positioning system, feeding back to its owner immensely valuable knowledge of competitive position, progress and direction.

The value of employee communications is finally beginning to get the recognition it deserves. When a company decides to achieve new efficiencies through re-structuring itself, it may feel like strong leadership – it may even feel efficient – to impose radical change overnight by means of a couple of all-staff memoranda sent down from the bridge. But employees who haven't been consulted, haven't been informed and feel that they haven't even been thought about can be immensely expensive obstacles to change: not because they're ill intentioned but because they're ill-informed. Ill-informed people quite naturally become apprehensive and resistant. And the consequential costs, though difficult to quantify, will always be high: in the greatly extended implementation process; in the loss of good people; in the general decline in morale. A sustained programme of listening, consultation, conversation and information can minimise confusion and hesitation, build trust through understanding, and contribute usefully to a sense of corporate unity.

The product that is sold is called *employee communications* or *internal marketing*.

The product that is bought is more like machine oil: lubricating the process of comprehension and willing compliance swiftly and smoothly throughout the organisation at small extra expense.

There are other marketing services that fulfil much the same function. Before you start doing business in a country unfamiliar to you, you will need to know how best to put your case. And that means getting to know the laws and customs of that country; the language of that country; the opinion formers of that country; and the media of that country.

The product that is sold is called *public affairs*.

The product that is bought is more like a mountain guide: an experienced Sherpa who's scaled that peak before and knows where all the crevasses are.

The central virtue of direct marketing – relationship marketing – is its ability to separate the more valuable consumers from the less valuable consumers, and concentrate effort and ingenuity on those with the greatest potential. It is an immensely accurate and efficient approach.

The product that is sold is called *direct marketing*.

The product that is bought is more like a prospector's sieve, screening out the mud and waste and exposing the few bright glints of gold for all to see.

All those, and there are many more, are examples of marketing services whose primary but not exclusive value lies within the broad category of contributing to efficiency through saving costs: in many cases, as a result of saving time.

But it's at least as much for the second category – for their ability to add value to brands and services – that client companies look to marketing services.

Wherever consumers have both money and choice, an intrinsically good product offering gives a marketing company no more than permission to compete. Winning will depend on its ability to add greater value than competitors can: and part of that value will come from presentation. To put a competitive case is to present your case – your company, your product, your idea, your policies, your proposition – as attractively as possible.

It's why people buy cosmetics, why window-dressers should be well paid and why costermongers polish their apples.

No competitive enterprise, in whatever field of endeavour, can leave its apples unpolished and still expect to win. There may still be a few who belong to the 'good wine needs no bush' school of marketing but they

won't be found amongst the winners and quite soon they won'
at all.

There are those who accept the need for pack design but believe that
its only function is to make the product 'stand out on shelf'. It should
certainly do that; but it should also do a great deal more.

There was much talk a few years back about the coming domination
of something called 'generic brands'. As a phrase, it was a contradiction
in terms. As a concept, it had limited consumer appeal. But it's instructive to remember just how institutional 'generic' packaging was: like
state-approved commodities in state-owned stores in corporatist
regimes.

A brand, to be successful, needs to be singular; needs to have a personality; needs to engage the heart as well as the mind. A good pack can
synthesise and express all this in a way that no other medium can – and
will continue to give added pleasure to its consumers throughout the
product's life.

What design companies sell is called *pack design*.

But what clients buy is more like a brand's identity card – its DNA, in
telling, graphic form.

For a company, its packshot will be its letter heading, its symbol: a
unique combination of words and design that comes to represent the
whole.

What design companies sell is called *corporate identity*.

But what clients buy is more like a national flag or football strip: an
instantly recognisable rallying-point, that can absorb and re-transmit the
values and achievements of the whole.

And then there is advertising, which has almost as many roles and
functions as it has users. But probably its most common use – and the
one most likely to puzzle both financial directors and social commentators – is that of supporting and promoting established brands and serv
ices. People can accept the need for advertising when launching a brand
or having made an improvement to a brand – but find it harder to see the
value in spending money to tell people about the existence of something
they very possibly already use. And it is here that we need to recognise
the value of celebrity.

Celebrity is recognised by theatrical agents and promoters and publi-
cists as having a necessary value for people. It has an equivalent value for
brands. Indeed, George W.S. Trow has written: 'The most successful
celebrities are products.'

Being around, being well known, being salient, being contemporary – in any market – are vital preconditions for sustained competitive success. But these qualities, like suntan, fade over time. They need, constantly, to be refreshed. And that is precisely what much of the best advertising for established brands is doing – year in, year out.

What agencies sell is called *advertising*.

But what client companies buy is more like a pool of spotlight on a stage; a trickle recharge for a brand's batteries; or a lasting place in the Hall of Fame.

The demand for communications services continues to grow: and so does the range of such services. Though existing media may be forced to re-position themselves with the arrival of new ones, no marketing medium has yet been totally extinguished. So the choice available to the enterprise with a competitive case to put grows ever wider and potentially more bewildering.

In evaluating the new ones, and in ensuring that the chosen disciplines work together with consonance and coherence, one final metaphor may help.

There are two forces at work when you try to make progress: thrust and drag.

Some marketing communications help their client-consumers reduce drag, and some help their client-consumers increase thrust – and some do both. If they are bought and evaluated not for what they are but for what they do, the management of marketing can seem a great deal less complicated.

Frozen lasagne and the future of advertising

It's now over five-and-a-half years since I first pointed out how much advertising agencies had to learn from frozen lasagne and as far as I can tell they haven't taken a blind bit of notice. So why do I go on, I sometimes wonder?

Only my own profound sense of responsibility and the news of the Great Nantucket Debate[1] drive me on.

The thing about frozen lasagne is this: the first three brands on the market all stressed their particular points of marginal difference and the market didn't get very far. Then along came the fourth brand, which decided to ignore conventional wisdom and dramatise the generic benefits of the sector as a whole. Not only did the whole sector prosper, but so did the brand.

Everybody who's written anything half-way useful about advertising has agreed that the most important decision a client company makes about advertising is the decision to advertise in the first place. The difference to a company's long-term prosperity between advertising and not advertising is infinitely greater than any decision it might make between two alternative creative approaches or two competing advertising agencies.

But that, of course, is a very generic point of view. And agencies, like all competitive brands, have little to gain from generic truths; so they

---

Marketing, January 1998. This piece replaces 'What are advertising agencies for? The lesson of the frozen lasagne', a presentation I made to an IPA Conference in 1992 which was reproduced in the second edition of this book. So it's now eleven years since I first pointed out how much advertising agencies had to learn from frozen lasagne

1   A debate featuring Professor John Philip Jones and Professor Andrew Ehrenberg, mainly about short-term vs. long-term effects of advertising and whether it is a 'weak' or a 'strong' force

compete at the margins. 'Come to us,' they say, 'and through our own proprietary creative alchemy, we will convert your modest budget into a force of fearsome power and effectiveness.' And so does every other agency. Nobody puts the basic case. Nobody says that the most important decision about advertising is the decision to advertise.

Meanwhile, Professors Andrew Ehrenberg at the South Bank University and John Philip Jones at Syracuse University continue their rigorous burrowing into the nature and value of advertising. They agree on many things, not least that the most important decision about advertising is the decision to advertise. Any client looking for independent justification for their advertising expenditure will find well-documented comfort from both of them. Yet when they meet and debate in Nantucket, the comment is all about their relatively minor areas of disagreement. Once again, the central, generic case goes under-represented.

Given all this, it should be no surprise that agencies continue to lose share of just about everything: from total marketing expenditures to senior client trust. And yet, still, few agencies bother to evaluate the fundamental worth of what they do, or even to keep abreast of the work of the academics. Agency case-histories compound the problem: they imply that all marketing problems are caused by inadequate creative content and all marketing solutions are to be found in a change of creative direction.

Professors Ehrenberg and Jones, while freely conceding the importance of creative content, have a more valuable view: but who's listening?

Agencies continue to behave like the first frozen lasagnes: loudly trumpeting their individual and peripheral advantages, totally failing to put the common case, and wondering piteously why nobody honours them for what they truly do.

One of many batty old observations about marketing

This is the first in an occasional series about batty sayings that have gone too long unchallenged, thus denying marketing persons many zillions of units of currency and inflicting upon them almost as many deeply tiresome dinner-party conversations. This is what Ralph Waldo Emerson (1803–1882) is famously believed to have said: 'If a man write a better book, preach a better sermon, or make a better mouse-trap than his neighbour, tho' he build his house in the woods, the world will make a beaten path to his door.'

To the financial director and the dinner-party didact, these are thrilling words. So who needs marketing? Who needs advertising?

I'll tell you who: that sanctimonious, pen-pushing mouse-murderer, that's who. And if you don't believe me, try this simple experiment.

Go into deep woods and build yourself a new house. As soon as it is completed, first write and then deliver a better sermon. Then wait.

The following day make a better mouse-trap. And wait again.

Only if you are still unconvinced should you bother to write a better book.

Because I am sorry to have to tell you that there will be no beaten path. Rather, such path as there was will soon be overgrown from disuse.

We know five things about Emerson's man. He writes books; he preaches sermons; he builds mouse-traps; and – despite living in the middle of a wood – he has a neighbour. (Eerily, this neighbour has precisely the same eclectic set of hobbies but apparently pursues them with less skill.) We also know that however great the books, the sermons and

the mouse-traps may be – and however much the world would appreciate them were the world to know of their existence – he is doomed to disappointment for as long as global ignorance persists.

The mouse-trap saying is a killer on two counts. For those who have
no time for marketing, it provides glib and authoritative support. And for
those who have too much faith in marketing, it is so transparently silly
that it even deters them from the wholly admirable pursuit of better
mouse-traps. Almost on its own, this potty apothegm has bred the belief
that, since good products sell themselves, only bad products need marketing. Among those who believe that the intelligent Emerson never
uttered these words may be counted myself and Elbert Hubbard. There
is absolutely no written record of Emerson ever having used them: and
the only attribution occurs in a book published seven years after his
death in which a lady claims to have heard him say them.

Elbert Hubbard, insanely in my view, vigorously contested this suggestion, claiming authorship for himself – much to the posthumous
relief, I would imagine, of Ralph Waldo Emerson.

And, no: I don't know who Elbert Hubbard was, either.

A Mickey Mouse solution to the problem of internet stocks

This column will be devoted to giving unsolicited and seriously flawed advice to venture capitalists. In the process, however, it's possible that some interesting reflections about marketing may surface.

First, some well-rehearsed facts about internet companies.

The price of net-related stocks continues to defy traditional analysis. It's said that the average length of time that such stock is held can be measured not in months or in days but in hours. Within 24 hours of one company coming to market, each of its shares had been traded five times. Companies that have never earned a cent in profit are worth billions of dollars. The net is the fastest growing medium in the history of media. There are hundreds of start-up (and upstart) companies seeking to provide faster, cheaper, easier, more interactive access to better organised information and entertainment.

Investors and commentators agree that whilst some of these companies will survive and prosper, most will not. What's harder to agree on, however, is which will do which. That is what perplexes the venture capitalists; and that is what, with becoming diffidence, I just may have the beginnings of an answer to.

Let me start with the man from whom I once, at the request of the WPP switchboard, took an unscheduled phone call.

The caller explained that he was a member of a family firm based near Reading and that for years business had been excellent. Recently, however, the pound had turned against them, a competitor had come out with a parity product at a barebone price and the workforce was demanding a pay rise. His father, he told me, had instructed him to ring a few numbers because he was beginning to believe that they might, after all, need some marketing. He wondered if we were in a position to provide them with some.

We made an arrangement to meet, but before we could do so I read in the *Financial Times* that his company had gone into liquidation.

Marketing people spend much of their time wondering wistfully why marketing never seems to attract quite the respect and affection they believe it deserves. This is partly because most trades tend to wonder wistfully why they're not more rapturously appreciated by their fellow citizens and partly because there's something in it.

The more successful the company, the more tempting it is for them to believe that they don't need marketing; to believe that marketing is a deeply dodgy modern substitute for manly, competitive performance. When de-coded, the proud boast 'We don't need marketing' means 'The success that we enjoy owes everything to the unrivalled excellence of our product offering and nothing whatever to spin and schmooze.' The 'good wine needs no bush' school of business is seldom articulated publicly these days, but I have little doubt that it sits complacently in many a corporate subconsciousness. An expert was once defined as a person brought in at the last minute to take the blame. Marketing often occupies the same role.

You might think that marketing case-histories might help but in fact they compound the problem. For obvious reasons, marketing case-histories are seldom about superior products. It would be a foolish person, for example, who tried to ascribe the success of Viagra to its imaginative marketing programme. Marketing case-histories tend to favour stories in which skilful marketing triumphantly overcomes product parity or worse. And so, through association, good marketing becomes indissolubly linked with undistinguished product. This is clearly what they think at Linux.

Linux is an operating system, in direct competition with Microsoft but with at least one important difference. It's free – you just download it. The Open Source movement was formed to promote the Linux cause and Eric Raymond, one of its leading figures, was quoted as saying: 'Our development community sees itself as having been persecuted for a long time. We have continually written better software and lost out to idiots with better marketing. It's made us very angry' (*The Times*, 27/1/99).

This might have seemed a compliment but of course it's not. Here's a heroic product that's been crushed by some idiot competitor's marketing.

No wonder marketing gets a bad name. Even when it works, it's at the expense of excellence.

Apart from their all being children of the net, the hectic new companies have one other thing in common: they are all founded on some functional, technological advance. And that is both their strength and their potential downfall.

As with the father of my caller from Reading, there will be many who believe, because they have a functional, demonstrable advantage, and therefore a superior product, that they don't need marketing; or at least, not yet. Those are the companies I would advise my venture capitalists to keep their distance from. And there will be other companies, also with a demonstrable advantage, also a superior product, who will know that their immediate need is to begin to build brand differentiation and brand celebrity. And those are the ones I would timidly suggest that the venture capitalists began to snuggle up to.

One model is Disney. Back in the beginning, Disney must have known more about animation techniques, and must have posted more animation-related patents, than anyone else in the world. And if that's all he'd done, it would by now be a forgotten company. But Disney invented not only animation techniques but Mickey Mouse and Goofy. From the beginning, he understood his ultimate audience; from the beginning, he built and sustained a brand. For him, marketing was a continuous and continual process that started with invention and never stopped. And it still hasn't.

One new company describes itself as being '...an Electronic Commerce infrastructure and service provider, offering a modular, turnkey solution for outsourced transaction processing and legacy system integration'. If I were a venture capitalist, I would nod sagely on hearing this information – and then question them closely about Goofy. And if they didn't understand, I'd move on.

Why New Labour is better than spray-on socks

Here is a test question for all advertising and marketing sophisticates. Who said this, and when?

> *This use of advertising – to add a subjective value to the product – becomes increasingly important as the trends in our technology lead to competing products becoming more and more the same.*

The answer: James Webb Young, over 70 years ago. And even he was probably not the first to express the thought.

Yet each marketing generation continues to believe that there was, until only very recently, some golden period when all products were not only demonstrably different from each other but also, wondrously, better than each other.

So we try all sorts of dodges in the hope of re-creating this golden age. We employ gap analysis to identify unsatisfied consumer needs. Stephen King, that most mordant of planners, once employed gap analysis to identify the absence on our supermarket shelves of left-handed margarine. As the saying goes: there may be a gap in the market; but is there a market in the gap? And when a major multinational client, in all seriousness, invited the agency to put aside all such practicalities as technology and cost and just come up with really unique ideas that would meet genuine consumer needs, the same Stephen King responded with joyful fecundity. Of his long and entertaining list, I remember spray-on socks and bed-making fluid with particular affection.

Next, of course, the R&D team having failed to come up with a functional product discriminator, we turn to the agency account planner and ask her to invent a non-functional one. This leads to a 30-page document, together with tapes and a mood-board, defining the precise and unique brand personality for the thirty-fourth imported lager to be offered to the drinking public. A work of Jesuitical ingenuity, it is wholly unactionable.

Even those who have been most dismissive of Rosser Reeves and his USP continue to behave as if some sort of competitive claim – functional or non-functional – is invariably necessary for competitive success.

In truth, I don't suppose there's ever been a time when competing products were anything but pretty similar: that's why they're competing products. Nor do I think that real people (as opposed to marketing people) even want their competing products to be sharply distinguished. Before getting too carried away with niche marketing, it's worth remembering what a niche is. It's a small hole in a wall: not often the most profitable place to park your brand. As the Labour Party has belatedly realised, if you want to be a mainstream brand, you'd better be in the main stream: and don't worry too much about being distinctive.

The person who understood all this best was the lady in the Persil focus group who said dismissively: 'Of course they're all the same – everybody knows that. It's up to you to decide which is best.'

Parity products: more and more of what isn't there

No two products are identical. Parity products do not exist. There are no exceptions to this truth. So it is surprising that, according to widespread marketing belief, parity products are becoming more common.

It is, of course, true that products may lose their functional advantages very quickly. It is also true that two competing soaps may wash equally well, smell equally pleasant and be equally good value for money. All this has been so for at least 70 years. But parity products exist only in the minds of the marketing and advertising community; they exist not at all in the minds of real people. The human mind both abhors and rejects the concept of parity.

Give a small boy two marbles and within an hour he will have formed a preference for one. They will not be absolutely identical: no two proper marbles are. But they will be a great deal more like each other than any two products we claim to have parity, and they will still be seen to be distinctive. So it is with products and consumers. I have never known any real person to find two competing products in all respects identical and interchangeable nor any research to suggest that such people exist.

It is marketing people, frustrated in their search for 'something to say', who bleat about parity. And they bleat because, deep down, they still think they should be looking for some profoundly motivating USP: some verbally expressed and unique difference in their product that will prove irresistible to millions of people. The concept of product parity serves as a valuable scapegoat for their failure to find it.

But if you have to look that hard for a functional advantage that can be verbally expressed and will be of significant value to the consumer, then the chances are it isn't there. It's interesting that the phrase Unique Selling Proposition is an input phrase: a phrase adopted by the marketer, the seller, the transmitter. I know of no evidence to suggest that the consuming public is looking for a response equivalent; for a Unique Buying Justification. They find it very easy to identify the differences; but then, people have always been better at understanding marketing than marketing people.

You would think that advertising agencies were parity products. With the exception of Ted Bates all those years ago, when the USP philosophy was its own USP, no agency to my knowledge has ever successfully promoted itself on the back of a unique, verbally expressed functional discriminator. They all do the same sort of thing in the same sort of way with the same sort of people. Their occasional attempts to differentiate themselves rationally tend to be deeply unconvincing. Yet clients, potential clients, employees and the trade press have no difficulty whatsoever in telling them apart.

The real giveaway, I think, is the phrase itself. It's always 'parity products'; never 'parity brands'. Parity brands sounds too much like a contradiction in terms – which of course it is.

That toothpaste is an imposter!
(But who cares?)

There's a poster up at the moment featuring an outline toothpaste tube, a question mark and the words: 'We're too busy improving our own to make it for anyone else.' It's signed off by Colgate.

National brand manufacturers who choose not to supply own-label feel themselves a lot more virtuous than those who do, and get much aggrieved when their virtue goes unrewarded. They long to out their competitors by name but never do. Instead, whenever frustration becomes uncontainable, they instruct their agency to come up with an advertising campaign to trumpet their own purity while strongly implying the duplicity of others.

Understandable, certainly: but it's hard to believe that people will dutifully respond: 'Now that I know that Colgate does not manufacture toothpaste for others to sell under their own names, I shall from henceforth use no other.'

I've always suspected that paranoia over this issue springs from the widespread folly of believing respondents.

Get consumers into a focus group and ask them why they buy cheaper, retailer brands and they grope around, not unnaturally, for some self-enhancing justification. Or to put it another way, they lie. 'Well, they're all the same really, aren't they? I mean, everybody knows that. I mean, they're all made by Heinz/Nestlé/Kellogg's/Cadbury's, aren't they? When you buy the brands, you're just paying for the adverts.'

And marketing directors study the transcripts and believe them, and decide that it's time to be proactive and set the record straight through advertising.

The challenge to the agency is to find an angle. In this case, the angle is that Colgate is too busy improving its own toothpaste to make it for others: and I have to say that I do not find it persuasive. Too busy? All day, every day, improving? A toothpaste? You have a simple choice: to disbelieve it; or conclude that there's more room for improvement than an established brand should wish to boast about.

These nervous little campaigns may make manufacturers feel better, but I can't remember one that's rung true. The basic flaw, of course, is that if people like the retailer brands enough to go on buying them – and they're cheaper – why should they care who makes them?

The real value of national advertising is as it's always been – to establish and maintain for national brands an unargued air of confidence, superiority and worth. To start getting peevish, and in front of the punters at that, simply diminishes the brand's stature.

Heinz withdraws national television support from its brands. A couple of years later, it starts making baked beans for its retailing competitors. Maybe the two decisions were unconnected but the theory of brands suggests otherwise.

Big brands should remain, at least in public, pretty lofty: which is why comparative advertising is nearly always unwise for a brand leader.

There may well be a case for making known the fact that Colgate doesn't make toothpaste for anybody else. But why not through public relations or perhaps on pack?

Don't forget the absence factor: or why fmcgs become smcgs

The problem facing a great many fast-moving consumer goods companies is that their goods move far too slowly. Fmcgs get a lot of attention – but there's at least as much to learn from a study of smcgs. They deserve a lot more recognition and perhaps even their own awards evening. My own nomination for the Grand Prix would probably go to Angostura Bitters.

Smcgs are usually slow-moving not because each unit takes an age to exhaust, but because consumers leave very long gaps between finishing one unit and starting another. If this is a symptom from which your own brand suffers, you may confidently diagnose it to be suffering from what we doctors call a low absence factor.

Some commodities have very high absence factors: petrol, for example; or loo paper; or cigarettes. You can't not know you haven't got them. But not all commodities, and even fewer brands, make their absence so tellingly felt. And the longer people manage without them, of course, the fainter the feeling of absence becomes until – the ultimate failure – you've got another lapsed user on your hands.

All ambitious brands should aim for a high absence factor but surprisingly few seem to do so. One of the most effective techniques has always been to couple your brand to a specific occasion. Only one kind of jam, for example, enjoys a high absence factor – and that's the one that's made from oranges and belongs to breakfast. Consumers invented bedtime drinks for themselves. Lemon Jif makes annual use of Shrove Tuesday. Turkeys may not vote for Christmas but their breeders certainly would.

But then, all too often, greed sets in. 'You know, Nigel, we're crucifying this brand by limiting its appeal to bedtime. If we re-positioned it as the Anytime Drink, we could up consumption potential by a factor of four.' This is not just greedy, it's ignorant. By disconnecting the brand from bedtime, there will now be no daily prompt, no regular reminder, no automatic trigger. The Bedtime Drink becomes the Anytime Drink – and within a very few years the No-time Drink. Unnoticed and unmourned, its absence factor at zero, it disappears forever from the nation's shelves.

Another good wheeze is to look for a permanent visual reminder of an object's absence. This sounds difficult until you remember kitchen towels. There sits the empty holder on the kitchen wall, day after day, radiating reproach, until the consumer cracks. I'd love to know how the consumption of paper towels differed between households with holders and those without.

Trying to calculate how much things are missed can be a more helpful way of assessing brand strength than how much they are appreciated. If your brand's absence factor feels low, think kitchen towels, turkeys, Creme Eggs and marmalade.

Why reality in advertising is to be avoided at all costs

Of all the time-honoured accusations levelled at advertising, its refusal to reflect a true picture of the real world is one of the most familiar. It is, we are told, a failure to face up to reality.

In fact, of course, advertising is absolutely right to avoid featuring the real world. Advertising's most common function is to bring out the best in things, to make its subjects as attractive as possible. The real world is full of dirty finger nails, derelict housing estates and dog turds. These are unwelcome associations for personal equity plans and freeze-dried coffee granules.

Advertising people should not see themselves as courageous chroniclers of gritty, social truths. Rather, they should model themselves on costermongers, cosmeticians, auctioneers, wedding photographers and taxidermists.

Apples look better when polished up a little. The lumpen husband will think it money well spent if the boil on his neck is away from camera and he comes out looking like Hugh Grant. An auctioneer who adopted the Roy Brooks school of advocacy ('this hideous painting is almost certainly a fake and would be over-priced at a guinea') might soon have to take his children out of private school. And who, in the interests of truth and documentary realism, wants their old, dead poodle to come back from the taxidermist looking like an old, dead poodle?

There is an innocent and valued role in life for those of us who try to help things look their best. We should not allow ourselves to be bullied into feeling guilty about it. We are most commonly mocked, of course, for our portrayal of families. There have never been families, our critics say, like the families we put in advertisements: daddy and mummy, he in jacket and tie, she in her pinny, sitting around the breakfast table with one small girl and one rather bigger boy, sunshine streaming through the window and milk decanted from the Tetra-Pak into a blue-and-white-striped jug.

What a travesty, what a parody, what a lie!

This month, as you must have noticed, research has once again revealed that the cause of our continued national decline is the disappearance of the British nuclear family and with it the structured meal.

But did you also notice the photographs that accompanied these stories?

They were all captioned 'The Family – as it used to be' and they showed daddy and mummy, he in jacket and tie, she in her pinny, sitting around the breakfast table with one small girl and one rather bigger boy, sunshine streaming through the window – and milk decanted from the Tetra-Pak into a blue-and-white-striped jug.

Look even more closely, and you could find a smaller caption: *Photo: Advertising Archives.*

So it seems that the cause of our continued national decline is the fact that we no longer have families of the kind that everybody knows we never had in the first place. A bit of a failure to face up to reality, if you ask me.

In praise of hypocrisy

It seems to be increasingly politically correct to adopt a curled and derisive lip about political correctness. That's probably a good thing; much of it is embarrassing and some of it sinister. But I wonder if we make a sufficiently thoughtful distinction between political correctness and socially valuable euphemism.

I once heard the marketing director of the American Rabbit Promotion Council (Eastern Branch) being interviewed on a New York radio station. He had, he said in bitter tones, an impossible job. How could he reasonably be expected to get families with children to eat rabbit when those very same children cuddled baby rabbits on their knees and brought them carrot tops home from the supermarket? He greatly envied his counterparts in the cattle trade. Little children could watch young calves gambolling in the spring sunshine yet be quite unaffected when confronted with a veal escalope. What was needed, said the marketing director of the American Rabbit Promotion Council, was a word for rabbit meat that didn't use the word rabbit. If the rabbit industry was to be expected to compete on equal terms, it needed an equivalent to the word veal; a word that acted as a sort of buffer between farm and table; an anodyne word that would be gratefully embraced by all those who might much enjoy a rabbit casserole but would rather not be reminded of its winsome origins.

He also spoke enviously of the words beef and ham for the same reason.

The interview finished with an invitation to the audience, presented by the marketing director and sponsored by the station, to submit non-rabbit words for rabbit meat which the American Rabbit Promotion

Council (presumably having changed its name) could then employ for marketing purposes.

As far as I know, the competition was never won; but it has occurred to me since that the idea wasn't nearly as ludicrous as I'd initially thought.

Not everyone does: but I like sweetbreads. If I see sweetbreads on a menu, metaphorical salivation begins. But would it, I wonder, if I saw calf's pancreas – or even, perhaps, cow's thymus gland?

A wise and canny colleague used to insist on the value of what he called emotional hypocrisy. No member of his team, however incompetent, would be allowed to leave the company without being the centre of a small drinks party and the subject of a short and affectionate speech. The canny colleague's reasoning was unassailable.

Everybody knew that Nigel had been fired and many felt it should have happened sooner. But they saw no reason for Nigel's self-confidence to be irrevocably dented, they all wished him well, any excuse for a free drink was welcome – and they quite liked the style of a company that could behave in this way. As a bonus, of course, the word that Nigel later spread about his former company would be surprisingly fond and favourable.

It was certainly a kind of hypocrisy; but universally recognised as such and widely appreciated. Compare and contrast with the all-staff e-mail, which might have read: 'Nigel has been fired for incompetence and will be leaving immediately.' Full marks for truth and openness; but not very many for management skills.

Not all hypocrisy is shameful, nor all euphemisms cowardly.

A good euphemism helps us entertain two incompatible thoughts simultaneously without imploding: a necessary ropetrick for anyone of any sensitivity. We know that Nigel is incompetent; we know that Nigel should be fired; we don't want Nigel to be hurt. There is a clear case for ambiguity. The little leaving speech may not contain lies; but the attentive will note what hasn't been said – and be glad.

Not long ago, I was telephoned by a journalist on a trade paper. He was writing an article on some new dotcom development and was seeking quotable opinions about it from a broad spectrum of people: 'From', as he rather nervously put it, 'young Turks to (and here he paused for a count of at least three) to those…at the more seasoned end of the scale.' And we both laughed. There are dozens of euphemisms for old; and I'd like you to know that I'm greatly in favour of all of them.

Militant vegans may believe that a week working in an abattoir would convert the majority of carnivores to their ranks – and they might be right. But unless you believe that rearing animals for food is intrinsically wrong, or unless you have reason to believe that the animals are subjected to avoidable pain and distress (both perfectly respectable positions), then to give up eating meat because you've been reminded that no meat can be eaten until an animal has been killed is not rational. Indeed, it's rather less rational than the harmless hypocrisy of continuing to enjoy food while choosing not to dwell on the precise manner of its provision. (And how's that for a euphemism?)

Just off the A303 in Wiltshire, there's a large and well-kept pig farm. The pigs have their own houses and plenty of territory. If ever you've seen contented pigs, these are they.

Recently, the farmer has erected an extremely large sign, round which the piglets innocently rootle. It reads: 'PUT BRITISH PORK ON YOUR FORK'.

I know it rhymes. I know the British farming industry is in serious trouble. And it's not as if I didn't already know that you can't make a sausage without killing pigs. But it has certainly strengthened my conviction that the American Rabbit marketing director was indeed a sound psychologist.

Fall guy wanted to save moronic chairman's skin

As a great many recent boardroom events have testified, not all top jobs turn out to be quite as desirable as they must have seemed at first sight.

I blame the executive search agencies. By following their traditional recruitment methods, they attract a great many candidates but all of the wrong kind. In my opinion, there's only one way to improve the failure rate of top job appointments – and that's to tell the truth about them.

As guide and inspiration, the executive searchers should turn to one of the very earliest examples of successful recruitment advertising.

Ninety-nine years ago, before setting off for the South Pole, Sir Ernest Shackleton placed this advertisement in the London papers:

> *MEN WANTED for Hazardous Journey. Small wages, bitter cold, long months of complete darkness, constant danger, safe return doubtful. Honour and recognition in case of success –*
> *Ernest Shackleton.*

Not only did Shackleton get the men he wanted but they were all made of the right stuff. When they started on the job, there were no nasty surprises.

But imagine how it might have been had Shackleton employed a professional placement agency:

> *TITLED ADVENTURER offers once-in-a-lifetime travel opportunity for would-be high-achievers. Challenge and comradeship await in exotic surroundings. Unusual remuneration package includes free transport and prospect of immortality.*

This would, of course, have attracted even more applicants; but every one of them would have been profoundly unsuitable. Just a few hundred yards into the first blizzard and they'd have been dropping like flies.

So in a spirit of helpfulness, and based on Shackleton principles, here are two draft advertisements for top positions in British industry. (The jobs, of course, are completely fictitious and bear no resemblance to any such jobs that may or may not coincidentally be vacant.)

> *CHIEF EXECUTIVE WANTED FOR THOROUGHLY DEMORALIZED MAJOR RETAILER. The successful applicant will be cunning enough to outwit a large board of self-important non-executive directors, energetic enough to compensate for two decades of corporate complacency, insensitive enough to shrug off the daily sniping of financial journalists, honey-tongued enough to placate disillusioned investors and pragmatic enough to know that any prospect of success is frankly minimal. The only really good thing about this job is the salary – but that, of course, may not last very long.*

> *FIRST-EVER MARKETING DIRECTOR wanted for famous financial institution which lost its way seven years ago and has been running on reputation ever since. Though not a member of the core management team, the successful applicant will be expected to deliver trading and margin improvements by the end of the first quarter so that the incumbent executive chairman can then take credit for them. A key requirement will be to work closely with the six board-level departmental heads, five of whom voted against the appointment of a marketing director on principle.*

There might, I grant you, be rather fewer applicants. But there'd also be fewer nasty surprises.

Should we all go barefoot for our children's sake?

This is a serious column about individual responsibility and socks.

It's not often that I find myself reading a sock label. In fact, I can't remember when I last read a sock label even once, let alone over and over again. So I've now decided to share the contents of this sock label with you and seek your help and advice.

The brand of sock is MS. Not M&S – just MS. And the headline (which, like any good headline, was what grabbed my attention in the first place) reads:

MS – the ozone friendly sock.

Here we will pause while I ask you to consider: in what way do you think that a brand of sock could be ozone friendly?

Thank you. If it's any comfort to you, I felt much the same.

Let us now read on:

100% cotton. Helps prevent foot odour…

Did you find that helpful? No, neither did I. So let's see how it ends.

…which is probably a major cause of the ozone layer.

Here, in uninterrupted form, is the full copy again:

MS. The ozone friendly sock. 100% cotton. Helps prevent foot odour which is probably a major cause of the ozone layer.

Now, I know what's going on here. I'm no fool. This is what's called cause-related marketing. It's the new way to make us feel good about buying things and guilty about not.

But let's read the copy yet again, even more carefully. It seems (a fact new to me) that foot odour is probably (only probably, mind you) a major cause of the ozone layer; and we all know that the ozone layer is a good thing. It is holes in the ozone layer that we have to worry about – as indeed it is with holes in socks.

But MS socks, perhaps by virtue of being 100% cotton, are positively inhibiting the generation of foot odour – and thus (if MS have their facts straight) denying us as robust an ozone layer as we might otherwise have enjoyed.

Far from being ozone friendly, these socks are a serious health hazard. Just what cause am I supposed to be relating to here?

Surely, if we care for the future of our children and our children's children, these socks must be stopped.

But here's my problem. MS make very good socks indeed and – at £3.99 for three pairs – they represent astonishing value. I do not want to have to give them up.

It is a very modern dilemma, this. Would one man's foot odour, if allowed to befriend the ozone layer unchecked, really make such a material difference? If all cotton socks threaten the ozone layer, why should MS alone be penalised simply for being honest?

Please help. This is not an easy one.

Why is my shaving cream more interested in other men than in me?

All right, all right, I'm convinced. But why isn't my shaving cream?

I have read almost as much as you have about relationship marketing and lifetime value and discounted cashflow. And I promise you: I understand and agree and accept that it is often a great deal more efficient and more profitable to concentrate time and tender loving care and precious resource on keeping a satisfied customer satisfied than on trying to find a new one. But then, as I do 365 times a year, I look at my shaving cream.

I have been using the same shaving cream for 20 years. This means that I have looked at the can my shaving cream comes in 7,300 times. In fact, of course, I look at it several times every morning: taking it from the shelf, applying nozzle to fingertips, replacing it on shelf and so on. So, conservatively, I have cast my eyes over this can *22,000 times*.

And yet, when that can looks back at me, it is as though we've never met before.

The design of that can has only one shameless purpose: to attract and inform new users. As for me – loyal, lifetime fan, serial purchaser, and worth a hundred times more to the brand than some wretched, first-time, adolescent shaver – I am ignored and despised.

The appearance of my can may well help it stand out on the shelf – but it does nothing for the suavity of my bathroom. Since it is as permanent a fixture in my bathroom as the taps and the light fittings, why has no thought been given to its appearance in home? And the words on the pack! I am told, for example, that it is 'smooth and comfortable'. Now, I have used this cream (as I may have mentioned) over 7,000 times.

I *know* that it is smooth and comfortable. If it was anything but smooth and comfortable, I would have stopped using it 7,000 days ago. And there are even lengthy instructions as to how to use it. It is possible, I suppose, that I was once quite grateful to be advised to rinse my face after shaving, though it seems unlikely; 7,000 shaves later, it forces me to find the brand absurd.

Proper marketing recognises that all brands have an after-sales responsibility. Proper marketing recognises that, if the daily experience of a brand is pleasurable, the once-every-six-months purchase decision is likely to be favourable. So why doesn't proper marketing recognise the after-sales potential of good pack design?

There are some distinguished exceptions, of course – most tissues now come in boxes that look good in the home as well as on the shelf – but the majority of packs continue to be blatant in their single-minded ambition. Like street traders, they care nothing for the sustained satisfaction of their customers. They do nothing to encourage or reward loyalty. They just want to make a quick buck, now: and then turn their rapacious attention to the next punter to pass their way.

Cheese rind and chicken shit – that's progress for you

Once upon a time, all cheddar cheese came with its rind on. Since you bought by weight and the rind was inedible, you incurred both cost and inconvenience.

Time passes. Market forces work. Consumer dissatisfaction is identified and a new, improved cheddar is made available: new, *rindless* cheddar. With waste eliminated and convenience enhanced, you are, reasonably enough, invited to pay a little more for it. Rindless cheddar represents progress.

So far, no problem. Rational man nods approvingly. Time passes.

Market forces move again. New dissatisfactions are identified. And a new, improved cheddar is made available: new, mature cheddar *with rind*. Both waste and inconvenience have been restored; but you are, nevertheless, invited to pay a little more for it. Farmhouse cheddar *with rind* represents progress.

Rational man's brow furrows. Hang on a minute. If cheese with its rind on used to be cheaper than cheese with its rind off, why is cheese with its rind off now cheaper than cheese with its rind on? How can it be progress to go from A to B and also from B to A? Unless going from A to B in the first place was a mistake in which case it wasn't progress. What's going on here?

Rational man may reach for one of two explanations.

First, that the cheese rind scandal is but an infinitesimal part of the Great Marketing Conspiracy. Vance Packard first exposed it over 40 years ago. Brilliant young men and women, many of them university graduates, first create and then exploit rampant consumer insecurity.

Virtual dissatisfactions are identified, promoted and then gratified by virtual product improvements. All change justifies higher price. Progress doesn't necessarily require forward movement; movement in any direction will do nicely, thank you. Bond salesmen call it churning.

And the second, much less interesting, explanation is this. Good marketing has no place for dogma or intolerance. Rind on cheese means different things to different people. People who like it off are right to want it off. People who like it on are right to want it on. And the people who make and market cheese are right to make and market both. So the cheese rind story is not scandal but parable. It explains why all monopolies are suspect and why centralism is doomed to fail the individual. And that's the explanation I prefer.

Once upon a time, eggs were sold loose, their shells often bearing unmistakable signs of their farmyard origins. Time passed, market forces worked, consumer dissatisfaction was identified and quite soon eggs came hosed down, scrubbed up, spotlessly sanitised. Clean eggs represented progress, and people were happy to pay for it.

But of course those university graduates were never going to be satisfied for long. So today, you can buy free-range eggs with a tiny, curly hen's feather in every box. It can't be long before we're offered, for very little extra, free-range eggs *now with genuine chicken shit.*

I don't expect to buy them but I'll be pleased to know I could.

New role for Mr Kipling:
e-commerce consultant to geeks and anoraks

Oh how I chuckled when I read these words in *Campaign* last year: '...some of Britain's oldest brands – Hovis, Mr Kipling and Bisto among them...'

And the reason I hugged myself is this: Hovis is 110 years old, Bisto is even older – while young Mr Kipling will not be celebrating his fortieth birthday until 2007.

Even pre-natally, Mr Kipling was an old brand: he was designed to be. J. Walter Thompson conceived him: name, pack, the lot. Much maligned focus groups (or group discussions as they were then quaintly called) had told us that the last thing the world needed was a new cake. A new cake, like a new whisky or a teenage neuro-surgeon, was a disturbing proposition. Much the best cakes were yesterday's cakes: yet the new range had to be launched.

So we invented a new concept. We called it 'retrospective lead-time'. And the idea, though undoubtedly self-explanatory, is this. Some new products, far from firing off rockets and drawing boastful attention to themselves, should do their best to tiptoe on to the market without anybody noticing. Or to be more precise: their presence should be noticed, but not their arrival. Under no circumstances should phrases like NEW! or AT LAST! be employed. In the case of Mr Kipling, the devilish intention was that cake-eaters everywhere should find themselves mildly perplexed: why did no one tell us about these exceedingly good cakes before now? The difference between 'new' and 'new to me' is an important one.

And it worked. Retrospective lead-time meant that, within minutes of launch, an entirely new range of cakes had established an entrenched reputation for longevity, consistency and trustworthiness. This, I'm happy to remember, infuriated competitors. And *Campaign* reporters under 30 believe Mr K to be one of Britain's oldest brands.

In the mad new world of e-commerce, mastering the art of creating retrospective lead-time may well be a critical marketing skill.

Everybody from Francis Fukuyama to the Henley Centre tells us that the brands of the future are going to be trust brands. In the jungle of choice and uncertainty that the internet presents, familiarity will count for more than ever. Yet the internet brands most likely to start trading first and fastest will be the new brands – if only because they need adopt no seismic change of culture nor undertake the cannibalisation forced on their old-established competitors. It's a great deal easier for Amazon.com to be exclusively obsessive about selling books on-line than it is for Barnes & Noble.

But the traditional brands won't lie down and die. As price and availability become less and less important as differentiators – because everyone will be able to make instant price comparisons – so the value of brand affinity will increase still further. The traditional brands, as long as they haven't left it too late, will still have a trump card to play.

So the upstarts – those brazen, rootless children of the net – will need to be very clever indeed. They will have to learn how to be both excitingly new and reassuringly well established. They will need retrospective lead-time.

In the pursuit of this policy, they could do worse than employ Mr Kipling as a communications consultant. At only 33, he's already one of the oldest brands in Britain.

If you make 'em laugh, do you make 'em buy?

In the 1970s, when I wrote this, there was more 'humorous' advertising in the US than there was in the UK – or so it seemed. During the 1980s, the position was reversed. In the early 1990s, as the recession hit advertising expenditure, there were those who blamed advertisers' inconstancy at least in part on the 1980s agencies' obsession with entertainment at, allegedly, the expense of effectiveness. The advertising business, so the argument went, by failing to fulfil its primary function of selling, had so devalued its own product that its clients deserted as soon as times got difficult. At the same time, there was new evidence that 'likeability' in advertising was a near-constant factor in successful campaigns. While people continue to discuss the question in general terms – as if it's all good or all bad for all tasks at all times – I expect we shall continue to see examples of extreme turgidity, examples of extreme facetiousness and quite a lot of reasonable stuff in the middle.

The question, 'Does humour sell?' belongs to that fine family of advertising questions none of which is likely to be answered definitively but all of which will continue indefinitely to be asked. Other favourites include: 'What is the optimum level of advertising expenditure?', 'How many times should a commercial be shown?', 'Is a 30-second commercial better than a half-page in the *Daily Mirror*?' and 'What about nudity, then?'

It is, however, both sensible and respectable to persist in asking these questions, so long as both questioner and questioned resist the temptation to establish or accept glib and all-embracing dogma.

With luck, and hedged about by inevitable questions such as 'What is humour?' and 'What is advertising?', it should be possible to begin to say how, in certain circumstances, certain kinds of humour may fruitfully be used in the advertising of certain products – at least for the time being. If anybody thinks that too inconclusive, hypothetical and unsatisfactory an objective, he should perhaps choose to earn his living in some simpler and more measurable occupation.

Humour can be kind or cruel; broad or subtle; largely visual or totally dependent on a collision of words. It can be trivial and facetious, or deadly serious in its undertones. Between the poles of satire and slapstick lie an almost infinite number of levels and variations of humour. And as with every kind of communication, each form of humour will be understood and enjoyed only if the listener (or looker) is capable of making that final and necessary act of completion.

A joke that nobody sees is not a joke. A joke that one person in a hundred sees is not a joke to the other 99. If the concept of irony is alien to the receiver, he may accept the irony at face value, and so not only miss the point, but interpret the message in a way diametrically opposite to the way the sender of that message had intended. (It would be interesting to know, for example, what proportion of the loyal viewers of *Till Death Us Do Part* accepted Alf Garnett as the long-awaited spokesman for all that was right and shrewd and sensible. And equally interesting to speculate just how much bigger that proportion might have been in the absence of studio laughter.)

Humour, then, has no universal and objective values. It will always be judged individually and subjectively. A man in a top hat slipping on a banana skin may strike almost everybody as fairly funny; but even that primitive incident relies for its humour on some prior knowledge, some prior attitudes, and some ability to contribute on the part of its observers.

Unless the top hat is known to symbolise the upper classes, unless the observer is already against the upper classes, and unless the observer is capable, however subconsciously, of seeing the undignified upending of a single figure as a comment on the fallibility of privilege, then not only will the incident fail to amuse but indeed it is likely to arouse sympathy and concern. (Few people are likely to be amused by the sight of a frail old lady slipping on a banana skin; but it's just possible that her best friend, slightly older but for years made to feel inferior, might.)

However, there is one characteristic that all forms of humour seem to share (and indeed without which they would fail to be humorous) and that is their *ability to reveal.* Humour, when it works, makes people think; it makes them see the familiar from an unfamiliar point of view. And it makes people think not only painlessly but pleasurably.

This pleasure comes not just from the revelation itself, but from the self-congratulation that derives from a contribution made. Just as a joke will fail if it asks too much of a recipient, so it will fail if it asks nothing.

If the point is explained, the recipient is denied the chance to participate: and there's no flash-moment of perception and pleasure.

So all humour, however broad and however universally understood, is implicit rather than explicit: an explicit joke is either not explicit or not a joke.

All good comedians, all good storytellers, all good makers of advertisements, entice their receivers into willing and constructive collaboration. It's a skilful, delicate and difficult thing to do – particularly in advertising where the pressures of committees and cost tend to favour the 'explicit', the 'unambiguous', the 'message that just can't fail to be understood'.

But the measure of a good joke is much the same as the measure of a good advertisement (judging it now purely in terms of its communications effectiveness). Has it asked enough, but not too much, of its selected audience? Has it allowed that audience to see something for itself? (Whether, in the case of the advertisement, what the audience comes to see is the most persuasive and relevant thing is clearly another question.) So the principles of humour and the principles of commercial persuasion are very close.

Many years ago, the Ford Motor Company wanted to tell American motorists that they sold more convertibles than did any other automobile manufacturer. They could perfectly well have said: 'America's bestselling convertible.' Instead they ran a headline that read: 'The only convertible that outsells Ford.' And the picture was of a baby-carriage. That is a kind of humour; and it's almost a joke. It certainly depends entirely on a contribution from its audience for the communication to be complete. But the contribution is a small and pleasurable one, well within the capacity of anyone in the market for a car. And what could have been a piece of self-congratulatory manufacturer's so-whattery became engaging evidence of confident leadership. The point had been seen.

In the pursuit of better advertisements, there is probably more to be learned from a study of the anatomy of humour than from any other subject.

When we come to look at the deliberate use of humour in advertising, it is as well to remember this basic similarity of principle. Advertising humour becomes discredited largely because of its misuse, mainly in connection with two great advertising misconceptions.

(1) *Television is an entertainment medium, therefore commercials must entertain.*

Not true, of course: first, television is not an entertainment medium. It's a medium, just as the telephone system is a medium, and twice as versatile. It is no more an entertainment medium than news print is a news medium. It can be used to educate, to carry news, to tell stories.

Second: even if a high proportion of television time is devoted to what sets out to be entertainment, it clearly does not follow that all commercials for all products addressed to all people should also seek to divert. Involve, yes; reward, ideally; entertain, not necessarily.

(2) *This is a low-interest product. Unless we do something funny, they'll go and put the kettle on.*

Any product good enough to be bought, and bought again, is of interest to the people who buy it. (It may, however, be of low interest to the creative people, in which case they should be trained or fired.)

This attitude leads to blind headlines ('Let's intrigue them so they just have to read the copy'), mindless use of borrowed interest ('Why don't we get Mick Jagger?'), and animated spokesmen with funny voices mouthing otherwise conventional copy-points. Such advertising may not bore, but neither will it persuade.

One of the most important and difficult functions of advertising is to show the familiar and the relatively mundane in a new light. Anyone in advertising who backs away from this inconvenient fact and relies instead on irrelevant and dissociated excitement is abdicating from one of his more important responsibilities.

If humour is to be used relevantly and effectively, a distinction should first be made between products bought from housekeeping money and those from pocket money. Most women buying most products from a limited housekeeping budget like to feel they've bought prudently and well. For them, shopping is part of their profession; possibly enjoyable, sometimes sociable, but serious.

There are certain kinds of humour – the clever-clever, the superficial, the transient, the slick, the over-sophisticated – that will, simply through association, begin to make the products themselves seem superficial and cheap. A repeat purchase product, bought out of housekeeping money, runs a considerable risk of losing its reputation for substance and quality if it's consistently promoted in a jokey manner.

This is still more true of proprietary medicines, even those bought for relatively trivial complaints. There can be a kind of seesaw in people's minds: when the fun end goes up, the effectiveness end goes down. That long-running series of highly entertaining commercials for Alka Seltzer in the States, having successfully jolted the product into the twentieth century, must surely, sooner or later, run the risk of sapping the product of its medicinal magic. And when the magic goes, so will the effectiveness of the product.

But there's another kind of humour which, significantly, we tend to call good humour. Far from being superficial, it can manifest a deep understanding of, and affection for, humanity. People are seen to be real people, with frailties and fallibilities and vanities and perversities. This kind of humour has practically universal appeal. It has permanence and substance and warmth. It reaches the heart as well as the head; evokes a smile rather than a laugh. This kind of humour is perfectly in keeping with the nature and function of everyday, housekeeping products.

Some products, though, are bought not from housekeeping money but from pocket money. The purchasers are more likely to be men than women – presumably because women aren't so easily able to give themselves pocket money. And pocket-money spending is an altogether different affair: freer, less regular, less responsible, more impulsive, more fun.

Schweppes, presumably, is a pocket-money product – bought if not by, then at least at the behest of, men. [*Perhaps true in 1971, but clearly no longer.*] And the style and the wit with which Schweppes presents itself to the public again seems true to the nature of the product and the circumstances of its consumption. Humour here, far from debasing the value of the product, is enhancing it; is giving it an extrinsic value that must make life very difficult for its competitors.

If you examine very closely all those very funny American commercials we view with such envy and respect, you'll find that a very high proportion of them are for products bought by or for men, from pocket money. Alternatively, they are for products aimed at a small minority of people. It is tempting, but ill-advised, to try to apply a style of wit and humour that is right and relevant for a pocket-money, minority-audience product to a mass-consumption, housekeeping-money product.

Much more could be written; but perhaps the main points to summarise are the following.

(1) The principles of humour and the principles of making good advertisements are similar: both should 'reveal'.

(2) Communication is most successful when the recipient makes the final contribution himself. Creative skill is needed to ensure that the recipient cannot fail to arrive at the desired conclusion.

(3) Economy is not just brevity but implicitness. And for the recipient to contribute, a degree of implicitness is essential.

(4) Humour will always be assessed individually and subjectively. What is funny to you may be incomprehensible to your target audience: and they are the only ones who matter.

(5) Humour, when used, should spring naturally from the product, or from the need the product is there to satisfy.

(6) Consistent use of irrelevant and superficial humour can call into question the intrinsic worth and quality of a product.

(7) Good humour can be affectionate and kind, and can be evidence of a human and understanding advertiser.

(8) Expensive products are not necessarily serious, nor cheap ones frivolous. It's more important to consider the kind of money with which they are bought: does it come from a restricted weekly housekeeping budget or from discretionary pocket money?

(9) Wit, irony, understatement and allusion may be understood and appreciated by a minority of people. For products designed for those people, such humour can add appreciably to their extrinsic value.

(10) The nature of the humour used must always be true to the nature of the product (or its desired nature) and to the nature of its present and potential users.

Don't shoot the packshot!

It's a pity that packshots are called packshots. The word reminds you what they are but stops you understanding what they do. So the age-old comic debate continues: clients want them in and preferably big; art directors want them small and preferably out. A compromise is reached. The packshot is included: big enough to disrupt the original script or layout (which had excluded it altogether) but too small to be of value. The daily evidence is there in every medium, perhaps most reprehensibly in posters.

There are lots of different kinds of packshot, many of which aren't packshots at all, but they all fulfil one central, priceless function. As David Ogilvy wrote 45 years ago, every exposure of every good advertisement makes an important if often immeasurable contribution to the competitive personality of the brand it features. Over time, these tiny, cumulative contributions can hugely enhance the distinction of the brand – but only if they are stored. And where they like to be stored is in some constant, visual symbol. It may be the pack itself; it may be a logo or an emblem (Michelin man or Andrex puppy); it may be consistent typography (Lloyds Bank, Tiffany's, Volkswagen); it may be the Rolls-Royce radiator. Occasionally, though rarely, it's not visual at all but a snatch of music or a distinctive voice.

Whatever the form, the purpose is common: to act as a receptacle for the brand's values; to be a rechargeable dry-cell battery which – like any battery – does two things. It accepts and holds a charge; and it releases that charge on demand. Again like any battery, its physical state is one of natural decay: it can't be left for long without recharging.

All new symbols start empty. Over time, and in the hands of skilful brand management, they take on meanings, values and associations – absorbed, cumulatively, from the contexts in which they appear. A fully-charged brand symbol, in the flicker of an eye, can re-transmit brand values that may have taken years to foster. And the advertising in which that symbol appears is simultaneously both exposing and recharging it.

None of this has much to do with on-shelf pack recognition. I have heard senior marketing persons speak solemnly of the need to increase the size of the packshot so that the aisle-cruising housewife is more likely to recognise the pack that she's had in her kitchen for the last 15 years. With fans like this, no wonder the packshot is held in such contempt by equally senior agency people.

Packshots are mugshots: they're the face of the brand. They're flags, they're football strip, they're anthems. When we see them, all the good feelings we've accumulated in our minds are instantly refreshed and released.

The best advertising for repeat-purchase brands works both immediately and over time. It both generates extra sales and, at least as importantly, keeps the brand's batteries perpetually charged.

To leave out a packshot is to condemn each advertisement to remain just that: a single, discrete and transitory ad. It will never play a bigger, longer role. It will never repay its cost. It will never be part of advertising.

The value of saying nothing

If you want to make sure that you never become President of D&AD…
if you're longing to be expelled from the Groucho…if you'd like to rule
yourself out as a candidate for all fifth-wave, cutting-edge, total-commu-
nications idea-incubators…here's all you have to do. Speak well of the
jingle.

Among sophisticated advertising practitioners, the jingle's been out
ever since it was first in. As long ago as 1960, it was my curled, dismissive habit to remark: 'If you've got nothing to say, sing it.' I don't know
who first coined the phrase – it was certainly not me – but I thought it
wonderfully wise and witty. Furthermore, David Ogilvy agreed with me:
good salesmen don't sing.

But now I wonder. It's now generally acknowledged that there are
some brands, in some markets, that have absolutely no need to find
'something to say' – at least in the literal, verbal, competitive sense.
Account planners, to their intense relief, no longer need to test our
credulity by identifying the unique functional properties of the latest
caramel countline.

A great many brands, at the competitive margin, are much less valued
for what they do than for who they are. You may debate what Nike actually does; but what makes Nike powerful is who it is. Try to put it into
words if you like; but you'll fail. That swoosh encapsulates and
represents a character, an attitude and a celebrity in a way that lame and
lumbering words could never hope to equal.

Poets Laureate (even the good ones) consistently fail to find adequate
words to mark work-a-day royal occasions. They always will. We should
put them out of their misery, and (if we really still need to commemorate

the birth of royal infants) instead commission original works from painters and composers.

Symbols and music share this huge advantage over words: you can't look them up in a dictionary. They can mean what you want them to mean – even if you can't begin to articulate it. Their effect is subjective, impressionistic, pervasive. And because, in a literal sense, their meaning is undefined, they are impervious to competitive challenge.

This much is known and agreed about symbols. So why have advertising agencies been so iffy about music? How can the very people whose formative years were defined by sound, who've personally experienced the potency of cheap music, who know from their own movie-going how an inspired music track can make predictable images sublime: how can these same people be so miserly and unimaginative in their use of music in advertising?

Well, you know the answer as well as I do. It's the word that's wrong, innit? No self-respecting, red-blooded, mould-breaking creative is going to put reputation at risk by suggesting something called a jingle. Jingle means Pepsodent and Murray Mints and Shake'n'Vac and terminal loss of self-respect.

But what about Brand Songs? Or Brand Hymns? Or even Sonic Brand Triggers for those who like to talk posh.

Non-functional, non-verbal brand discriminators are already worth as much as any secret ingredient – and their patents never lapse. A unique brand sound, instantly expressing the brand's rich essence, soaring effortlessly over frontiers of age and language, and even binding together all those tiresomely fragmenting media, could soon be the most prized of all a brand's properties.

When doing a little is better than doing a lot

Not all marketing people understand the difference between doing nothing and leaving well alone. As a result, doing something is perceived as good, doing nothing is perceived as bad and doing lots is a lot better than doing a little.

The only corrective may be a vast new annual marketing ceremony at which the Leaving Well Alone Awards would be presented.

The winners would have to demonstrate that, faced with a range of irresistible opportunities – a new all-the-family positioning, seven new flavours including elderflower, a new, squeezable dispenser, distribution on cross-channel ferries, a joint venture with Alton Towers, tailor-made packaging for theme pubs and a brand stretching extension into first-time mortgages – they not only decided to do absolutely nothing; they prospered.

It may usually be better to do something than nothing, but it isn't always. For a company to be very well known for doing one thing superlatively well – and to keep it that way – is a significant achievement; and it used to be enough to satisfy companies when companies were run by their owners.

But companies – and brands – are now run by passing traffic; and passing traffic wants to make its mark before passing on. Building up a formidable reputation for doing nothing is no way for thrusting young marketing executives to get on to headhunters' shortlists.

So a year's brand activity that does not include the introduction of five new variants and a change of pack design becomes evidence of sloth. And, as every marketing document makes clear, what is needed in today's cut-throat marketplace is not sloth but aggression. (It was once enough to get your prices right. Today, you must commit yourself to an aggressive pricing policy.)

It would be both informative and hugely entertaining were a major marketing company to conduct a five-year brand experiment: frenetic activity in 75 per cent of the country; and Leaving Well Alone in the remainder. At the end of that time, I wonder, what would we find? What differences in share, in volume, in margin, and in costs? Not many executives would have enhanced their personal career prospects; but I suspect the brand would be at least as healthy in the Special Area of Diminished Marketing.

Leaving well alone does not, of course, mean doing nothing. Leaving well alone means being so sure of the nature of your particular patch, and re-investing in it so assiduously, that it remains impregnable to marauders. It means continuously strengthening the core values of your brand rather than diluting them through volume-driven peripheries.

For many years, there's been an admirably single-minded petshop on 3rd Avenue in New York called *Doggie-Do*. But I noticed last month that it's now called *Doggie-Do (and Pussycats, too!)*.

So far, perhaps, so good. But the moment Doggie-Do gets into gold-fish, house-plants and humidifiers is the time that you and I should think of opening up a specialist dog-shop on 3rd Avenue.

Never use irony in Chicago

Prompted first by Marshall McLuhan and later infamously championed by Theodore Levitt, globalism (terrible word) started to get the marketing and advertising worlds over-excited in the mid-1970s. In its more extreme interpretations, global marketing was alleged to mean that you could now sell the same products in the same way all over the world. Levitt once claimed that the needs and wants of the world's consumers had become 'irrevocably homogenized'. It was always absolutely apparent that this was not the case but people in marketing – particularly people in multinational companies – are curiously afraid to challenge new wisdoms. To question globalism was to run the risk of seeming out of touch and parochial. Besides, most large companies were attempting to expand internationally and to have global ambitions made them feel good. The nearest the world has yet come to a truly global product is probably Coca-Cola, which to this day is beyond the reach of more than half the world's population. Though globalism is now to a large extent discredited, the word 'global' continues to be freely used. It should be interpreted as meaning 'in as many as two other countries apart from its country of origin'. The following piece appeared in Commercials *13 years after the events it describes, to coincide with the 1989 Screen Advertising Film Festival in Cannes.*

It was in 1976 that Chicago first discovered the rest of the world. Every year, Advertising Age *organises its well-attended Advertising Workshop and in 1976 it decided to devote it to the sexy new phenomenon of global communications.*

The people from Advertising Age *got in touch with J. Walter Thompson in New York – just who they talked to I never discovered, but I'd still like to know – and asked if the agency would take part. All they wanted was a three-hour presentation with examples of international advertising in all media, from all over the world, accompanied by definitive views and conclusions.*

J. Walter Thompson New York, anxious as ever to oblige an influential trade paper, said of course, only too pleased, no problem, thank you for thinking of us.

There was then a gap of some weeks while J. Walter Thompson NY glowed in the gratitude that had beamed its way from Chicago. Advertising Age *then wrote asking for details of the presentation: title, names of the participants and so on. They were, they explained, finalising their first mailing shot. For the first time, J. Walter Thompson NY realised that, in agreeing to undertake the presentation, they had not actually completed their obligation.*

It's a well-established fact that the word 'international' is a synonym for foreign. What Advertising Age *wanted, therefore, was a presentation about foreign advertising. It followed that it would be quite wrong (so went the reasoning) for J. Walter Thompson US to undertake the task of putting together a three-hour presentation of foreign advertising in all media within two months. Quite improper. But they had, they remembered handily, some foreign branches.*

It was then that I got the telephone call to say that my name had been enthusiastically accepted by the Advertising Age *organisers as the team leader and would I please let them (J. Walter Thompson US) know if there was anything at all they could do to help, such as make hotel reservations? In the meantime, good luck and goodbye.*

When I got the mailer from Advertising Age, *it spoke excitedly about the new tidal wave of globalism. It told me that ideas were now crossing national frontiers with the speed of jet planes and that the needs and wants of the world's citizens were now irrevocably homogenised and a lot more stuff along similar lines.*

The mailer then went on to say that the J. Walter Thompson presentation would illustrate the truth of all this, which I noted with interest since I'd never been sold on its existence let alone its value.

Having had the project so deftly delegated to me, it was clear that I needed to do a bit of the same. So I recruited my J. Walter Thompson equivalents from four other cities: George from Frankfurt, Bob from Toronto, Tony from Sydney and (confusingly) Hans from São Paulo. In itself, this was a good idea. What I suggested we did, however, was not.

Whenever I had visited other J. Walter Thompson offices around the world and been shown their work, I had been struck by one recurring comment. Whoever was introducing the work would say: 'Now this next one's probably not going to mean a great deal to you because you won't know that our most popular national leisure activity is earwig racing and this commercial uses the language of earwig racing to imply that only Bard's beer makes you virile though of course in this country you aren't allowed actually to show the beer which is why we use this famous comedian who you won't recognise because unfortunately he's unknown outside this country but the catchphrase he uses is as good as saying Bard's to most people because of a sponsorship programme he did for them five years ago. Anyway, see what you think. It's been amazingly successful and since it started sales have gone up by nearly 26 per cent…'.

And sure enough, I'd look at the commercial and it wouldn't mean anything to me at all. But I did believe the sales figures so I had to believe that what I'd just looked at was a piece of successful advertising.

I also believed them because whenever, in turn, I was showing the London reel to visitors I would find myself saying, 'Now this next one's probably not going to mean a great deal to you…'. (Have you ever tried to explain the nature and appeal of mushy peas to a Californian?)

Convinced, therefore, that much of the world's most original and effective advertising was quite incomprehensible except to those to whom it was addressed, I encouraged George, Bob, Tony and Hans to bring with them as many examples of obscure and effective national advertising as they could find. At the same time, I asked them to bring examples of equally effective work that they believed could be understood just about anywhere.

We all pitched up at the Conrad Hilton in Chicago. The Conrad Hilton in Chicago is the world's friendliest hotel. I know this because it says so outside in 30-foot-high neon lettering.

There were just four days to go before the presentation and we had nothing written down. We had several hundred commercials, but no idea which we were going to use, let alone in what order — so they were all still on their separate 16mm spools. We worked in a large room which had been set up by an immensely helpful crew from J. Walter Thompson Chicago as editing suite, viewing room, typing pool and fast-food joint.

Each of us started by showing the others the work we'd brought with us, and at almost every turn we found ourselves saying, 'Now this next one probably won't mean a great deal to you, but in my country…'.

We then assembled the best of these into an obscure/national reel and started to write a linking commentary. This consisted mostly of finding different ways of saying, 'Now this next one probably won't…but in Germany/Japan/Yorkshire/New South Wales it's long been a tradition that…'.

We then assembled the commercials which, we all agreed, did communicate readily to all of us, with little or no explanatory introduction. Hardly surprisingly, we discovered that they all set out to appeal to what we chose to call global tribes – a word we came to prefer to target groups.

An advertiser offering beauty to women, or rebellion to teenagers, or masculinity to smokers, or luxury to business travellers, could successfully use common stimuli to evoke universal responses: as long, of course, as those stimuli were universally and consistently recognised.

We were reminded that many of the (relatively few) global campaigns owed much of their universality to the common denominator of the movies. Very few people, even Americans, had ever seen a real cowboy: Marlboro's campaign could never have travelled if the Western hadn't been there first.

So we divided our presentation into an examination of different tribes. We found tribes which contained members from all countries, and tribes which contained members from only one country. We also found tribes which contained members from only one region. And we found, hardly surprisingly, that the advertising that worked best was that which understood those tribes best.

I then wrote the introduction. Into eight minutes, I packed every cliché I could retrieve about the new globalism. I raided McCluhan and Levitt and Advertising Age *itself. I talked about the world getting smaller and ideas crossing frontiers with the speed of jet planes, and the aspirations of the housewife in Nicaragua being identical to those of her counterparts in The Netherlands and the electronic village and new universalisms of communications.*

And to demonstrate the validity of what I was saying, I showed a very recent commercial from Great Britain. In Welsh.

This idea was not too clever by half. It was not clever at all. Nobody understood it. Irony is a dangerous game at the best of times. On a hot August day in Chicago, I'm now in a position to tell you, it is terminal.

As I discovered later, it was at this point that one of the journalists left the room, never to return. He later wrote an appreciative report of the full three hours which was headlined: 'World Growing Smaller Says JWT Staffer.'

Do not believe the old saying that good advertising speaks for itself. Good advertising speaks for itself only to those for whom it is intended. Much good advertising speaks quite deliberately in code, or uses a secret language, and excludes the rest of us. That's one of the reasons why it's good.

Being exposed to things you don't understand is very bad for the self-esteem. For many hours, we showed that Chicago audience things they didn't understand, having told them beforehand that they weren't going to understand them, and then explaining to them afterwards why they hadn't. They didn't warm to us.

About the only piece of work they did understand was the Australian commercial which showed a dog called Kevin peeing on the wheel of a Leyland truck.

The radio version went: 'Kevin may have done it on a Leyland truck but Kevin never done it on me.' When I say they understood it, I suppose I mean that they understood what *was happening rather than why it was happening. I don't think any of us understood that.*

Around this time of the year, international juries drawn from the outstanding advertising talent of all nations gather in darkened screening rooms to pass judgment on thousands of other people's commercials.

There's nobody there to say to them: 'Now this next one probably won't mean much to you but in my country…'. Sometimes there's a synopsis: 'In this scenario the goblin robs the children of their porridge. A light-hearted tune punches home the sales message.' Synopses are not always of great value.

How can these juries, however well intentioned, understand commercials that were cunningly devised to be generally incomprehensible? Of course they can't – and sensible national agencies won't have entered them.

If they are wise, they will enter just that work which genuinely does speak for itself – to everyone. You've only got to sit in the Cannes cinema on the final night to know that such work exists. Within a split second of the end of a commercial, there's a sharp crack of applause from absolutely everybody present – irrespective of age or nationality.

Something has worked for all of them, instantly – and that something, of course, is a universal something. All round the world, dogs pee on truck wheels. All round the world, children fart in baths. It is far more often visual demonstration than verbal assertion.

The commercials that are recognised by international juries almost by definition deserve to be: they've proved that they can communicate immediately with many different people from many different countries. What an international jury can never be expected to do is recognise a piece of work it doesn't understand – particularly one that hasn't been entered in the first place.

As the global gospellers begin to sound ever less persuasive, it is the coded tribal messages we should increasingly look at with respect.

Part Three

Understanding brands

Elastic brands

As the cost and risk of launching orphan brands continue to increase (see'
What sort of family does this Jaffa Cake come from?' page 102), so does the
attraction of stretching the authority of existing brands. Since the piece
appeared, Prudential has retreated from estate agency and Wilkinson is into
skincare. The article prompted a telephone call from the secretary of the
managing director of Jockey Ltd who wanted to know what size underpants
I wore. It turned out that Y-Front is one of their registered trade marks and not
available at Marks & Spencer. I'm happy to make this clear.

*There is also the possibility that M&S, which has had shaky
success in North America so far, will nudge its own products into
Brooks Brothers stores. (The Times, 3/5/88)*

Good morning, sir. May I help you?

*Thank you. I would like one button-down cotton Oxford, size
15–33, in the solid blue; one pair of cordavan loafers, size 8E; and
two cod-and-prawn fishcakes suitable for the microwave.*

With pleasure, sir. Charge or cash?

Just how far a brand reputation can be stretched without diluting the
value of the original is one of the constantly fascinating debates in marketing. Cadbury's must have thought hard before it gave its name to milk
powder; and even harder before going into instant mashed potato. Mars
is surely right to use Pedigree for its petfoods. I haven't yet got used to

Prudential as an estate agent, though that may be the fault of the boss-eyed cherokee.

Dunhill was clever to recognise that a reputation for classy cigarettes and lighters could be extended beyond smoking into classiness generally. It was a lot more logical to go from tobacco to tailoring than it would have been to launch a Dunhill roll-your-own.

Retailers' names have much greater elasticity than those of manufacturers: presumably because their skill is known to lie in selection rather than in making. Wilkinson Sword could go from secateurs to razor blades to (just) shaving cream. But not, I think, to aftershave to eau de toilette to challenging Poison. Harrods could, and does, stock the lot – and so could Boots.

Many people are so acutely conscious of the risks involved in attempts to (as we say in marketing) optimise a brand franchise, that timidity sets in. Parker Pen, at least in this country, agonised for some years before deciding to market a ballpoint; and even then it was called not a ballpoint but a ballpen to distinguish it (a subtlety lost on the public) from the Bics and the Biros. Parker's hesitation was prudent. All ballpoints at the time were cheap, plastic and disposable, and Parker was selling not writing instruments but expensive and lasting gifts. Until recently, cheques signed with anything other than a fountain pen had been invalid. In the event, it was in part the authority of the Parker name that brought respectability to the entire category.

The best way I know to test such timidity is to play a game christened, if not invented, by Doug Richardson. It's called Brandicide and its rules are so self-evident that I'll explain them to you.

Take any powerful brand – and mentally extend its name to a new venture of such a kind that the parent's brand values are not just diluted but killed outright. It's not as easy as it seems. After Eight Chewing Gum seemed a likely starter, but on reflection it seemed that the Parker effect might come into play and legitimise the sector: an adult, sophisticated chewing gum is not an impossibility. But After Eight Bubble Gum is another matter. Brandicide has been committed.

For an instant, the paragraph from *The Times* (above) conjured up the vision of a double death: two duellists killing one another simultaneously. Mariner's Bake and Madison Avenue: the immediate extinction of both Brooks Brothers and St Michael. But I expect all they had in mind was Y-Fronts.

The clipboard and the copywriter – and why the uncalculable can be of incalculable value

Many years ago, when cost accounting and efficiency experts were enjoying disproportionate popularity, a man with a clipboard interviewed an advertising agency copywriter.

'Tell me,' said the clipboard, pencil poised, 'How long does it take to write a 30-second commercial?'

The copywriter, a seasoned survivor of difficult client meetings, didn't hesitate.

'Two hours and 23 minutes,' he replied.

The expert nodded, made a note and moved on. He later counted up the number of commercials written by the agency in the course of a year, multiplied the figure by two hours and 23 minutes, divided the total by the number of copywriters on the payroll: and concluded in his written report that 48 per cent of them were surplus to requirements.

He may well, of course, have been right – but if so, through chance rather than calculation.

The book that you now hold in your hand, the WPP Group annual report and accounts for the year 2000, contains approximately 7,500 numbers. They attempt to do far more than comply with the company's legal and fiduciary obligations. They strive to convey, with forensic accuracy, the anatomy of the business that its shareholders own; its scope; its competitive performance; its 80-plus component parts; and all this broken down by region and discipline.

Essay from the WPP Group plc Annual Report and Accounts published in 2001

It is absolutely no criticism of these figures, nor of those who pain-stakingly compiled and audited them, to say that, while they accurately quantify the bone-structure of the company, they fail almost completely to evoke its essential character.

Of course we need numbers. Without numbers, incoherence reigns, progress goes uncharted, comparisons become impossible and a company's value is literally incalculable. The danger of numbers is not that they exist but that we become mesmerised by them; that we come to believe that the importance of things is directly related to their susceptibility to measurement.

In his book *The Tyranny of Numbers*,[1] David Boyle quotes the economist Robert Chambers:

> *Quantification brings credibility. But figures and tables can deceive, and numbers construct their own realities. What can be measured and manipulated statistically is then not only seen as real; it comes to be seen as the only or the whole reality. And Chambers summed it all up like this:*
>
> *'Economists have come to feel*
> *What can't be measured isn't real.*
> *The truth is always an amount –*
> *Count numbers; only numbers count.'*

Coming to feel that only numbers count is seductive. Numbers seem so safe and scientific. Numbers protect us from making subjective judgments that may be open to challenge. Numbers are like security blankets. But in our heart of hearts, we already know that not everything that matters can be quantified: so we look for ways to measure the immeasurable. In certain competitive sports, judges ascribe a score to something called artistic excellence. You might as well mark a Monet out of ten.

We look, in other words – however uneasily – for ways to quantify quality. Today there are numbers being attached to ethical behaviour and corporate citizenship. It's probably better than ignoring them altogether, but the numbers are not true numbers, like the number of metres in a kilometre; they are metaphors disguised as measurement.

In our lives as citizens and consumers, we are far less reluctant to make judgments. When we choose a car, we may calculate the amount of

---

1   *The Tyranny of Numbers*, David Boyle, HarperCollins, 2000

baggage space we need, the future cost of fuel, our projected annual mileage, our disposable income; but crucially, and often critically, we also respond to style, design, personality and how they contribute to our own self-image: immeasurable factors, every one of them. Perhaps the most important decision we ever make is who we marry; but only if we prudently elect to marry for money does any element of quantification enter into our decision-making process.

The way we choose brands baffles many commentators. The whole of Naomi Klein's bestselling book *No Logo*[2] is predicated on the assumption that brands are imposed on people by the brand owners. The first paragraph of her first chapter reads:

> *The astronomical growth in the wealth and cultural influence of multinational corporations over the last fifteen years can arguably be traced back to a single, seemingly innocuous idea developed by management theorists in the mid-1980s: that successful corporations must primarily produce brands, as opposed to products.*

(That 'seemingly innocuous' is a nice touch.)

But you can't, of course, produce a successful brand without producing a good product first. And a successful brand, of course, exists because people want it to exist. People differentiate between objects, people, animals instinctively and voluntarily – and rarely on a totally rational basis. People invented brand values in their own heads centuries before the first management theorist dared to try and classify them. Entities that can't be said to market themselves in any conventional sense are perceived by their supporters and detractors to have clear brand characteristics: newspapers, political parties, football teams, schools and universities.

The human brain performs an astonishing act of computing when it does something as apparently simple as choosing a brand of petfood. It takes into account the quantifiable: price, availability, pack size, ingredient list; and the totally immeasurable: style, character, familiarity and a wild projection of the animal's personality. When making brand choices, the human brain has no trouble at all in reconciling the measurable and the immeasurable, the rational and the irrational, quantity and quality. It understands that even price is not a simple matter of low = good,

---

2   *No Logo*, Naomi Klein, Flamingo, 2000

high = bad. To the despair of rationalists, a high price may be seen as evidence of greater quality and therefore greater worth.

(When that very same brain is invited to explain to a researcher the reason for its choice, it should come as no surprise that the brain will favour the rational over the irrational, the quantifiable over the emotional. As we've noted before, numbers, with their beguiling precision, provide a much more respectable justification for behaviour than woolly old subjective affection.)

It may be doing her an injustice, but there seems to be a distinct note of disappointment in Naomi Klein's voice when she recounts the events of Marlboro Friday and its aftermath. According to Klein, the decision of Philip Morris to cut the price of its brand by 20 per cent sent the pundits nuts – 'announcing in frenzied unison that not only was Marlboro dead, all brand names were dead'. Surely the day of the brand – of all brands – was over? Surely 'the whole concept of branding had lost its currency'? 'Study after study showed that baby boomers, blind to the alluring images of advertising and deaf to the empty promises of celebrity spokesperson, were breaking their lifelong brand loyalties and choosing to feed their families with private-label brands from the supermarket'. After all, she reminds us, 'Marlboro had always sold itself on the strength of its iconic image marketing, not on anything so prosaic as its price.'

In fact, as it happened, not all the pundits were in unison. The saner ones knew perfectly well what consumers have always known: that value and price are not synonymous; that value is an individual and subjective equation, of which price is only part; and if price is perceived to outweigh desirability, then any sense of value goes into steep decline.

Even in times of recession, when the concept of value is most likely to tilt in favour of the rational, it is hard to find examples, in any developed market, where the brand leader by volume is also the cheapest.

Marlboro quite simply modified its recipe of appeals; and today prospers.

So we are faced with a bit of a conundrum. In our private lives as real people, choosing things and getting married and deciding which vacation to take, we confidently embrace both the functional and the emotional; that which we can measure and that which we can't.

But when we come to business – to the business of making money (quantifiable), gaining brand share (quantifiable), building margins (quantifiable), maximising shareholder value (quantifiable) – we seem to lose our nerve a bit.

As long ago as 1965, David Ogilvy wrote: 'The majority of business-men are incapable of original thought because they are unable to escape from the tyranny of reason.' Yet these same people, in their personal lives, shuck off the tyranny of reason on a daily basis.

In other words, it seems that those who buy brands have a more instinctive sense of worth and value than those who provide them: even when they're the same people.

The reason, of course, is the inevitable business need to argue a case, to gain support, to attract investment from a finite source. We reach, because we have to, for numbers. And we really do have to. Imagine a business plan which read in full: 'When I look at this design, my heart fills with wonder and my soul soars. Please grant me $2bn to build a prototype.'

For WPP, for its companies and its competitors, numbers are just as necessary: yet their product – that which clients buy – is more often than not unquantifiable.

A 30-second commercial may take two hours and 23 minutes to write; or three weeks; or half an hour. But there will be no correlation between its time of incubation and its value to client.

Nor, indeed, is it possible to put a tape measure on that value to client: either before its exposure or – with any precise certainty – even afterwards.

While it is true that some disciplines find it easier than others to put a reassuring figure on return on investment – direct marketing, for example, may find it easier than public relations – it is in the nature of marketing communications that they will, infuriatingly, remain activities requiring a departure from pure rationality to invent and the application of judgment and subjective instinct to approve and support.

The reason is simple. In the recipe of appeals that any brand offers, the rational ingredients will by and large come from the core product itself: from its performance, its price, its distribution. They will be invent-ed and selected by a rational process. In contrast, the emotional ingredi-ents will by and large come from its communications: its messages, its look, its design, its voice. And the invention of each of these demands, at least in part, an excursion into irrationality; into inspiration and creativ-ity; into a field of fantasy where numbers have no place. Were it to be oth-erwise, they would fail in their appointed task to transform that core product into an object of even greater value to its users.

There is probably no other area of business life that makes such per-sonal demands on business people as the purchase and evaluation of a brand's communications. Deprived of both measurement and precedent (if it's been done before it's probably no good), struggling to find words to describe the non-verbal, buffeted by the winds of passionate advocacy and vehement condemnation, only judgment serves.

We may long for the comfort of the clipboard; but we need the copywriter more.

Never underestimate the critical importance of the trivial

I still treasure a letter I received a couple of years ago from Hillier Parker May & Rowden, estate agents, of Grosvenor Street, W1.

The letter was addressed to Mr Jeremy Bellmore. Nothing very surprising about that: I'm very rarely Bullmore; far more often Bulmer and very, very frequently Bullimore. In New York, I've been Jerry Bullwink. Bellmore was a refreshing variation. The address on the envelope was THOMPSON J WALTER CO LTD – a company, when deciphered, I'd left 12 years earlier. But none of the above would have been in any way remarkable had it not been for the bold (in every sense) announcement of the subject-matter. After an introductory Dear Mr Bellmore, it said:

FIRST IMPRESSIONS COURT

Well, yes, I thought. First impressions certainly do court. And the impression you've made on me so far courts heavily against you. Had it not been for this unfavourable first impression, I might very well have expressed keen interest in the grade II listed building providing 16,000 sq ft of modern air-conditioned office space within three minutes' walk of Reading station which Hillier Parker was thoughtfully offering me on extremely attractive and flexible terms.

In case I'd missed the point of the headline, the first paragraph of the letter spelt it out: 'Projecting the right image in (sic) your business is a must in today's difficult economic climate.' I have (as you can see) given their offer deep thought; and I have still to identify the chain of reason that led Hillier Parker May & Rowden to believe that a Mayfair-based advertising agency might choose to project the right image in itself through occupying 16,000 sq ft of office space within three minutes' walk of Reading station.

I looked out this letter again quite recently, hoping to be reminded exactly how long ago it was sent – but unfortunately I'd thrown away the envelope and the letter itself simply says Date as Postmark. Second impressions court, too.

Last week I got another letter, also undated. This one started: 'Dear John, It is no coincidence that world-class companies are world-class communicators.' True, very true; which neatly explains why the business communications specialists who sent me the letter, despite having a stand at this year's CiPD exhibition in Harrogate, are not a world-class company.

Most competitive businesses continue to behave as if trivial matters of detail are trivial matters. They are not. Tiny instances of ineptitude can provide all the evidence we need that the largest of enterprises is comprehensively incompetent. Faced as we are, in almost every decision we make, with multiple options, we seize upon reasons for rejection just as avidly as reasons for preference. It may be wholly irrational of us to resist the overtures of a mighty financial concern simply because of a single unhappy encounter with its call centre: but that's our right and we will increasingly exercise it.

The first time you walk into another company's reception, your eyes are supernaturally observant. You will note every smallest detail, from the hairstyle of the receptionist, to the selection of magazines on offer, to the state of the flowers. If there are discarded polystyrene coffee cups still on the side table, you will not only notice them but draw from them disproportionate conclusions.

But familiarity breeds a kind of blindness. You walk into your own reception maybe 20 times a week and notice nothing; quite forgetting that to others – applicants, perhaps, or potential clients – that untidy pile of video tapes and that temperamental clock of yours will be seized upon, in the absence of any deeper knowledge, as evidence of the kind of company you are.

Not only are most business letters written by people who can't write; they're written by people who can't read. They never seem to pause for a moment and ask themselves: how will this letter seem to the *reader*? What will it be like to open and receive? Just as they never ask themselves: how will my reception area seem to the first time visitor?

Hillier Parker were right to remind me: first impressions court. And, just as the smallest gravy stain on the corner of a menu can cause you to doubt the chef's career credentials, so that only-very-slightly unpolished name plate can incline you to choose another solicitor. Or, as it might be, estate agent.

So much is obvious, if often neglected. There's much more fun to be had in inventing apparently trivial things that can have an equally disproportionate but positive effect.

I know of one client who stayed loyal to his agency through thick and thin largely because the receptionist always had change for his parking meter. Don't mock. To him, this was more than casual convenience: it was evidence that his agency could successfully put themselves in his shoes; could look at life through his eyes; *was on his side.*

Any good supermarket throws away the outside leaves of lettuces before putting them on display. Only one supermarket that I know of puts the discarded leaves in plastic bags, calls them BunnyBags and gives them away free. Any child with a rabbit hutch at home will be a loyal customer of that supermarket for the next 40 years or so.

A while ago I was taken to lunch in the Connaught dining-room by a friend not noted for extravagance in his entertaining. I expressed my pleasure – and my mild surprise. He told me that, several years earlier, on his own first visit to the Connaught, his host, having forgotten his reading glasses, was peering distractedly at the wine list. No word was spoken; but within a minute, a waiter appeared at his elbow with a velvet-lined tray on which, neatly aligned in slots, were displayed ten pairs of reading glasses of different levels of magnification.

It cost, perhaps, £200; a trivial sum. But what that tray delivered was not just a pair of spectacles; it delivered hard and symbolic evidence of meticulous thoughtfulness, of immaculate innkeeping. I do not know how many Connaught regulars have found their loyalty cemented by that trivial tray – I have since heard of two more – but few £200 investments can have earned a more satisfactory return. And, please note, it was not my friend who even needed the glasses.

First impressions court, OK: and there's little more important than the detail.

Would Odorono smell as sweet by any other name?

Madonna is calling her daughter Lourdes. Perhaps she hopes that, as a result, her daughter will command respectful attention throughout her life. If so, she'll be disappointed. In common with a lot of other people, Madonna seems to be ignoring the unequivocal lessons of Odorono and the Earls Court Road.

New brand names come in two broad categories: full names and empty names.

Full names are favoured because they come furnished with ready-made relevant connotations: either descriptive or emotive. Ready-Brek, Band-Aid, Oven Pad and I Can't Believe It's Not Butter are all descriptive; Phileas Fogg, Fisherman's Friend, Golden Churn and Legendary Harley Davidson are emotive. So is Lourdes. Empty names are favoured because they are sterilised and virus-free. Since they come with no baggage, they carry no undesirable overtones and can also be more easily registered in today's obligatory 293 countries. Ariel, Andrex, Kodak, Zantac were all, once, empty names. (They may have explicable origins, like Tesco and Amstrad, but no instant significance.) Numerals as names are just about as empty as you can get.

But once a brand is established, these pre-natal distinctions very rapidly disappear. Empty names, for good or ill, begin to fill up. They absorb the brand's values and begin to represent them. And full names show an even more disturbing tendency. Much to their godparents' dismay, the original carefully chosen, rigorously researched emotional associations are ruthlessly replaced with associations the brand actually deserves. They are rarely the same.

One of the most socially desirable residential areas in London should be the Earls Court Road. (If Earls Court Road had an apostrophe, where would it be? Is it the road where one Earl lives or dozens? And which, I wonder, would make it the smarter?) But its take-aways and bed-sits and kangaroo valley immigrants have re-colonised the name completely. Earls Court would not, now, be a good name for a new premium-priced aftershave.

New, earned meanings can invade the emptiest of names. Just say XJ or XK to a serious car person and watch the pupils dilate. (Then say C5 and watch them glaze over again.) It took me 50 years to realise that the long-established deodorant had been hoping to get us to think 'Odor? O, no!' It can only be good news for the brand that we don't.

As names, whether initially empty or initially full, simply come to stand for earned brand values, those carefully contrived double meanings get completely lost along the way. In the end, it is context, and only context, that counts. Drive half a mile south from Earls Court and you get to Chelsea. What does Chelsea mean?

Chelsea means the King's Road and swinging London. Chelsea means Stamford Bridge. Chelsea means the President's daughter. Chelsea means pensioners. Chelsea means the flower show. Chelsea means the Chelsea Arts Ball. Chelsea means buns. Context tells us which is which. There's no overlap and, astonishingly, no confusion.

Whatever daughter Lourdes turns out to be like, that's what her name will come to mean; as it would had she been called Winifred or Trixie-Belle. (But not, I grant you, had she been called Odorono.)

What sort of family does this Jaffa Cake come from?

An edited version of a speech given to the British Direct Marketing Association in May 1985. Eighteen years on, direct marketing has grown in size and salience – becoming relationship marketing and one-to-one marketing in the process – and the recognition of the value of the corporate brand has also increased. But I see little sign of corporate values being built more commonly into direct marketing campaigns. Since most experts agree that the key to success in future direct marketing – and particularly in electronic commerce – will be the establishment of trust, I find this strange.

I want to take this opportunity to focus on one element of marketing, advertising and business strategy, which we all know about and in my view neglect. It applies to conventional marketing through retailers; to the marketing *of* retailers; and, I'd suggest, at least as much to direct marketing.

To make this single point, I want to call as witnesses the Oxford University Press, the coffee spoons at Langan's, Len Heath's new car, a pile of underpants in a street market, the Sinclair C5, Lexington Avenue, the instant custard market, Hugh Johnson, the Bank of Kuwait and high rents in Harley Street.

I'm sure I've already made my point.

On Tuesday of this week I was given lunch at Langan's. My host and I had apparently identical coffee spoons. But when we looked at their backs – and I've no idea why we looked at their backs – his said 'Made in Japan' and mine said 'Made in Taiwan'. His suddenly seemed the better coffee spoon.

Len Heath once sold his share of an advertising agency and bought an Aston Martin. He told me he'd chosen an Aston Martin because of an advertisement he'd read. 'Fancy that,' I said. 'But the point is,' Len said, 'I saw that advertisement when I was 14.'

I was once at an open-air market on a Saturday morning in the north of England. From one stall, a large pile of gents' underpants was selling briskly. The sign behind them read: 'Genuine Marks & Spencers Rejects!'

The cheapest mortgage you could obtain last week, by one-quarter of one per cent, was from the Bank of Kuwait.

My own company's offices in New York are at 466 Lexington Avenue. The owners obtained access to the west, so the building could legitimately be called the Park Avenue Atrium.

All these trivial facts have one thing in common: they illustrate, in one way or another, that *source, parentage, heritage* can and do significantly affect our perceptions of value – up or down. There may or may not be logic or justice in this truth: but truth it is.

The first instant custard to be launched in this country came from Brown & Poulson. It was very successful until the second instant custard came along, from Batchelors. Which was very successful until the third instant custard came along, from Birds. And Birds wiped the floor with both of them.

Where things – objects or services – *come from* matters to us all.

Until very recently, anything from Sinclair was looked at with optimistic respect. I hate to think what the reception of the C5 has done to the authority of the Sinclair name.

A specialist in Harley Street tells you there's nothing wrong with you and sends you a bill for £500. The same man in Surbiton would have been lucky to get away with £50.

In many of the marketing battles of today, everyone is competing for the same money from the same audience. Retailers are competing with their own suppliers with their own brands. Direct marketers are competing with both, and, of course, with each other. The cry is efficiency. Be a low-cost producer. Enjoy economies of scale, in manufacture and distribution. Pick the right products. Fulfil fast. Price it right. And of course, these are all essential conditions for survival, let alone success.

But, *all other things being equal,* the biggest prizes will go to those marketers, manufacturers or retailers who recognise the value of *source*; who create such a respect for source that people will choose *their* products rather than identical products from an unrespected source or from no source at all.

The balance of power between the retailer's brand and the manufacturer's brand has been analysed and debated at more conferences even than the growth of globalism. But if you come to think of it, retailers have an almost accidental advantage which many of them are now quite consciously exploiting to the full. They are perceived as a source. They are perceived as selectors. They can build a *general* reputation for a very wide range of goods. Marks & Spencer can add its authority to goods that range from fresh foods to gents' underpants. What manufacturer could do that? The greater the reputation they acquire as a source the less dependent they are on the niceties of highly competitive pricing; and the healthier their margins are likely to be.

Some manufacturers have traditionally followed this strategy as well – but a surprising number haven't. Look at your newspapers and magazines and television and you will see that the majority of brands being advertised are still what I will call *orphan brands* – because they appear to have no parents. They have no source. They don't come from anywhere.

Look through the MEAL figures of ten years ago and the MEAL figures for today and you'll find that few of these orphan brands are receiving anything like the same level of media support they once enjoyed. On their own, these lonely brands simply don't justify it.

But do they really have to be on their own? Can you imagine a car manufacturer advertising his models but not even mentioning his company name? If they'd followed that policy, the Ford Motor Company would have died with the Model-T and Len Heath would never have bought his Aston Martin.

Publishers – some of them – understand this simple truth. The current dictionary battle between Penguin and the Oxford University Press is at least as much a battle between *sources* – which is what the publishers are – as it is between the intrinsic quality and price of the two dictionaries. However comprehensive it was, which of us would put serious personal money behind a dictionary from Mills & Boon?

I find readers' offers interesting – because the newspaper is stretching its authority to something totally different from the traditional purpose of a newspaper. But it can work. I'd be much more likely to order a case of wine at £50 from Hugh Johnson's *Sunday Times* Wine Club than I would from PO Box 173, Loughborough.

This failure to enhance corporate, parental, source values concerns me in conventional retail marketing – and it concerns me in direct marketing as well.

I sense that direct marketing is *so* measurable, *so* quantifiable, *so* accountable – and so immediately so – that the opportunity to build longer-term values into the source of the offers is seldom being seized.

I am not, please note, talking about empty corporate advertising. I am not implying that any sacrifice needs to be made in return on media investment behind any particular product. I am not even talking about range advertising or 'umbrella' advertising. I just believe that real people – even including you and me – do like to know where things come from. And in many cases, that familiarity and trust and knowledge can be the one discriminator that turns a near miss into a certain sale.

It is also one of the few factors in marketing that is both wholly within your control and costs nothing.

Had you held precisely this conference, chairman, with precisely this programme on precisely this day – and you'd held it not at the Grosvenor House Hotel but at the Edgware Road Assembly Rooms – I wonder just how many delegates you would have attracted?

Why every brand encounter counts: seductive, anarchic or catastrophic

You read a compelling advertisement for a piece of electrical equipment and you buy it. And then you open the instruction manual.

It is incomprehensible in seven languages.

The advertisement understood the reader; the manual does not. In design and empathy, the brand of the advertisement and the brand of the manual have nothing whatever in common. For the purchaser, those first moments of ownership are crucial. Critical faculties are on full alert; apprehension lurks; reassurance is anxiously awaited. And that's exactly when the dreaded manual strikes.

Not only has a perfect opportunity been lost to confirm new users in the wisdom of their choice, but a perverse and wilful act of brand mutilation has been committed.

For the best part of 50 years now, we've spoken confidently about brand image and brand reputation. Nobody has seriously challenged the view that people hold opinions about products and services that are based on more than function and direct experience. This shared understanding has helped shape and improve all conventional marketing communications: no one much doubts that advertising, direct marketing, promotions, public relations and pack design, among others, can enhance the reputations of competitive enterprises (they don't have to be objects) to the benefit of buyers and sellers both.

Where we've been less assiduous – perhaps because we sense the quest would be such a nightmare – is in trying to identify the less obvious sources of a brand's reputation.

An essay from the WPP Group plc Annual Report and Accounts published in 2000. Slightly edited

Imagine for a moment that it was possible to scan the human brain, isolate the cell that contained that particular brain's opinion of a particular brand – its image – and then trace and log its origins. Not for one second should we expect to see just a few strong, clearly differentiated wires labelled Experience, Advertising, Word-of-Mouth, Presentation. If we successfully traced and identified every encounter that had contributed over time to that brain's view of that brand, the resultant three-dimensional map would be like a huge bowl of multi-coloured spaghetti: too complex, too confusing, too inter-related to be of any immediate value.

But that's no reason for pretending that they don't exist. The non-conventional contributors to brand reputation are already more important than we admit – and every social and technological change is making them more so. With a greater understanding of these less famous brand ingredients, and some canny management, a real opportunity for competitive advantage presents itself; and at virtually no cost.

In surveying the entire range of brand encounters, we can identify two clear and coincident scales: one of simplicity and one of control. The communications we favour – and will rightly continue to favour – are relatively simple both to manage and to monitor.

Advertising, direct marketing, pricing, promotions, public relations, sponsorship, packaging, the brand website, in-store display – all in different ways and at different times affect any single individual's impression of a brand. As marketers, we take them all seriously, pay more than lip-service to the concept of integrated communications and strive hard to see that the signals that each activity sends out are consistent, coherent and complementary.

All these activities, diverse as they are, have much in common. They are all planned, paid for and executed by the brand's owners. Control, of both quantity and content, lies with the company. They are all *transmissions*: broadcast from the company to its consuming public. They are deliberately engineered brand encounters; and, as encounters go, they are seductive in nature. Their primary intention is to court custom. This form of brand communication is at least a thousand years old: as old as the town crier and probably older.

Town crier publicity brings news to the people. It may be difficult to plan and expensive to execute but its value has never been more widely recognised. Demand for all forms grows in real terms, year by year. It will continue to be the basis of reputation for any competitive enterprise, from candy bars at 25c to executive cars at $100,000. It will continue to be the first serious marketing investment made by every internet debutant.

So valuable are these simple, controllable conventional encounters that it is tempting to believe that they are the only contributors to brand reputation and all that efficient brand management entails is sitting high up in the corporate palace monitoring brand transmissions worldwide for relevance and consistency.

But there are other sources – many other sources – from which we as consumers derive our opinion of brands. Some of them are within the control of the company (though not necessarily of brand management); and some of them lie almost completely outside management control and influence. They're getting more numerous and more important with every day that passes – but so fragmented are they, crossing and challenging traditional corporate structures and budgets, that many companies choose not to think about them at all.

So, first, a look at some of those brand encounters that technically lie within the company's control, yet only rarely seem to be consciously directed or monitored. It is as if we believe that only conventional communications will be noted by our public and that all other encounters will be screened out. But no manifestation of a brand is ever ignored; and all will make some contribution, positive or negative, to that brand's reputation.

The ill-conceived and incomprehensible instruction manual is one such example. But there are many other brand encounters that differ from seductive encounters in that they all have a reason for existence other than the courtship of the consumer. It's just such a pity that this primary function so often seems to blind companies to their potential for simultaneous (and free) brand-building.

It is odd how little brand use is made of trucks. Vast travelling billboards, already paid for, thunder up and down the highways being seen by hundreds of thousands of people; yet with little or nothing on their sides to promote or enhance the company or the brand. Can it be, in the corporate structure, that trucks come under transport rather than communications? And who is a transport manager to know about brand values?

The contribution of architecture to corporate brands is widely debated but infrequently practised. At a time when all are agreed that corporate brands need to be as clearly differentiated one from another as repeat-purchase consumer goods, tens of millions can be committed to buildings and internal design without a single reference made to the likely effect on the ultimate customer. It is as if senior management believes that creating a competitive reputation can safely be left to the hired hands in the marketing department and is nothing whatever to do with them.

Financial services companies were slow to understand the need for simple brand distinction – but they're catching up fast. Savings schemes and pension plans are now packaged far more attractively and the language in which they are described is sometimes even coherent. But then you get a letter from head office – and your conclusion is immediate. The presentation was a sham, no more than cosmetic. Behind that glossy package lies a company as bureaucratic, self-obsessed and insensitive as we always knew such companies to be. In its advertising – in its planned, seductive encounters – a large British financial institution makes much of its friendliness. But a recent head office communication from the same company contained the following sentence: 'This is a computer-generated message and therefore has no signature.'

The fury provoked by poorly trained people in call centres and by interminable pass-the-parcel voice-mail systems has been widely reported. But until somebody quantifies the cost of that fury and the damage it does to a company's bottom line, little improvement is likely.

These are wasted opportunities: contacts between brand and brand user which have to happen, which are within the company's control, but because their primary function is other than brand communication, are thought to have no brand effect. The majority of marketing companies do not think of them as media; do not monitor them as media, and therefore make no attempt to integrate them with more conventional media. Their customers, however – their buying public – make no such distinction. And so substantial sums of money, which could have reinforced brand values from unexpected directions, are at best under-utilised and at worst counter-productive. There are many more brand encounters of this kind – all essentially anarchic in nature. By failing to confirm the brand's true spirit, they challenge it, and so brand authority is needlessly diminished.

Even more slippery to deal with, but with even greater future implications, are the chance encounters.

Just as we bump into friends and relations, so we bump into brands. These accidental interfaces are almost completely outside the control or influence of the brand owner – but their effect on the public can be significant. Because they are so disparate and diffuse, chance encounters seldom earn a mention in a communications strategy document. Because they are almost impossible to foresee, control or orchestrate, they tend to be totally ignored.

Here are just a few examples.

A story in the press about racial discrimination at a brand's factory; a meeting with a friend who has a friend who's just been sacked by the company that makes the brand; a crusading website devoted to your company's pay policy in the Middle East; a product recall for safety reasons; a cardboard outer, bearing the brand name, in an untidy corner of a supermarket; dangerous driving by a clearly branded truck; rumoured financial problems at the holding company; a scare story started by an industrial blackmailer; a discarded wrapper in a well-tended park; a widely reported case against the company for sexual discrimination; two cars, of the same make, broken down at the roadside within a mile of each other.

You could add another hundred: the majority trivial, a few potentially catastrophic. Most chance encounters are negative in impact; and every single one of them will have some lasting effect on people's aggregate belief in a brand – and therefore on its success and profitability.

Every change that's taking place today increases both the number and the effect of such unhappy accidents.

Today, to a marked extent, all brands are service brands. Other than street traders, few businesses now see their only function as being simply to make a sale. After-sales service, relationship marketing, the concept of lifetime value, the growth of interactive media: all these trends and developments mean that a few unfortunate chance encounters can poison a consumer's mind forever – and undo the effect of all those seductive encounters so expensively engineered by the marketing department.

The one great certainty about all long-term relationships, of course, is that they go through rocky patches. The maintenance of immaculate service standards is even harder to achieve than the maintenance of product standards. Errors are inevitable. But if chance encounters are really chance, and lie well outside a company's sphere of control, surely that means there is no sensible corrective action the company can take?

But there is. In this new and open commercial world, future prizes will go not just to those who make the fewest errors – but also to those who recover, apologise and make amends most gracefully. There is ample evidence that a brand that takes corrective action quickly and sympathetically will not only be forgiven but may well, as a result, find itself even more thoroughly trusted.

And it is here that the great neglected army of the workforce demands new attention. When nearly all brands are service brands; when it is the people behind the brand who provide the long-term reassurance; when news and information about brands is freely accessible from the internet and elsewhere; and when the gracious correction of inevitable error becomes a competitive necessity: that's when an intelligent, informed and trusted staff can turn even the catastrophic brand encounter into a reinforcement of brand loyalty.

This means opening up the whole marketing strategy to absolutely everyone. It means confiding in them and training them and asking them for constructive suggestions. It means trusting them to respond to customer dissatisfaction both immediately and personally, without cowering behind head office instructions. It means as conscious an application of internal marketing – internal communications – as we give to our external marketing.

Sometimes mesmerised by the new media, we neglect to make full use of the old. Whether seductive, anarchic or catastrophic, the number of brand encounters can only multiply. Each one is an opportunity. But to make the most of them, the function of brand management needs to be radically redefined.

Posh Spice and Persil

In 2001, in the person of John Noble, the British Brands Group invited me to give the second of their Brand Lectures – and it is reproduced below, with few alterations, much as I gave it in December of that year. It was later distributed by BBG in printed form and a few months later reprinted in WPP's Annual Report and Accounts for 2001.

It is the longest single piece in the book. (A speech can be short; a lecture, it seems, is required to last for at least 40 minutes.) For me, it was a bit like that apocryphal exam question: 'Write down everything you know.'

As a result, much of the thought and a few of the examples occur elsewhere in this book. A few instances of duplication have been edited out, but some, necessarily, remain.

> *Right from the beginning, I said I wanted to be more famous than Persil Automatic.*
>
> *Victoria Beckham*[1]

In his British Brands Group inaugural lecture this time last year, Tim Ambler set a depressingly high standard.[2]

He raised a number of critical questions about the nature and value of brands and answered many of them. He left us with one perplexity.

If brands are as important as they are to business – and he left us in absolutely no doubt that they are all-important – why do chief executive officers and their boards devote such a curiously small proportion of their time to their health and nourishment?

---

1   Victoria Beckham, *Learning to Fly, The Autobiography*, Michael Joseph, 2001
2   Tim Ambler , British Brands Group Inaugural Lecture, 2000

With seemly diffidence, I'd like this evening to put forward a possible explanation.

And as a sort of hors d'oeuvre to the main course of my lecture, I offer you these 13 deeply disturbing brand facts.

- Products are made and owned by companies. Brands, on the other hand, are made and owned by people, by the public, by consumers.
- A brand image belongs not to a brand – but to those who have knowledge of that brand.
- The image of a brand is a subjective thing. No two people, however similar, hold precisely the same view of the same brand.
- That highest of all ambitions for many CEOs, a global brand, is therefore a contradiction in terms and an impossibility.
- People come to conclusions about brands as a result of an uncountable number of different stimuli, many of which are way outside the control or even influence of the product's owner.
- Brands – unlike products – are living, organic entities: they change, however imperceptibly, every single day.
- Much of what influences the value of a brand lies in the hands of its competitors.
- The only way to begin to understand the nature of brands is to strive to acquire a facility which only the greatest of novelists possess and which is so rare that it has no name.
- The study of brands – in itself a relatively recent discipline – has generated a level of jargon that not only prompts deserved derision amongst financial directors but also provides some of the most entertaining submissions in Pseuds' Corner.
- It is universally accepted that brands are a company's most valuable asset; yet there is no universally accepted method of measuring that value.
- The only time you can be sure of the value of your brand is just after you've sold it.
- It is becoming more and more apparent that, far from brands being hierarchically inferior to companies, only if companies are managed as brands can they hope to be successful.
- And as if all this were not enough, in one of the most important works about brands published this year, the author says this: 'Above all, I found I had to accept that effective brand communication…involves processes which are uncontrolled, disordered, abstract, intuitive… and

frequently impossible to explain other than with the benefit of hind-sight.'[3]

All of the above, I believe to be fact. For the sake of economy, and to some extent for effect, I have made some half-truths into whole truths and presented them more starkly than perhaps a more conscientious lecturer would have ventured to do.

But all of the above statements are more or less true.

So, in answer to Tim Ambler's implied puzzle – why do CEOs devote so little of their time and intelligence to the care of their most important asset? I advance the following explanation.

Brands are fiendishly complicated, elusive, slippery, half-real/half-virtual things. When CEOs try to think about brands, their brains hurt.

And I sympathise. Given the nature of brands – and the persistent perversity of consumers – who wouldn't choose to concentrate executive time on simple, rational, quantifiable things like gross margins and case rates and return on capital invested?

I believe it to be an increasing human instinct – and an entirely understandable if highly dangerous one – to over-value that which we can measure and to under-value that which we can't. There is a comfort to be found in figures: they give us a sense of certainty, however false, in an otherwise chaotic world.

Perhaps the time will come when the mysteries of brands will be no more; when everything about them can be measured, valued, predicted and replicated. Perhaps. But not in my lifetime; nor even, I think, in yours.

So, with the hors d'oeuvre behind us, my aim for the main course of this lecture will be to explore most of those 13 deeply inconvenient brand facts rather more thoroughly – not to provide answers or solutions but more, I hope, to shine a little light on these murky matters. Thinking about brands should be a productive rather than a painful occupation – and should lead to a greater confidence in taking intuitive decisions. More often than not, such decisions turn out to be gratifyingly simple.

First, my thanks to Victoria Beckham for the title of this lecture.

If her early ambition to be more famous than Persil Automatic seemed to you surprising – or even laughable – it shouldn't have done. It was very astute of the young Posh Spice to choose not Robbie Williams nor

3   Robert Heath, *The Hidden Power of Advertising*, World Adverising Research Center, 2001

Sir Cliff Richard nor Madonna as her benchmark of fame but the country's best-known washing powder.

Because just about the only thing that successful brands have in common is a kind of fame. Indeed, it's been suggested that brands are the real celebrities. And for most human beings, fame not only holds a powerful fascination but bestows an incalculable value on anything that enjoys it. We value the famous far more highly than the little known.

I do not think, as is often suggested, that this is a new phenomenon. Nor do I think, another social theory, that we the public have invented celebrities as a replacement for the vanished aristocracy. Rather, I think that the aristocracy were of interest to us peasants not because they were aristocratic but because they were the most famous people around. We should not assume that everyone who stands in the rain to catch a glimpse of Her Majesty the Queen is a royalist. The Royal Family continue to engage the interest of us peasants at least as much because they are celebrities as because they are royal.

And then, as Andy Warhol so memorably observed, with the arrival of mass media, particularly of course television, fame became technically available to everyone, if only for 15 minutes.

It is one of the peculiarities of fame – whether for people or products – that real fame appears to be spectacularly untargeted. By that I mean, that the most famous people in the world are known to an infinitely greater number of people than their particular talent or profession would seem either to demand or to deserve.

Victoria Beckham is one such example. So is Madonna. Real fame implies being known to millions of people who have never bought your records and never will. Stephen Hawking is known to millions of people who will never understand a word he writes; and to ten times as many who will never even try to.

To the consternation of media planners and buyers in advertising agencies, the same is true for brands. A brand, if it is to enjoy genuine celebrity, must be known to a circle of people that far exceeds what we in the business so chillingly call its target group.

It is not enough for BMW to be known only to that 5 per cent of the population wealthy enough even to contemplate buying one. For BMW to enjoy real fame, it needs to be known almost indiscriminately.

I do not know why this should be; I only know that it is.

There are those who believe that it's all to do with envy and one-upmanship: what's the point of your driving about in a £50,000 BMW if 95 per cent of us peasants don't realise just how successful you must be to own one? There may be a bit of truth in this theory, but it surely can't explain the value that Persil derives from being universally famous? And doesn't it seem improbable that we pop a six-pack of Coke or a packet of Oxo cubes into our shopping basket in the hope of arousing envy and admiration in the hearts of all the other others at the checkout counter?

There are thousands of great and public brands that virtually no one is debarred from buying on the grounds of price – yet they possess a value that lesser-known products lack.

For manufacturers, for brand marketers, I don't think the question of *why* matters very much. It only matters that it is. Fame is the fundamental value that strong brands own.

You do, of course, have to be famous *for* something: and we come to that later.

The matter of fame takes us naturally to the matter of brand ownership.

Of course, in a legal sense, the company owns the brand. But for a company to *feel* that it owns its brands is to tempt it to believe that it has total control over them – and it does not.

Forget the marketing-speak. The image of a brand is no more nor less than the result of its fame: its reputation. And, like a reputation, it can be found in only one place: in the minds of people.

Lord Archer, Sir Richard Branson, Victoria Beckham, Rudolph Giuliani, Harry Potter and the Prince of Wales are all public figures; and like all public figures, they have reputations. But you will not find these reputations neatly defined and filed away in Companies House, nor lodged with their respective solicitors. The only way you will find a reputation is by opening up other people's minds and peering inside. The same is true for the image of the brand.

Nor, of course, does a public figure have a single, constant reputation, shared by everyone. One of the most potent political reputations over the last 30 years has been that of Mrs Thatcher. Not only has that reputation changed dramatically over time, but it has never been remotely homogeneous.

This very same person, *indisputably* the same person, at exactly the same point in time, has been seen as both tyrant and liberator, and a thousand variations in between.

Her views, actions and achievements have been known to everyone. The stimuli have been common. But the response to those stimuli has been as varied as the characters of those who have known of her existence. Mrs Thatcher's reputation does not belong to Mrs Thatcher; it belongs to the 50-odd million people in this country who know of her existence – and many more abroad – and it comes in as many different shades.

Tiresome though it may be to accept, the same is true for brands. The most valuable part of a brand…the added value bit…the bit that protects respectable margins and fills up the reservoir of future cashflow…the bit that distinguishes a brand from a mere product…*doesn't belong to it*. It belongs to its public. And for those who are loyal to brands, this sense of ownership, of possession, is strong and often overtly recognised. It's 30 years or so since I first heard real people in group discussions talking openly and quite unselfconsciously about their favourite washing powder. But they didn't just talk about Persil: they talked about *my* Persil.

So the image of the brand – its brand reputation, that which makes it the shareholders' most valuable asset – doesn't belong to it. It belongs to all those who give thought to it.

No wonder CEOs prefer to spend their time counting things.

But the fact that the image of the brand doesn't reside with the brand is not quite such a depressing truth as it may seem. Because it leads us to wonder how exactly these images – these brand reputations – are formed in the first place.

Many marketing companies, and even more of their marketing advisers, pride themselves on their ability to build brands. But of course neither group builds brands, because brands are built in people's heads.

What the most skilful of marketing companies do, with great sensitivity and unceasing vigilance, is provide some of the raw material from which brands are built. There is an enormous difference.

Many years ago, I wrote that people build brands as birds build nests, from scraps and straws we chance upon. The metaphor remains a useful one but it needs to be both modified and amplified.

I said earlier, as one of my 13 unpalatable brand facts, that 'people come to conclusions about brands as a result of an uncountable number of different stimuli'.

That's true – but we can count some of them. These are some of the scraps and straws from which people build brands.

Let me start with the *product*. It's often said that a brand is a product with added communication; but it seems to me that the intrinsic product – its delivery, its function – must itself be the primary brand communication. No washing powder that fails to deliver high standards of detergency will survive – however skilfully marketed. No beer that fails to please the taste buds – however great its advertising budget – will survive. Function is the first and permanent requirement for brand success. I shall talk much this evening about brand reputation and added value: but let me first echo a warning issued earlier this year by Niall FitzGerald in his Marketing Society annual lecture.[4]

He identified the manufacturer who starts out by being technologically very advanced – and is deservedly very successful. As his market gets more and more competitive, he comes to realise that he needs both product performance *and* brand character in order to stay ahead. Brilliantly, an image is built for his brand – so that users not only respect it but feel loyal to it as well. He is even more successful.

Then comes the critical stage. He becomes such an enthusiast for the notion of brand personality – and falls so deeply in love with his own – that he comes to believe that competitive product performance is no longer his highest priority. So he neglects to innovate, he neglects to invest in R&D, he stops listening intently for those first faint murmurs of discontent – and, for a month or two, or even a year or two – his success continues and his profits mount.

And then, with savage suddenness, his once-healthy brand becomes an invalid: losing share and reputation with precipitate speed.

Because when people discover what's been done, that a once-loved brand has taken its users for granted, those users will be totally and brutally unforgiving. And their desertion will have something of vengeance about it.

I shan't talk a lot more about function for the rest of this lecture: not because it's of little importance but because it's so self-evidently central to brand success that reiteration of that truth should be unnecessary.

The next most obvious clue to brand character is *advertising*; often claimed to be the greatest brand-builder of them all. I spent over 30 years in advertising; but unless you define advertising in an unusually liberal way, I wouldn't necessarily support that claim. That there has to be some *communication* between a brand and its public is obvious; but its name, its packaging, its stores if it has any, its vans, it news value can all give people important clues to a brand's character: and in some instances, these non-advertising communications media will be the all-important ones. This evening, we are principally concerned with manufacturers' brands, offered for sale in a competitive marketplace. But let's not forget the great schools, the great newspapers, the great football clubs; all of

---

4   Niall FitzGerald, Marketing Society annual lecture, 2001.

which not only perfectly fit the definition of brands but help us understand their nature. In few if any instances do brands of this kind owe their power and influence primarily to advertising.

Then *price*. Price is a wonderfully deceptive item. 'Look at me,' says price: 'I'm a number. So you can compare me to the prices of all my competitors and find out which is best.' For a second or two, would-be rational man may feel a surge of hope: at last, the comforting feel of ground beneath the feet.

But of course, as everybody knows, price offers no such universal reassurance. Price is both an objective fact and a stimulus likely to elicit any number of very different subjective responses. The same low price can simultaneously lower the barrier to entry and increase suspicions about quality.

It is only commentators who confuse price with value for money; consumers never do.

Consumers know that value for money is a calculation that they make, as individuals, often intuitively; and that price is just one factor within that calculation. Like the image of a brand, and for the same reason, value for money is an individual concept, individually arrived at – however widely shared it may turn out to be.

From time to time I try to identify a significant consumer market sector – detergents, toilet tissue, beans, packaged cakes, confectionery, cigarettes, canned beer – where the brand with the lowest price is also the market leader. In countries where choice is still a distant concept, there are of course many such examples. But in our more fortunate world, accustomed as we've been for 50 years or more now to a range of options in everything we buy, I can still think of none.

And this is not, as the rationalists would have us believe, because the gullible masses are lured into paying for some intangible image; it's because the masses are made up of individuals, each of whom is perfectly capable of determining which price demanded most accurately matches which set of satisfactions delivered: not universally, of course – but for himself or herself.

One of the many functions of price is famously encapsulated, and with great marketplace success, by Stella Artois: 'Reassuringly expensive'.

Promotions are almost as deceptive a stimulus as price and for much the same reason. Surely a two-for-the-price-of-one, a banded offer of that new CD, the chance of a free holiday in the Caribbean – surely such bargains must lead to more sales and therefore be good for the brand?

Maybe the first; but not necessarily the second.

People – in which I continue to include you and me, not some remote and alien consuming body – people interpret all brand clues with instinctive intelligence.

Marketing people give a great deal of thought to what people think of brands. What brands appear to think of people is at least as interesting.

When brands make clear and often impertinent assumptions about us, we notice. When I get yet another invitation to apply for a platinum credit card, I know exactly the assumption that this brand has made about me. It has assumed that I will enjoy flashing a platinum card in front of head waiters; that I will appreciate an automatic if expensive overdraft facility of £10,000; that I drive a car with a personalised number plate and wear open-backed driving gloves while doing so. I resent these assumptions deeply. And I would, of course, resent them at least as deeply if they were absolutely accurate.

Most promotions fall neatly into one of two categories: bribes or bonuses.

The bonus makes this assumption about me: that I will appreciate some token of gratitude for my continued custom.

The bribe makes this assumption about me: that I will buy something I never wanted in the first place because it's now cheaper.

The first congratulates and flatters me; the second insults me.

The signal that the bonus sends out is one of generosity and confidence; the bonus enhances the brand. The signal that the bribe sends out is one of insecurity and desperation; the bribe diminishes the brand.

So the promotion – the offer – is more than a short-term sales incentive. It's another clue to brand character, one of those many scraps and straws from which people build brands inside their heads.

Advertising, packaging, price and promotions have this in common: they are all within the control of the marketing company. To be rather more accurate: the *transmission* of these brand stimuli is within the control of the marketing company. Their *reception,* however, is not.

Among all my deeply disturbing brand facts, this is the one most calculated to cause distracted CEOs sleepless nights – which is probably why they choose not to think about it.

I said at the start: 'The only way to begin to understand the nature of brands is to strive to acquire a facility which only the greatest of novelists possess and which is so rare that it has no name.' The last part of that sentence is not quite true.

In her 1996 Reith Lecture,[5] Jean Aitchison wrote: 'An effective per-
suader must be able to imagine events from another person's point of
view. In fashionable jargon, he or she must have "A Theory of Mind".'

A Theory of Mind may be fashionable jargon among academics and
psychiatrists but it's far from fashionable anywhere else; nor does it
deserve to be. It is a hopelessly inadequate term for a rare and priceless
facility. And 'empathy' is in its own way worse, since we think we know
what it means but don't.

The ability 'to imagine events from another person's point of view', to
see things through other people's eyes, to put oneself in someone else's
shoes – it might be a more respected skill were it only to have a decent
name.

I've been brooding about this rare ability for a very long time.

When I was about seven years old, I was taken to have tea with the only
rich relation we had. As we were about to leave, she reached for her
purse, took out five £1 notes and gave them to me.

I was, at the time, on two shillings a week pocket money. What I held
in my hand was one year's gross income.

Then she peered at the notes and said, 'Oh dear. Those two are *very*
dirty. I couldn't possibly let you go away with notes like that.' And she
took back two of the £1 notes – and didn't replace them.

My aunt did not possess a complete understanding of the Theory of
Mind. There was no meanness in her action; only a kind of blindness.
She saw those two notes through her eyes only.

We were both looking at the same notes. They had a measured, agreed,
universally accepted worth: they were worth £1 each. But to me they
represented riches beyond imagination and to her they were a Boxing
Day tip for the milkman. There is, I believe, no commonly accepted
name for this form of blindness but it is widespread – and not only in
marketing.

Most of us in the rich and fortunate West are genuinely bewildered to
discover that the way of life we know with such untroubled certainty to
be civilised seems, with an equivalent certainty, to be the epitome of blas-
phemy and greed to others.

Jean Aitchison is right. The ability to imagine events from another's
point of view is the first qualifying talent of the would-be effective per-
suader. Those scraps and straws over which we painstakingly pore have
no universal significance. Through different eyes, a single bank note can

---

5   Jean Aitchison, 1996 Reith Lecture

represent enough Smarties for the entire summer holidays, with a balsa wood glider thrown in; or a handy wedge to stop the table wobbling.

The poor old focus group has had a thoroughly hostile press in recent years – unfairly, I believe. And the reason for that hostility is a confusion in the minds of many commentators between the knowledge you gain from a focus group – and the use you put that knowledge to.

If focus groups tell you that the single European currency is regarded with deep hostility but that corporal punishment has acquired a new popularity, you will deserve every bit of odium hurled at you if, with absolutely no further thought, you pull out of Europe and bring back the birch.

But it is irresponsible government – and potentially suicidal management – deliberately to stay ignorant of the content of other people's minds.

You do not have to agree with what you discover. You should certainly not expect people to tell you what to do next. Nor should you be surprised if what people say they want turns out to be very different from what they subsequently choose. But you should never find yourself ambushed.

I cannot believe that Marks & Spencer was anything other than astonished by the severity of its fall from grace; yet neither can I believe that the signs weren't there for years before it happened.

Marks & Spencer has competitors; and the tiresome thing about competitors, other than their very existence, is that what *they* do has a significant effect on your own reputation.

We all have invisible maps in our heads, on which we plot the position of competing brands. Every brand is allocated its own, unique space. There may or may not be such things as parity products; there are certainly no parity brands.

Some 15 years ago, our mental map of the daily broadsheet newspaper market in this country would have allocated clear positions for the *Daily Telegraph*, *The Guardian* and *The Times*. And then *The Independent* was launched with considerable effect, and all the existing co-ordinates subtly changed: because reputations, as well as being subjective, are also relative. A brand is defined in our minds at least as much by its competitors as by its own behaviour.

These changes to brands take place all the time. A new competitor may occasion a perceptible change – but the really dangerous changes are the daily, tiny, immeasurable, imperceptible changes that accumulate invisibly over time until they've gained often unstoppable significance.

It is all this that leads me to say that brands are living, organic things – because all the time, those with knowledge of a brand are changing. They may grow richer or poorer and will certainly grow older; and as the perceiver changes, so inevitably, does the perception. If a marketing company closes both its eyes and its ears; if it relies on the single dimension of current sales; if it believes that yesterday's successful strategy is an infallible guide to tomorrow's profit: then it's heading for disillusionment of barometric severity.

A commitment to monitoring changes in brand perception demands constant vigilance – and an unusual degree of corporate humility. But it's an absolutely essential procedure for all brand stewards anxious to protect themselves from extremely unwelcome surprises.

The means by which these scraps and straws infiltrate the human mind remain something of a mystery.

The advertising world, in the teeth of instinct and much evidence, insisted for years that brand choice was the result of persuasive argument consciously processed.

Consumers were assumed to notice an advertisement; become engaged by its overt promise or proposition; and be thereby consciously persuaded to buy. It was a neat, linear, deterministic model that brought great comfort to disorientated advertisers and communications researchers alike: it offered consistency, rationality and some deeply desirable opportunities for measurement. The model put much emphasis on both attention and memory: and, what luck, both could readily be quantified.

It was always a deeply unsatisfactory model and, in practice, was widely ignored by advertising practitioners. But despite the occasional guerilla attack on its underlying premise, it remained the least worst respectable model in town.

This year, Robert Heath has published an important monograph: I quoted from it earlier. It's called *The Hidden Power of Advertising* but its subtitle is a much more accurate label: *How low involvement processing influences the way we choose brands.*

I will not attempt to take you through his own processes of thought; it is enough for you to know that it's a rigorous work and draws on new understanding from the worlds of neuroscience and psychology. But I will quote at some length from his own summary.

> *Consumers in general regard most reputable brands as performing similarly and because of this they do not regard learning about*

brands as being very important. Brand decisions tend to be made intuitively rather than rationally.

Because it is not seen as very important, most brand information tends not so much to be actively 'sought' as passively 'acquired'. Brand communication, such as advertising, tends to be processed at very low attention levels and we generally do not work very hard to learn or understand what we are being told about the brand.

Mostly we process brand communication using an automatic mental process called low involvement processing. Low involvement processing is a complex mixture of semi-conscious and subconscious activity. Much of it involves what is known as 'implicit' learning – learning that takes place without you knowing that you are learning.

The way our long-term memory works means that the more often something is processed alongside a brand, the more permanently it becomes associated with that brand. Thus, it is the perceptions and simple concepts, repeatedly and 'implicitly' reinforced at low levels of attention, which tend over time to define brands in our minds. And because implicit memory is more durable than explicit memory, these brand associations, once learned, are rarely forgotten.

To me, that makes absolute sense. It feels right.

When I examine the inside of my own head, and look at some the brand reputations that reside there, I cannot for the life of me trace their source.

I have learnt without knowing I was learning; I have absorbed, by some unconscious osmotic process, a range of stimuli – and from these, equally unconsciously, I have constructed a coherent brand character.

So let me return to these scraps and straws from which we, as individuals, infer so much.

And let me move from those brand communications over which the marketing company has theoretical control – product, advertising, packaging, price, promotions, for example – to brand encounters of a far more accidental nature.

You see a truck, boldly branded, driving badly on the M25. You see a pack in the house of someone you dislike. You read that the company that makes the product has been taken to court for racial discrimination. The daughter of a friend is fired by the parent company. You receive an illiterate and ill-spelt letter from head office. After holding on for 25 minutes, you have still to speak to a human being at the company's call centre.

Like people, brands have body language; and it's a language we understand. Every time we encounter a brand, we make an infinitesimal and subconscious adjustment to our personally constructed brand picture: and in each of the instances mentioned above, those adjustments will not be in the brand's favour.

And the reason it matters is this. The luxury of choice that we all enjoy; the fact that, however crassly sometimes, competitive companies are fighting for our cash and our custom; all this means that, in allocating our loyalty, we welcome reasons to reject a brand almost as eagerly as reasons to prefer it.

As Andrew Ehrenberg and others have long demonstrated, and as Robert Heath reminds us, what is called brand loyalty is very rarely a truly exclusive matter. We assume all alternatives to be broadly acceptable; we all have favoured repertoires within each brand category; and we all want to make brand decisions with a minimum of anguish. So however infinitesimally negative a brand encounter may be, the damage it may do to that brand's competitive standing may be serious.

The way we interpret the body language of brands means that the apparently trivial can be greatly significant.

In the performing arts, or so I'm told, they preach something called 'transitive action'. And what this means, or so I'm told, is that good writers and directors encourage an audience to deduce character and motivation not from what is explicitly said but from what that audience observes being *done.*

The best brand stewards, too, encourage their potential customers to deduce character not just from claim and assertion – from presentation – but from transitive action: from brand behaviour.

I have long admired a supermarket in the States. Proud of their reputation for fresh produce, they had always removed the outside leaves of lettuces before putting them on display. One day, a lowly member of staff made a modest suggestion: and from then on, those outside leaves, instead of being consigned to the garbage bin, were popped into plastic bags and given away free at the checkout – to families whose children kept pet rabbits. Naturally, they called them BunnyBags. I don't think it absurd to suggest that, as a result, 15 years on, those children will choose to take their own children to that very same supermarket.

Some years ago, a friend of mine was a lunch guest in the Connaught Hotel dining-room – and noticed his host first of all patting his pockets ineffectively and then peering miserably at the menu. No word was said: but within a minute, a waiter had appeared with a velvet-lined tray on which were displayed ten pairs of reading glasses of different levels of magnification. My friend, the guest, has been a loyal Connaught user ever since; and remember – it wasn't even him who needed the glasses.

BunnyBags and reading specs: two very small examples of brand behaviour with much in common.

Both showed an understanding of A Theory of Mind: they put themselves in the place of their customers; they understood what it was like to be a small child with pet rabbits or an embarrassed businessman finding small print difficult.

Both understood the importance of transitive action, of brand body language. They invited their customers to infer, from behaviour, rather than to accept from boastful claim or assertion.

And both realised – or simply, perhaps, instinctively felt – that the apparently trivial can, in interpretation, take on quite disproportionate and positive significance.

I believe the best brand stewards of the future will recognise the potential power of such body language; and demand much more in the way of brand action and rather less in the way of empty self-praise.

They will also, I believe, have to come to terms with perhaps the most daunting proposition that I endorse this evening.

There was once a time when most brands had no publicly recognised parents. You bought your packet of Persil or your jar of Marmite and knew absolutely nothing, and cared rather less, about the company behind them. For two quite different but converging sets of reasons, that is changing fast – and will continue to do so.

The age of the free-standing brand is nearly over. For reasons widely understood, most brands now – and nearly all new brands – trumpet the name of their parent. The parent may be a company or an already established brand but the reasoning is the same: let's leverage our brand equity; let's trade on the trust we've already so painstakingly and expensively built.

But of course, just as the good news can be shared and spread through such linkages, so can the bad. Free-standing brands – orphan brands, with no known parents – may be non-contagious. But when brand relationships are not just public but widely publicised, bad news from one can rapidly become an epidemic.

The effect of the internet is to accelerate the chances of brand contagion. The internet means that there is nowhere to hide. You cannot charge $350 for a pair of chinos and pay third world workers $3.50 a day to make them and hope to go unnoticed. You cannot deprive your own workforce of knowledge of your company's performance when they have ready access to it elsewhere. You cannot ignore the conversations that your networked employees are having with your networked customers. For more on this, consult *The Cluetrain Manifesto*:[6] a splendidly anarchic rant, of internet origins. Once you have read it, feel free to ignore quite a lot of it; but don't fail to read it and don't ignore it all.

And – as Tim Ambler pointed out – Naomi Klein's book *No Logo*[7] is not, as is widely supposed, an attack on brands; it's an exposé, as she sees it, of the double standards of multinational corporations and the risks they run.

This convergence of company and brand, this reckless openness of communication, this threat to general reputation that any specific transgression now poses, is quite enough reason for the chief executive to take a very close interest indeed in the management of his brands. Or perhaps I should say, his brand.

But there's another, more positive reason.

Today, to a marked extent, all brands are service brands. Other than street traders, few businesses now see their only function as being simply to make a sale. After-sales service, relationship marketing, the concept of lifetime value, the growth of interactive media: all these trends and developments mean that the creation and maintenance of a valued brand should now quite clearly be the responsibility not of some relatively lowly brand manager but of the chief executive of the enterprise itself.

This is not just a defensive measure: the competitive opportunities presented by the deliberate creation of a corporate brand are immense. They are described in detail, with impressive case-studies, in a book called *The Masterbrand Mandate* by Lynn Upshaw and Earl Taylor.[8]

The extension of the principles of branding from product to company means opening up the whole marketing strategy to absolutely everyone within that company. It means recognising that every corporate action, every corporate decision, every corporate communication will be seen as a clue – as one of those all-important scraps and straws from which people build brands.

6   Christopher Locke, Rick Levine, Doc Searls & David Weinberger, *The Cluetrain Manifesto*, Perseus Publishing, 2000
7   Naomi Klein, *No Logo*, Flamingo, 2000
8   Lynn Upshaw & Earl Taylor, *The Masterbrand Mandate*, John Wiley, 2000

If you want to get a feel for the corporate brand, think of some successful first-generation companies – companies such as Dyson or Pret à Manger. Still led by their forceful founders, they embody and broadcast a single-minded and unifying set of values. And that which is done instinctively and obsessively by such pioneers can be done equally well by the chief executives of long established companies; but only if they are prepared first to understand and then to undertake the role of brand steward.

The value to the company, of course, if they get it right, extends well beyond sales levels and profit margins: it extends into labour relations and press relations and investor relations; it helps in the retention of valued executives; it gives them a competitive edge when recruiting new graduates.

But while recognising and recommending the masterbrand strategy, let me return to the Niall FitzGerald warning. However brilliantly reputation management may be masterminded, and however much that reputation contributes to differentiation and competitive success, if there's anything fundamentally wrong with the product, then ultimate failure – I'm extremely happy to report – remains inevitable.

The authors of *The Masterbrand Mandate* devote a whole page of praise to a giant American company which was 'transforming itself into a brand-based organization'. They report that 'Messages about creativity and innovation are sent to employees through their intranet, via T-shirts, in print and television advertising, at employee meetings, in self-training programs.' This is the corporation that won *Fortune* magazine's 'Most Innovative US Company' award four times in the mid-1990s – and it's called Enron.

It's stories like this that give immense comfort to brand-averse CEOs. 'There you are,' they say, 'it's all smoke and mirrors stuff. Only charlatans rabbit on about brands. All puff and no substance. Never lasts. Now let's get back to counting things.'

But of course, the authors weren't wrong to recognise what Enron was doing. If the fundamentals of the Enron operation had been solid, what Enron was doing would indeed have been admirable. An obsession with the management of brands must never be at the expense of functional efficiency. Indeed, as I hope I've stressed, and stressed indelibly, functional efficiency is a strong brand's first prerequisite. But that simple thought seems to get forever lost.

I was very happy to accept your invitation to give this lecture this evening. I was even foolish enough, as I began to write it, to believe that

I might be able to bring a little enlightenment to the subject – and encourage some of those hesitant CEOs to take on their rightful mantle of chief brand steward.

Instead, as I now realise, I started with 13 daunting brand facts and ended by inviting you to admire Enron. I must have put the brand cause back by at least ten years.

The new Stella Artois:
unnervingly inexpensive

I've always believed that 'reassuringly expensive' was one of the great positioning statements of our time. Now a promotional 12-pack (to which I shall return) has made me try to work out why. It's been a brain-damaging business, as you'll soon see.

With the exception of Stella (and the occasional dismissive reference to a competitor) the words cheap and expensive are never used in advertising. Critics believe this is because copywriters are a slimy lot who can't bring themselves to be straight about anything, but for once that's not true. The reason the words aren't used is because none of us much wants to buy either cheap things or expensive things. Nor, even, do we want to buy middle-priced things. What we want is good things at the 'right' price. This simple concept used to be called value; but value has now been so thoroughly debased through its use as a euphemism for cheap that we need something else. Language, like money, is a currency extremely susceptible to inflation.

What we want is for things to be worth it: worth the money, worth the price. And worth is made up of satisfaction – which is subjective – at an acceptable pain threshold of price.

This, of course, does not mean that the lower the price the higher the satisfaction because we don't always know how to judge worth. Estimating worth involves making competitive judgments about elusive concepts such as quality. So, confusingly (are you still with me?), we look to price to help us. Price has to be both low and high; but not too low or the possibility of worth becomes improbable; and not too high or the satisfaction snaps.

Furthermore, what you think is good is different from what I think is good; and what I think is expensive you regard as dead reasonable. When advertisements tell me that the object on offer costs less than I think, I become enraged. How can they know how much I think it costs when I do not know myself how much I think it costs and they decline to tell me?

I hope this has clarified things a bit. What it means is that most advertising for above-market-price items is trying to raise belief in (and perhaps even contribute to the delivery of) worth, to the point where the price, when finally revealed, meets both requirements: low enough to be acceptable and high enough to act as confirmation of quality. And that, of course (which you knew all along), is why 'reassuringly expensive' is so brilliant.

Somebody, however, seems to have forgotten. There's this promotional pack of Stella Artois in the off-trade at the moment – 12 for the price of 10 – and the legend on it says: 'Reassuringly Good Value.'

I hope for the long-term prosperity of the brand that I'm the only person to have noticed it. And I certainly wouldn't dream of passing it on.

High noon at Elkhart, Indiana

The drive for new business obsesses agencies. New business presentations combine tension, expense and absurdity in roughly equal proportions. This one happened in the 1960s but I didn't write about it until 1987, when the following article appeared in Campaign.

Unwisely, as it turned out, I told one or two people what I was going to do before I went. 'There's this very important new business presentation in Elkhart, Indiana,' I said. 'Six of us will be going down from New York on Wednesday. Henry, Tom, three or four others from the New York office – and me, representing The World.'

Henry was President and Tom was International Director. I'd never been asked to represent The World before and was naturally gratified. As it turned out, The World was all those bits that weren't the United States but that still left quite a lot.

I'd been told we'd be rehearsing for most of the Tuesday in New York. We had a lot to cover and only a couple of hours for the presentation. Rehearsal was essential. It was going to be slick and seamless. A great many millions of dollars were at stake worldwide. I flew to New York with a 16mm reel of commercials (in those days, they could only show 16mm in Elkhart, Indiana). It was very cold indeed when I walked to the office at 8 am on Tuesday morning and I was glad of my new overcoat. I went first to Tom's office. He was in a meeting. So was Henry. And so were Kevin, Bob and Bill. They were all in different meetings, but were planning to meet mid-afternoon at La Guardia. We were to fly to Chicago, then to South Bend where we would spend the night. We would rehearse there before going on to Elkhart the following morning.

I went out to La Guardia with Tom, who was going to write his bit on the plane. It had been a very hectic week. For the first time we all met and Kevin, who was in charge of administration, handed out the tickets. There was a ticket for everyone but The World, so I went off and bought one for myself. Outside it started to snow.

We were the last commercial flight to be allowed to land at O'Hare that day. We had to wait an hour while they chipped the snow away from the gate before we could get off. The connecting flight to South Bend had been cancelled so we checked into the Ramada Inn. Outside it was still snowing and getting colder.

We had dinner and much imported burgundy in the baronial dining room, where the waiters wore wigs and knee-breeches and there was a dance band. The band-leader's wife was very decorative and Henry, who looked not unlike Cary Grant, asked her to dance. The band-leader went on leading the band but with his head facing the dance floor. I'd never seen that before.

At 1 am we had a final stinger and started to go to bed. When I told the receptionist that my new overcoat had been stolen from the cloakroom, he very kindly gave me a raincoat instead. Its hem stopped just short of my shoes, it was stained all the way down the front and it had no buttons. The receptionist also apologised for the absence of water: the mains supply had frozen.

As I was getting into bed, the phone rang. Henry had booked rooms for the two of us at the Flying Carpet, where they had water. The taxi was waiting. I got dressed, put on the raincoat and joined Henry, leaving my watch on the bedside console.

Soon after 2 am we checked into the Flying Carpet Motel and Henry discovered the piano bar. We ordered stingers and Henry got into conversation with three lawyers. One had made an air hostess pregnant, one had been caught importing yen illegally into Canada and the third was drinking along with the other two out of sympathy. Henry, not a lawyer and knowing nothing of tax, began giving them advice on tax law. Impressed, they began calling him sir and buying him stingers. He was still accepting them graciously when I went to bed again at 3.30 am.

On Wednesday morning, I phoned Bob at the Ramada Inn to ask if he could find my watch. He, Tom, Kevin and Bill had already spent an hour trying to find Henry and me. Henry hadn't told them we had moved. In the airport bus Henry told me that, in his experience, after a certain hour it was better not to go to bed at all. He then fell silent. We took off for South Bend in a gentle blizzard and Tom returned to his speech. It was exactly the time we should have been starting our presentation in Elkhart, Indiana, but Kevin had called the client to explain.

After 20 minutes, the chief stewardess brought us all up to date with the news. The airport at South Bend had closed. Normally we would be returning to Chicago. However, our pilot hadn't obtained the necessary qualifications for landing that type of aircraft in the conditions then prevailing at O'Hare, so instead we'd be landing at Fort Wayne, where conditions were much the same.

We were the last commercial flight to be allowed to land at Fort Wayne that day. Henry sat in a corner with his eyes shut and Kevin went to call the client. Tom went through his notes, lips moving slightly as he did so.

Kevin came back with the news that the client was sending the company QueenAir to fetch us. It could fly under the weather at 800 feet.

Henry opened his eyes and told us that he was to begin a vacation in Jamaica the following day and would wait at Fort Wayne until the first proper aircraft left for anywhere. He would not be going to Elkhart. The QueenAir slithered in.

There were five of us and four seats so Kevin sat on the lavatory at the back.

We arrived at Elkhart, Indiana, were issued with security badges, walked through the factory and were shown into the meeting room.

The ashtrays were full, the projector was unmanned, there were no windows and no clients. We were seven hours late.

Bill put his slide tray on the carousel. He was going to tell them how he had co-ordinated Pepsi-Cola advertising in Latin America. I fed my reel into the projector.

Two clients came in. Bob and Kevin, who had met them before, introduced me as coming from England. One client, beyond surprise, nodded and said: 'England'. He'd heard of it.

Tom, leader in Henry's absence, started. He bent his head and read slowly from his reminder cards. 'At J. Walter Thompson,' he read, 'we are international, resourceful.' Here he stopped, having reached the bottom of his first card.

After only a moment's hesitation he realised that he should turn over to the next, which he managed at the first attempt. His head bent lower. 'And dynamic,' he said doubtfully.

Bill had reached Chile when the first client left the room to make a telephone call. As Bill finished, the second and last client left the room without explanation. It was my turn.

Tom looked at his watch and then at me. 'I think you'd better start anyway,' he said. For 12 minutes, I spoke about The World to Tom, Bill, Bob and Kevin.

They looked at me loyally and nodded from time to time. One client returned when I was showing an After Eight commercial. The second never returned.

Tom asked if the client had any questions. The client said: 'Are you hoping to get back to Chicago tonight?'

As I picked up the raincoat, Tom said: 'Your suit's split down the back.' It had.

Back at work in London the following Monday, I got into the lift. 'How did it go?' they asked.

Part Four

Marketing and people: how advertising works

The consumer has a mind as well as a stomach

Being the creative director in an advertising agency means spending a great deal of time discussing and evaluating work done by others. Much of the development work you are shown seems wrong; either strategically wrong or executionally wrong.

When it is strategically wrong, it is relatively easy to explain why you want it changed but when you feel the execution is at fault, the problem becomes a great deal harder. It never seemed satisfactory – or fair – simply to say, 'This isn't good enough, start again.' I always felt the need to try to explain why; to try to relate the specific rejection to a more general principle. In this way, disappointments could at least be part of a learning process – and, besides, it was good for me to try to explain and justify my decision.

The problem was, there were (and are) few sensible and well-articulated theories about how advertising works. There are some 'rules', some sets of beliefs about what is good or bad, but very little communications theory, however inadequate, on which to build and against which to test a particular instinct about a particular proposal. Again and again I found myself having to explain that *saying* something did not mean that you had communicated it; and almost as often, that not having said something didn't necessarily mean that you had *not* communicated it.

The first time I put these thoughts together in public was in 1972 to a Kraft International Management Conference in Switzerland. The first two editions of this book carried the presentation more or less exactly as I first gave it. Since then, I've made similar presentations on a great many occasions in the course of which I've dropped the almost totally irrelevant original introduction and added a few more examples and illustrations. That is the version printed here. It's probably best known as *Stimulus & Response*. I remain extremely grateful to Terry Hamaton for the illustrations.

There seem to be curiously few books about the nature of communications that are of practical help to those working in advertising. But those that do exist seem to be unanimous in believing the communications process to be composed of four distinct component parts.

There's a Sender:

A Receiver:

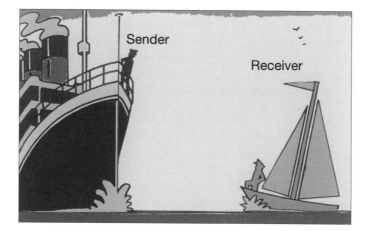

A Medium:

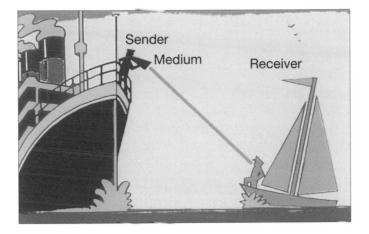

And a Message:

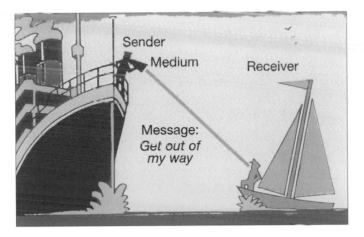

The man in the big boat says 'Get out of my way!' to the man in the little boat. The man in the little boat dutifully gets out of the way, and the communication has been successfully completed. It all seems very simple, doesn't it? But let's see if the same model can be applied to other forms of communication.

Here's another sender – an advertiser (or rather, an art director's mental picture of an advertiser):

He, too, has his receivers – his potential customers:

Again, there's a medium – in this case, television:

But what about the message? Well, that's not particularly difficult because the advertiser knows exactly what he wants the consumer to do. He wants the consumer to buy his product. So the message, obviously, is:

You may think this slightly unfair since little advertising these days is quite as blatant and aggressive in its tone. But read your newspapers and watch television and there's still a lot of advertising instructing us to 'buy some today'. And no election campaign is without bald injunctions to VOTE CONSERVATIVE (or indeed any other party for that matter).

The main question arising here is this: if the man in the little boat responds so obediently, why aren't consumers and voters so thoughtfully compliant? Either we hold the view that all consumers are irresponsible and should be subjected to heavy fines if they fail to consume – or we look for some other explanation.

So let's look at another communicator – another sender:

A comedian, a funnyman. He, too, has his receivers:

...a typical British family on a night out, determined under no circumstances to enjoy themselves.

The comedian's medium, of course…

…is his voice. But what's his message? Well, he knows what he wants his receivers to think, all right. He wants them to think he's funny. But I very much doubt if any comedian, at least more than once, would get up on stage and begin by saying: 'Ladies and gentleman…

…the first thing you should know about me is that I am funny.' And I very much doubt if that audience would leave the theatre still chuckling and tell their neighbours the next day just what a funny person they'd seen the previous evening: 'We knew at once he was funny because he told us so.'

The comedian is a far more skilled communicator than that. He knows that if his audience is to think he's funny, then he's got to make them laugh; he's got to tell them what we call a joke.

So he tells the joke…

…and the audience laughs. It is *their response* that he's funny. *They* come to that conclusion; it's their contribution, not the comedian's.

And it's this illustration that begins to cast serious doubt on the usefulness of the normal communications model of sender, receiver, medium and message. The real flaw in that theory is that it *in no way allows for the participation – the creativity – of the receiver.*

And like it or not, all receivers do participate. They resolutely refuse to sit there with minds like empty sponges, accepting all that they're told without question or modification. For example, at the moment, I'm a sender; and you, unfortunately for you, are receivers. Suppose I were to tell you in all seriousness that I was a man of many remarkable qualities – so many, in fact, that I found it difficult when asked to say which of my qualities was the most remarkable. My integrity was certainly widely admired, as was my compassion; but if forced, I'd have to say that of all my qualities, the most remarkable had to be my modesty. 'I'd like you to know,' I'd say, 'that I'm an extremely modest man.'

Well, that's my message. But do you accept it? Do I see you turning to each other and murmuring respectfully, 'What a modest man! Did you hear him tell us he was modest? I never knew before that he was modest!'

I suggest you don't. I suggest that, in fact, you arrive at a diametrically opposite conclusion. You conclude that my most pronounced characteristic is that, not of modesty, but of conceit.

In his book *Human Communications*,[1] Professor Aranguren says this: 'The emission does not always and inevitably lead to the simple quiet and passive reception of a message, but frequently excites an active response: and for the same reason, this response may be in opposition to the emission instead of conforming with it.'

But with due respect to the good professor, I don't think he's got it absolutely right even yet – because he's still using this word message. And the word message is a very dangerous word because we use it to stand for two quite different things and we don't always distinguish between them. Sometimes we use the word message to mean that which the sender *puts into* a communication; and sometime we use it to mean that which the receiver *takes out* of a communication. And however inconvenient and untidy it may be, we have to realise that these two can be – indeed, almost always are – completely different. How can the same word, message, be applied to that which I put in, '*I am modest*' and that which you take out, '*He is conceited*'?

It seems to me, therefore, that if we are to avoid all sorts of problems when creating or discussing communications, we need to think of them as being composed not of four standard component parts, but of five:

Sender:

1   J.L. Aranguren, *Human Communication*, McGraw-Hill, 1967

Receiver:

Medium:

Stimulus:

...and Response:

And the key words here, obviously, are the two words 'stimulus' and 'response' replacing the single word 'message'.

'I am modest' is not a message: it's a stimulus. Just as 'He is conceited' is a response. There's no longer any conflict or confusion.

The most effective communicators don't rage at their receivers' insistence on contributing to communications; they welcome it and turn it to their advantage.

In 1960, in the United States of America, the young John F. Kennedy was challenging Richard Nixon for the Presidency. Though long before

Watergate, the Nixon reputation was not altogether without blemish – and it was part of the Democrats' strategy to bring into public question the Nixon integrity. If this was their 'message', they might well have been tempted to publish an advertisement like this:

Had they done so, they would have run the serious risk that at least some part of the electorate would have found such an unsubstantiated slur unacceptable. Their response, therefore, would have been to challenge it.

Instead, both famously and infamously, they published this:

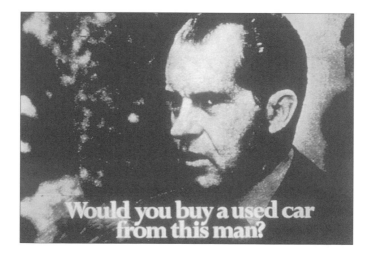

Here is a deliberate invitation to the audience to participate. Making effective (if disreputable) use both of Nixon's slightly dodgy reputation and his slightly shifty appearance, the creativity of the receivers is actively sought and utilised. Not entirely coincidentally, perhaps, Nixon lost by a narrow margin.

So receivers do not receive passively, with empty heads; they receive actively; and it is up to senders to turn this contribution to their advantage.

In his dense but thoughtful book, *The Act of Creation*, Arthur Koestler says this: 'Language itself is never completely explicit. Words have suggestive, evocative powers; but at the same time they are merely stepping stones for thought. The artist rules his subjects by turning them into accomplices.'

That seems to be as good a definition as I know of the role of creative people in advertising. We have to try to turn our audience into accomplices; because if they aren't our accomplices, they will be our challengers.

Here is a real advertisement:

How primitive, we think. How touching and unsophisticated! Some elderly smallholder, no doubt, eking out his pension. He'll probably do all right as long as he doesn't try to expand.

But imagine if he did, and called in a sophisticated London communications consultancy. It's not totally impossible, in the interests of

modernity and legibility, you understand, that they might recommend
their client to adopt something like this:

There's been no change of strategy, please note; nor even of copy. Just
the introduction of a familiar typeface, Helvetica.

They might even think it worth testing something along these lines:

Because responses to common stimuli are subjective, they are also
individual – so I can't be certain how each of you may have responded
to those three different advertisements. But I'm reasonably confident
that most of you, and indeed most urban egg choosers, would think less
well of the eggs offered in the second two advertisements than of those
offered in the first.

In fact, of course, if you look back, that original Fresh Eggs sign is a little masterpiece of brand communication. However inadvertently, everything about it triggers the right sort of response: the meticulously hand-lettered sign (but clearly not by a professional art director); not a weed in the flowerbed; the sign not quite straight; the carefully cut grass.

Each of these tiny triggers leads to a rich, internal, coherent composition: a small number of happy, organically fed, free-range hens looked after personally by a compassionate owner. The word 'fresh' here is redundant: how could they be anything else? Whereas in the second two examples, the typography has not only decided to fight the word 'fresh', it has comprehensively won.

The great skill in designing brand communications is in selecting those tiny triggers, because those that are uniquely right for one brand will by definition be wrong for another. Here is another brand looking for your custom:

I have repeatedly said that consumers'/receivers' interpretation of brand stimuli is active – is creative. This sign says, factually and accurately, what service is on offer. And that's all it says.

But what does it *imply*? What does it *communicate*? A very, very old flying instructor? A very, very old aircraft? A grass landing strip with molehills? Decomposing World War II tarmac? Not much maintenance? An open cockpit? Again, each individual receiver will have constructed a slightly different internal mental picture. But I don't think many of you would have chosen this brand. A bit of boring old Helvetica here would not have come amiss.

Wise communicators spend at least as much time thinking about their receivers – about what's in their heads already, about how they might interpret, mis-interpret, decode, modify any given stimuli – as they do on the creation of those stimuli. Here's one communicator who failed to think hard enough:

To the sender, the farmer, an entirely reasonable and accurate statement about the availability of two items of farm produce. To the squeamish receiver, mind as ever active and inventive, a deeply off-putting association. Irrational, certainly, but senders should never be surprised by receivers' irrationality.

I've left, of course, one question unanswered. If you can't *tell* people what to do; if you've got to rule your subjects by turning them into accomplices; then why did this work?

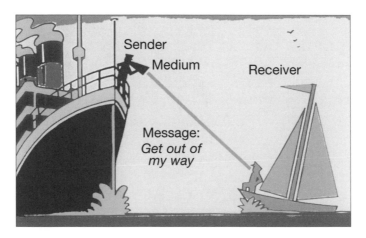

Why did the man in the little boat get out of the way of the man in the big boat?

The answer, of course, is that he had to; because if he hadn't, he'd have been dead: a motivation more powerful that those normally available to advertisers. The stimulus here resides not in the message but in the relative sizes of the sender and receiver. This sort of communication has nothing to do with persuasion; it is coercion. It depends for its success on the ability of the sender to penalise the receiver for disobedience. It is the communications equivalent of gunboat diplomacy.

The advertiser, fortunately, is never in such a position of power. He is always less powerful than the sum of his potential customers; and his potential customers know that they can always go elsewhere.

The advertiser can only succeed if he seeks and earns the willing complicity of his audience.

Why a pointless relaunch may be just the ticket

Brand owners, it seems, simply cannot leave well alone. Every few months there's a re-fit, some added jojoba essence, a new flash on the pack or a relaunch. The dispassionate observer finds it puzzling.

There are two different explanations for all this frenetic activity and only one of them is respectable. The first is all about marketing directors and brand managers needing to be seen to be doing something (*anything*) before making their next confident move up the corporate stepladder. It is entirely possible that the kind of management from which a brand would benefit most would be minimal management or even zero management; but this, of course, is not how career paths are blazed. 'Congratulations, Dennis. I note that in your three-year term of office as Brand Manager on VitaGel you've taken not one single marketing initiative. The job of Marketing Manager Substrates is yours – but only on the strict understanding that you pursue precisely the same policy.'

The respectable explanation is all to do with cognitive dissonance. And to clarify matters, here is the world premiere of the communications equivalent of 'Have you stopped beating your wife?'

Let us pretend that you are my friend. And I say to you: 'I have a theory about human communication. I believe that everyone, on being presented with a proposition, is initially moved to challenge it. Do you agree?'

At this point, please stop reading and think. How will you respond? Do you agree – or do you not?

You see? Aha! Gotcha! If you said 'yes', you do agree to this proposition, then of course you failed to challenge it. That which you said and that which you did were diametrically opposed and irreconcilable.

And if you said 'no', you don't agree to this proposition, then of course you did challenge it. That which you said and that which you did were diametrically opposed and irreconcilable.

The point, of course, is that it's quite impossible to answer this question sensibly with a simple 'yes' or 'no'.

Though the instinct to challenge is common, it is by no means universal. It depends on whether you find my proposition consonant or dissonant; or in other words, whether I'm proposing something that confirms your existing views or challenges them.

We do not like changing our minds. We do not like admitting to having changed our minds. Cognitive dissonance is a painful condition.

And that's why half the apparently pointless relaunches aren't pointless at all. A brand we have chosen to spurn for many years suddenly turns up with jojoba essence. We can now try it with untroubled conscience. We do not have to admit that we were wrong because the brand has admitted that any mistake was theirs. We were right not to like it before, and we're right to like it now. 'See – I was right all along!' is one of the great orgasmic cries of cognitive consonance.

So if you find yourself in the business of trying to encourage re-trial of a brand that research tells you many people are strongly negative towards, look first for what we professionals call an NCFS – or New Consumer Face Saver.

And if you don't believe me, why did you vote New Labour?

A new neurosis: too many people may be seeing your advertising

Here is a very short seasonal quiz.

Question: What does gift advertising have in common with Michael Portillo, June Whitfield and the Labour Party?
Answer: They all have multiple audiences.

I once saw a notice on the outside window of an extremely pretentious restaurant, which read: 'Staff Wanted. No Experience Necessary.' If I'd fancied a go at being a wine-waiter at *Chez Gourmet*, I'd have been pleased by this news. As someone who was thinking of eating there, I wasn't.

Even after 30 years, political parties still haven't worked out how to deal with television cameras at party conferences. The audience in the hall, the party faithful, united in their allegiance and emboldened by their numbers, is ready for more or less anything as long as it's unreasonable. Labour leaders at the Sheffield rally just before the 1992 election gave them premature triumphalism. Michael Portillo at the last Conservative conference gave them a heady whiff of xenophobia. On both occasions, the audience in the hall became inflamed with love and eternal commitment.

But the cameras were also there, snooping and eavesdropping and relaying these hot responses to another audience at home. And the audience at home was altogether cooler: remote and heterogeneous; composed of many hundreds of thousands of small, sceptical, half-attentive domestic units. The audience at home loved neither the Labour leaders nor Mr Portillo. Stoically uninflamed, they registered instead severe disapproval. And between them they accounted for a great many votes.

Both the Labour Party and Mr Portillo learned the hard way that you forget about multiple audiences at your cost.

Convenience foods had already learnt it. They used to think that their only audience was buyers and servers: 'Makes a dishonest woman of you' promised the domestic caterer that she could get away with it; but the promise was made in front of the family, the eaters, the real consumers. These days most convenience foods wisely take their convenience for granted and go all out on quality. Quality's of interest to all audiences – another lesson, perhaps, for Mr Portillo.

And then we have gifts.

Gifts are different from every other purchase we make. Gifts have only one initial function: to occupy the space within a parcel. We buy gifts not because we want them but because we want to get rid of them.

The point of giving is to earn gratitude and affection. We want recipients to open our parcel and look at us with wondrous, shining pleasure. We want them to think that we have been imaginative and thoughtful; that only we, in our sensitive, perceptive way, could have conceived of that particular present for that particular person.

So why then, I sometimes wonder, does anybody ever choose something that's been advertised as an acceptable gift ten times an evening on national television since early October? And even more puzzlingly: why do some peddlars of gifts put all their emphasis on how astonishingly cheap their products are?

I can only suppose, like Mr Portillo and *Chez Gourmet,* they've forgotten about that other audience.

Giles and the end of admass (which never existed in the first place)

I just can't wait for you to meet Giles. His mother comes from a famous New England family and his father is one of the world's most respected physicists. Giles himself was educated on three continents and has honours degrees in both business and the history of art. He played chess for Harvard and rugby for Oxford and speaks fluent French with a very slight Provençal accent. He's by no means conventionally good-looking but he's hugely attractive. And astonishingly, none of this seems to have gone to his head. I just can't wait for you to meet him.

You have never met Giles and have heard nothing but praise for him. Yet (if you are a man), the chances are you already dislike him intensely. Why should this be?

Yes, of course, envy, jealousy and petty competitiveness come into it; but that's not the whole story. What the whole story demonstrates is that perverse creativity of the human mind which most communicators continue to ignore.

And the reason they ignore it is because of a lingering belief in the existence of a mass audience.

The first falsely identified mass was the one created by the emergence of widespread literacy in the nineteenth century. The second was the one created in the twentieth century by that literate mass now acquiring serious spending power.

In 1955, in a book called *Journey Down A Rainbow*, the British writer J.B. Priestley described his recent tour of Texas. He found that a surge in national productivity combined with conspicuously increased personal affluence had produced a new phenomenon called marketing: and he found it horrible. Mass media carried massive amounts of advertising and high-pressure salesmanship to persuade mass audiences to conform to mass behaviour. The entire country was being presented with the same food, the same movies, the same songs and the same products: 'the creation of the mass mind, the mass man'. And the word he coined for this soulless, homogenous, wholly materialistic set of values was admass.

A couple of years later, Vance Packard published *The Hidden Persuaders*. It was not, as in popular belief, about advertising. It was about the emergence of people he called merchandisers who, in their dubious drive to appeal to their consumers' subconscious, were employing another new breed of professional called motivational researchers.

Both books, and many more like them, painted a deeply depressing picture. Individuality was in danger. Conformity was king. And the needs, wants and wishes of millions were being invisibly manipulated to enrich the coffers of a few omnipotent corporations.

With all the wisdom of hindsight, it is possible to see that both books gravely underestimated the wit, intelligence and cussed individuality of those consuming millions.

Today, and far less forgivably, the owners and users of mass communications risk making exactly the same mistake.

At least in North America, and in much of Europe and elsewhere, the 1950s were a time of a largely unremarked revolution. That new affluence and vastly increased productivity that had so alarmed Priestley between them engendered the most complete reversal in the balance of power that, to this day, producers and consumers have ever experienced. For at least a century, if you were a good producer, you had only to make something in order to sell it. And as a consumer, you had no choice but to accept your subordinate status; if you could afford a new car, you were touchingly grateful when granted a place on a waiting list. 'Any color you like as long as it's black' perfectly encapsulated the prevailing producer/consumer relationship – and was a totally justified attitude for any successful producer to hold. Two world wars both protected and protracted this state of unchallenged producer sovereignty.

And then came that gradual progression from under-capacity to over-capacity; from low disposable incomes to high disposable incomes; and almost imperceptibly, it was no longer enough simply to make in order to sell. Competition intensified. Consumers needed to be identified, courted, wooed and won; and, when won, retained. The emergence of marketing, and specialist marketing people (Packard's merchandisers), was as inevitable as it was necessary.

At exactly the same time, and for much the same reasons, mass media became available: for producers to buy into and for the public to consume. All Priestley's component parts were now in place: mass production had solved problems of under-capacity; mass marketing became a condition of survival; and the mass media meant that the mass producers could reach their mass audience extremely easily and, on a per capita basis, inexpensively. Admass achieved; or so it was widely believed.

But what seems to have gone unrecognised at the time, by both the manufacturers and the growing army of concerned social commentators, was that this was not a revolution complete and permanent in its outcome but rather a relatively short-lived period of transition. While it was true that the balance of power had swung overwhelmingly in favour of the consumer, consumers were still tightly restricted for choice: in both their choice of product and, even more so, their choice of broadcast media. In the United States, in 1960, the three biggest national television networks accounted for 94% of all television watched. Today that percentage is 39%.

Mass audiences existed not because tens of millions of people had been conditioned to respond identically to common stimuli but because when they turned on their television sets, there were only three significant buttons to press. Yet the very existence of these mass audiences – however involuntarily composed – encouraged the mass manufacturers and their advisers and agents to cling to their convenient belief in the existence and efficacy of mass communication.

For producers, after a century or so of ascendancy – of graciously releasing limited product to their patient public – it had been a painful enough process adjusting to their new role of supplicant. It is perhaps unreasonable to expect them to have come to terms immediately with the full implications of the revolution; indeed, there was no immediate compelling need to do so. But there will be soon.

To believe that 20 million people regularly watching the same programme at the same time is evidence that those 20 million people are identical in all important respects is to choose to ignore the most significant and also the most inconvenient truth about mass communication: it doesn't exist.

Mass *transmission*, of course, exists. Mass reception does not. And it is here that we return to the subject of Giles.

Long before interactivity became a hot word in marketing circles, it's been known that the act of reception – of even the humblest commercial message – is not a passive act. At some level of consciousness, every act of reception involves participation. Furthermore, receivers demand the right to participate: no transmission is complete until it has been received, challenged, modified and filtered through that individual's mental honeycomb of existing knowledge, misconception and prejudice.

As cited earlier (page 151), in *The Act of Creation* Arthur Koestler (often rather heavy-handedly) uses the example of humour to illustrate the communications process.

> *Economy, in humour as in art, does not mean mechanical brevity but implicitness…the listener must fill in the gaps, complete the hints; by doing so he…is compelled to co-operate, to repeat to some extent the process of inventing the joke, to recreate it in his imagination. Language itself is never completely explicit. Words have suggestive, evocative powers; but at the same time they are merely stepping stones for thought.* **The artist rules his subjects by turning them into accomplices**. *[Emphasis added.]*

And what is true for words is just as true for sounds and images and any other stimulus: they all evoke a subjective response in the mind of each individual receiver.

As Koestler hints, the greater the contribution made by the receiver, the more deeply the communication is likely to take hold; because to contribute to a communication is to become, in part, author of it. When I am told about Giles – and his distinguished parents and his two degrees and his ability to feel at home on three continents and in four languages including French which he speaks with a very slight Provençal accent – my need to contribute mounts. And since my informant – the transmitter – has been so relentlessly laudatory about Giles, my only available contribution is one of challenge and rejection. As a result of being told ten intensely complimentary things about Giles, not one of which I seriously doubt, I reach the unshakeable conclusion that Giles is a jammy toad.

The reception of every communication is active, participatory – and out of the immediate control of the transmitter; and nothing illustrates the widespread neglect of this truth more hilariously than the quaint and continuing use of the asterisk. It remains the dogged belief of censors that, when it comes to communications, input and take-out are the same thing; that imply and infer are synonyms; that audiences are passive and unquestioning. So it is, when censors choose to replace the letters uck with ***, they believe themselves to be protecting the young and the sensitive.

In fact, of course, the inevitable effect is to provoke the receiver into cracking the code, into completing the word. And those to whom the word is least familiar – and therefore those theoretically most susceptible to shock and outrage – will be precisely those who strive most actively to complete it. By demanding attention and participation, the censor has brilliantly ensured that the word has far greater potency than it would have had if left in its original form.

The receiving public's refusal to be passive and uncritical absorbers of messages infuriates politicians. 'We have made it perfectly clear' is one of their favourite phrases, usually uttered with some petulance.

They tell the world repeatedly that interest rates are down, employment figures are up, direct taxes have been cut by half, reported crime figures are too small to show up on the computer, and are upset and bewildered when all the world does is complain about the price of beer. The politicians may find this obduracy infuriating; we should find it liberating.

As we finally accept the disintegration of admass (which was never a reality anyway); as channels of commercial communication splinter irreversibly into smaller and smaller proportions of the whole; and as people's instinctive individualism finds new opportunities for expression: it is precisely this receiver insistence on taking an active part in the creative process that presents the world of commercial communications with its greatest opportunity.

It is today more widely recognised than ever before that every company has multiple audiences. There are consumers and customers; there are financial analysts and social commentators; and – hallelujah! – there is the company's own workforce. For years they were ignored with something close to contempt: yet, if kept well informed and encouraged to participate, they are now almost universally recognised as being management's most valuable (and most necessary) allies.

Whichever audience it is (and we need to remember that several overlap) the future rules are constant. See each audience not as adversaries but as potential accomplices. Invite and reward participation. Have faith in the implicit. Leave enough space for each receiver to complete the communication in his or her own individual way. Expect to be judged more by your actions than by your rhetoric.

It is commonplace now to apply all such sentiments to the internet. But the 'old' media have never in truth been one-way media. They've served us well for a hundred years; and if we employ them with wit and skill and understanding, they'll be serving us well for at least as long again.

As long as we remember, when it comes to provoking receiver response, that there's all the difference in the world between *'I can't wait for you to meet Giles'* and *'Giles can't wait to meet you.'*

> *The 'mass' is, of course, a fiction. Its function, as a linguistic device, is to eliminate the human status of the majority of people – or, at any rate, to deprive them of those distinctive features that make users of the term, in their own esteem, superior.*
>
> *John Carey*[1]

---

1   John Carey, *The Intellectuals and the Masses*, Faber & Faber, 1992

Never underestimate the value of bathwater

Here is a ridiculous prediction, but one which I feel more and more confident about making. This is partly because I get more reckless with age and partly because I'm beginning to think that it might be right.

The prediction is this: *For consumer marketing companies in the next century, there will be a serious scarcity of wasteful media.*

For the whole of the present century, we've known that buying mainstream media necessitates the acceptance of waste. When a brand of disposable nappies buys time in *Coronation Street*, no more than 5 per cent of that audience will own a malodorous brat. Even allowing for grans, mothers-in-law and the New Man, 80 per cent of those to whom we are so expensively talking will receive our message with implacable indifference. Of every ten seeds we scatter, eight will fall on barren ground.

We've accepted all this because there's been no alternative; and anyway, the economics of mass media have been such that the per capita cost of planting the two productive seeds has remained, if only just, acceptable.

Now, as we all know, things are changing. Divide the hyperbole by five; and we can still expect a lot more people to have access to a lot more television channels. Forget the glibbery about convergence, and we can still expect many more people to spend more time at their computer screens. Discount predictions about the end of the shopping-mall, and we can still expect e-commerce to become significant. Producers will know more and more about consumers, and will be presented with ever-more personalised ways of doing business with them.

For brand advertisers, most of this sounds encouraging. It may be confusing at first; but surely what it means is the beginning of the end of media waste? For the very first time, there will be channels and programmes directed exclusively at the owners of malodorous brats. Our disposable nappy commercial may not reach all the people we want to reach – but it will certainly exclude all the people we don't.

All baby. No bathwater.

What accuracy. What science. What efficiency. What frugality. What professionalism. What self-deception.

We have taken it as self-evident that advertising to those who will never buy is a waste of money, and so we have neglected to study them. And because we have selected mass media only reluctantly, we have taken it for granted that we will desert them as soon as we prudently can.

We have failed to recognise that, because the success of a brand resides in the strength of its reputation, there is a significant value in its being known to those who don't buy it as well as to those who do.

Very belatedly, we may well discover that what the baby's immersed in is not bathwater at all.

I'm encouraged in this view by two recent sightings.

There's a shop in Seoul called Masters Golf & Ski Center. Over its door it displays the slogan: 'WORLD FAMOUS BRANDS'. And these are the principal brands it stocks: Cleveland, Maruman, ENA, Daiwa, Yonex, S-Yard, Honma, Salomon, Nordica, Nicole and Goldwin.

I cannot tell you if these brands are indeed world-famous in South Korea. What I do know is that they are not world-famous in the world.

But Masters Golf & Ski Center has concluded that, to the citizens of Seoul, that doesn't matter a jot; and Masters Golf & Ski Center is right. Being thought to be world-famous is what brands need to strive for. Being thought to be world-famous is what makes people value them.

Real celebrity involves – indeed, demands – spillage. The Prince of Wales meets the Spice Girls. Bishops know about Pampers. There is a value in this – as Masters Golf & Ski Center instinctively recognises.

And for further support, I turn to my second sighting. This is Tom Wolfe, as quoted in the London *Evening Standard*:

> *I might just be tempted by television or movies. Not by the*
> *internet. Talk about a blind alley! I've known two outstanding*
> *young people, with creativity and talent and good backgrounds,*
> *who've gone into the internet thinking they are on the new frontier,*
> *and they are, but it's a frontier that seems to be made of ether.*

It's almost impossible to make a name for yourself on the internet unless you do something scandalous like Matt Drudge. It's a ghostland. It's not there.

The internet is a medium with almost no spillage. It is used, by choice, by several hundred million people daily – yet it has still to create its first celebrity. Wolfe cites Matt Drudge; but Drudge's notoriety is based on public media reports of his Lewinsky website. Amazon.com is (relatively) famous because it has been widely written about.

Private media, closed media, are very poor indeed at the crude creation of simple fame, which is what most brands need. 'It's almost impossible to make a name for yourself on the internet.'

As network television declines in share, and as people increasingly watch different things at different times, it will become harder and harder to reach mass, indiscriminate audiences, simultaneously, through broadcast media. None of the new media, brilliant though they are in their own respects, will be able to help.

And that's why there will suddenly be a scarcity of wasteful media.

This will be good news for the outdoor industry. It will be good for sponsorship and stunts. It will encourage others to say things like ''Tis the Season to be Tango'd' in 20 foot lights in Oxford Circus at Christmas time.

But it may not be good news for the owners and developers of brands.

Bet you can't remember how to tie the bow on your life-jacket

Marketing people like to believe that whatever it is they do, it's a great deal more difficult doing it now than it was when it was done by their predecessors. Standard whinges include: increasing competition; the virtual disappearance of functional product advantages; the fragmentation of media; the increased sophistication (i.e. canniness) of the consuming public; and the huge increase in the number of commercial messages to which these highly sophisticated persons are daily exposed.

Since all these developments affect our competitors at least as much as ourselves, I've never been able to understand why the job therefore gets more difficult: but in social commentator circles, of course, the development that causes the greatest concern is the last one.

You can open almost any work on marketing and find a figure. Let's not quibble – they're all guesses, anyway. Let's just agree that the average British adult (that's us, OK?) is confronted by well in excess of 1,000 commercial messages every week. Or is it every day? Or every morning before breakfast? Anyway – it's lots.

How do we cope with all this? Why don't we go mad? Where will it end? There are many wise and useful pages in Winston Fletcher's new book,[1] not least the ones that tackle this specific question.

He reminds us of the existence of selective perception, or what psychologists call 'perceptual defence': a protective mechanism the human brain has developed to screen and reject stimuli that are of no interest or relevance to it. By definition, we'll never know just how many stimuli we reject – but our capacity seems to be limitless.

1   Winston Fletcher, *Advertising Advertising*, Profile Books, 1999

To confirm this theory, I have long been tempted to conduct a two-part experiment. I calculate that the average global marketing director has taken 2.7 flights a week for the last 23 years. This means that he or she has been told how to find the life-jacket, how to tie the bow, when to pull the toggle and when (if at all) to blow the whistle 3,229 times. So for the first part of my experiment, I would conduct some in-depth interviews designed to establish just how accurately your average global marketing director can play back the information to which they've been so relentlessly exposed.

For the second part of my experiment, I would take the global marketing directors up to 35,000 feet over the Atlantic, at which point the Captain would announce that in exactly 14 minutes the aircraft would be ditching 500 miles west of Shannon.

The cabin crew would then, for the 3,330th time, run through the familiar emergency procedures – after which I would conduct a second set of interviews.

My hypothesis is this: that this particular transmission would be more attentively listened to than its countless predecessors, more accurately remembered – and therefore far more likely to be acted upon.

Some 40 years ago, James Webb Young wrote: 'People select advertisements they will give attention to just as they select the news items they will read in a newspaper. They make an immediate classification of both as "Of Interest" or "Not of Interest".[2] They still do.

---

2   James Webb Young, *How to Become an Advertising Man*, API, 1963

And so to Tracey Emin's bed

For me, the real value of the Turner Prize lies in the annual reminder it delivers of the phenomenon of framing.

By framing, I mean the singling-out of things: the italicising, the hi-lighting, the spotlighting. Year after year, objects on the Turner shortlist are singled out for mass attention; they are framed to attract our concentrated interest. We may like to think we judge things for themselves alone, uninfluenced by fashion or context or external commendation – but in that, of course, we deceive ourselves.

Our interpretation of just about anything – humble object, work of art, language – is crucially affected by its surroundings, by the frame in which it finds itself or into which it has been placed.

Pick an image – just about any image – and put a frame round it. Then draw it to the attention of others. By emphasising the image, the frame immediately gives it a higher rank of importance, greater prominence, an implied significance. As observers, we may well not know what that significance is, but we assume there must be one. And over time, if the frame is retained and the image consistently reproduced, then that image does indeed acquire significance. It has become significant because it is now familiar; and its familiarity is shared by millions. We say of Tara Palmer-Tomkinson that she is famous for being well known (as if we'd just thought of it ourselves) but we don't ask how. In fact, of course, she got like that because of the phenomenon of framing.

Frames are contexts. They carry their own baggage and are charged with their own values. They nudge us into different modes of interpretation. Depending on the frame, we may interpret and value precisely the same object in many different ways.

There is only one length of celluloid called *Carry on Camping* – but its audiences see many different films. Is it screened by (framed by) Channel 5 or by BBC2? At 3 pm or at 3 am? Is it opening a season at the National Film Theatre? Each different frame affects interpretation: from Donald McGill to post-modern irony.

A small ad reading 'Ex-governess seeks occasional evening work' would go largely unremarked in the chaste personal columns of *The Lady*. Exactly the same words in the window of a Kings Cross newsagent would prompt different expectations.

Context – the framing of things – critically determines how the brain deduces meaning.

Sentences form frames for single words – and have such a powerful influence on interpretation that the same single word can carry, quite unambiguously, a multiplicity of meanings. Does any of these sentences pose serious problems for you?

'President and Mrs Clinton left the White House with their daughter Chelsea this afternoon...'; 'In a London grudge match, Chelsea meet Fulham this evening...'; 'Early this morning police arrested seven revellers after scuffles broke out at the Chelsea Arts Ball...'; 'Rock cake's, Bakewell's & Chelsea's – all 10p each...'; 'It was at New York's legendary Chelsea Hotel that Sid Vicious first...'

There's no confusion. We don't even hesitate. Simply because of context, we know precisely how we are expected to decode each of those five usages.

I have been going to Shaftesbury in Dorset for about 40 years. Yet I've only just consciously registered the fact that it shares a name with London's nearest thing to Broadway. Shaftesbury is an unusual word; yet so distinctive are the respective frames, so discrete are the respective usages, that it simply never occurred to me that there was a connection. And of course, there isn't. However unusual, no single word, on its own, can be expected to carry significance from one frame to another.

Sponsors and sponsorship promoters forget this truth at their own risk. In the early days of sports sponsorship, it seemed logical to assume that the inclusion and promotion of the sponsor's name was all the return the sponsor needed or deserved. It may have seemed logical but it was undoubtedly wrong. When the name John Player is framed by a packet of cigarettes, it means cigarettes. When it is framed by the John Player League, it means cricket. Any transfer of fame or values will be brief and tenuous; and as the new frame gains currency, the connection will disappear completely. Unless the relationship is consciously and consistently (and expensively) kept alive, the two John Players will soon be as unrelated in people's minds as the two Shaftesburys are in mine.

And so to Tracey Emin's bed. I do not know whether this is art or not and I do not greatly care. But I do know this: had you and I, a year ago, chanced to find ourselves glancing through the open door of Tracey Emin's bedroom, we would not have stopped and gasped and confidently predicted a hot contender for next year's Turner. Unframed, such tableaux are invisible and so have no significance. But it is entirely possible that an exceptional photographer, glancing through that open door, would have seen the potential frame, would have selected and detached the image, and created a work of power and interest. That is what exceptional photographers can do that you and I cannot. And when the frame is called the Turner Prize, carrying all the weight and baggage that that implies, then Tracey Emin's bed – irrespective of intrinsic merit and by a process not dissimilar to that of Tara Palmer-Tomkinson and the Indian Rope Trick – does indeed become of singular interest.

As with those that go round spectacles, frames come in an infinite number of guises. The *Oxford Dictionary of Quotations* frames some thousands of quotations. Once enshrined, they enjoy a different status from all those other quotations still lurking undiscovered in great works. Harley Street forms a frame round medical practitioners, conferring weight and authority upon them. An Oscar frames a film forever. All lists, however arbitrarily compiled, frame their constituents. Booker shortlist books become instantly different from other books. And the world's most breathtaking example of framing is surely the Honours List. This supremely cynical device transforms its subjects from nonentity to nobility at the whisk of a chequebook.

It seems to be agreed that, to build a business on-line, you need to advertise off-line. As the new internet companies breed like gerbils, fighting for living space on limited territory, the canny ones will be looking for framing: hoping to be singled out, emphasised and highlighted. And as always, the most potent frames will be found in the crude, old-fashioned world of public media. It is not by chance that the word publicity starts with the word public.

Avoid criticism: write ads that nobody reads

Much bad advertising is bad not because it's off strategy or unpersuasive but because it's invisible. Absolutely nobody sees it, and so it represents the ultimate in waste.

This is the sort of advertising that should be regularly and publicly roasted yet very seldom is. And the reason, of course, is that it's invisible. Nobody roasts it because nobody reads it.

I may be the only person in the world to have read and noted the following copy:

> *In every era, the few who make the difference are those who dare to imagine a world beyond the horizon. A world in which old truths are enriched with new ones. The greater the resources, the greater the possibilities.*

Superimposed on this gibberish are two much bigger words at right-angles to each other. One is OBLITERATE and the other OBSTA-CLES. If you look very closely indeed, you will notice that a vertical rule in the left margin is in fact a legend listing the number of employees, offices and billions of dollars of assets that the bank in question can boast.

Yes, as you will already have guessed, this work is for a bank. And since I'm the only person to have read it, it falls to me to roast it.

I've no idea which language this advertisement was translated from or even which language it has been translated into. But as it happens, it doesn't matter. And it doesn't matter because – even had the words made sense and expressed something of interest to the reader – *nobody could ever have read them.*

The words above appear not in a newspaper but on one of those illuminated panels in international airports. Reasonably so, you might think: you are an international investment bank; your audience is international; international people may be expected to use international airports.

But these displays are on the walls of walkways. People walk along them. Being international business people to whom time is money, they walk along them briskly. Quite often there are moving belts, along which people also walk briskly. Even for the curious and the preternaturally keen-sighted, maximum reading time available is four seconds, or two if you're on the moving belt.

I cannot believe that this bank would spend money on any other purchase with such a total lack of common sense. Several people in the bank must have read the words; were they too embarrassed to ask what they meant? Somebody must have authorised the acquisition of the illuminated panels; did it not occur to them to ask how a busy person moving at ten miles an hour could be expected to read and absorb 40 words of gobbledegook from a distance of several feet?

The clients themselves must be international business people. They must be exposed to their own advertisements many times a day in many cities. How can they let them survive?

Or is it, perhaps, that they've just never seen them?

Consumer identification: the PG chimps and the novelist's mother

The reason why so many television commercials are stuffed with so many boring people is because of a theory called consumer identification.

The theory goes like this: if you want to get millions of very ordinary C2 people to buy your brand, you must cast your commercial with very ordinary C2-looking people. Those watching will then respond thus: 'Aha! I see that this brand is used by very ordinary C2 persons not unlike myself. I will therefore from henceforth buy this brand and no other.'

As a theory, it's flawed for several hundred reasons but I will concentrate on two; the first being best illustrated by the case of the novelist's mother.

He was a good friend and had just written his first novel, which was transparently autobiographical. His mother was a perfectly frightful woman and in his book he had portrayed her with an accuracy made effortless by 23 years of closely observed loathing. It was only as the book was published that he began to worry – but there was little he could do. So he inscribed a copy with some well-fashioned insincerity, sent it off to her and waited. A week or two later they met.

'Darling,' she said. 'What perfectly frightful people you do seem to know.'

That's the first flaw: people don't identify with people like themselves.

When I come across holiday advertisements featuring late-middle-aged gentlemen with wispy white hair in cardigans and garden chairs,

I am often in a cardigan and a garden chair myself. I know exactly what I am supposed to do: I am supposed to identify. In fact what I do is distance. I can't be the only person who doesn't want to go on holiday to meet people like myself.

Predicaments and problems, ambitions and emotions: that's what people identify with. You don't have to be black to identify with Othello, just jealous.

The second flaw is to think that the function of people in advertisements is to define the brand's users. It is not. It is to define the brand. And that's what they'll do whether you mean them to or not.

I do not know how many people there are in Great Britain who talk, dress, and entertain as people in After Eight commercials talk, dress and entertain. I do know that there aren't enough of them to eat 127 tons of After Eight every week.

One of the many reasons for the longevity and success of the PG chimps is that they portray reality, reassuringly, at one remove. Transpose in your mind all those chimp people back into real people and you've got a series of patronising situations with which nobody would have identified and which would have plunged the brand irreversibly down-market.

Clients and casting directors form an unholy alliance. They want ordinary people – but not too ordinary, you understand. So they choose people with no personality but preternaturally clean finger-nails.

Perhaps it's only people who earn their living portraying ordinary people in commercials who really do identify with the people they see in commercials. But then, as we know from the case of the novelist's mother, that doesn't happen either.

Brand loyalty: irrational affinity vs. the golden manacle

On Monday of this week, John Kenneth Galbraith, now aged 90, was given an honorary doctorate by the London School of Economics – and was invited to use the occasion to give a lecture.

Reflecting on the achievements of this century, he said: 'More important, there has been an escape from the worst feature of modern existence – hard, tedious, boring toil. This has not been eliminated, but one of the greatest accomplishments of the century has been the reduction in the proportion of people so engaged.

'The word "work" is our most misleading social term. It designates the occupation of those who would be very unhappy without it. And we use the same word for hard, repetitive, even painful toil. No word in the English language stretches over such different conditions. There is the further perverse fact that most of those who enjoy what is called work are those who are best paid. And they are also allowed the most leisure.'

Because English is such a rich language, with such a huge vocabulary, we allow ourselves to believe that we can trust it; that we are always using the precise and appropriate word to convey the precise and unambiguous meaning that we intend. But we often are not – and it's important that we recognise it.

I've long been fretting about this word work – and am delighted that Galbraith has opened it up.

If the only way you can support your family is to go every day to a petfood factory and strip the remnants of flesh off animal carcasses: that's called work. And it's work you dread; work that tyrannises you. The kind of work that the sooner you can chuck the happier you'll be.

An edited version of a speech to a Research International seminar, London, July 1999

At the other end of the spectrum, there are men and women of huge talent, well rewarded and much applauded, who will say – and mean – 'I live for my work.' And they will – quite voluntarily and with enormous pleasure – hope to go on working until they die.

And in between these two extremes, there are millions of lucky people such as most of us, who – by and large, most of the time, are delighted to have a home life and a working life; and however much we might pretend otherwise, view the prospect of a life without work with mixed emotions. And I don't mean a life without income; I mean a life without work.

That the single word 'work' should be expected to cover all these vastly different conditions is not only ridiculous but dangerous: because it inhibits understanding and communication. How can the same single, apparently unambiguous word be expected to describe that which some people live for and that which some people would almost rather die than go on doing?

Galbraith is probably right when he says that no word in the English language stretches over such different conditions. But a word that needs to be looked at with almost equivalent suspicion is the word of this morning. We have begun to use the word loyalty with reckless imprecision.

Let me take two extreme examples: the Case of The Husband's Best Friend and the Case of the Golden Handcuffs.

Maybe it never happened to you – but it's happened to lots of people I know. You, a man, have a best friend. He, this friend, has absolutely nothing whatever to commend him. He is a shambles of a person; shifty, unreliable, drinks too much and is chronically indiscreet. And he is your best friend. Then you get engaged. And your bride to be is totally baffled by this friendship. When they meet for the first time, he's clearly been drinking, he looks a mess and he makes several unfunny references to several other women from your past.

This is your best friend – and you want him to be your Best Man.

There is absolutely no logic in all of this. Your wife-to-be is right to be baffled. You can give her absolutely no reasons, however feeble, for your affection for this creep. This is loyalty; blind, irrational loyalty that brings you no credit and offers no joy. And, let it be said, exactly the same can be true of the Chief Bridesmaid.

And then there's the Case of the Golden Handcuffs. Your company rates you very highly; you have a particular skill that competitors long for; and so to guarantee your continued commitment, your company fixes you up with a handsome pair of golden handcuffs. Share options, perhaps, that cannot be exercised until 2005. So there you are, not real-

ly enjoying yourself very much, not really respecting your own company
– yet aware that any decision to leave would entail severe financial penalties.

And this, too, is called loyalty: achieved, after all, as a result of what is
called a loyalty programme. But this loyalty and the loyalty towards the
appalling best friend not only have almost nothing in common, but in
many respects are diametrically opposite.

The first is irrational, the second is not. The first contains no demonstrable self-interest, the second nothing but self-interest. The first is from
the heart, the second from the head. The first sees the subject in a state
of voluntary commitment; the second sees the subject in a kind of cap-
tivity. Yet we use – dangerously – the same word, loyalty, to signify both.

All this, of course, has a great deal to do with *brand* loyalty – which is
why I've gone on about it.

The marketing world has done much to confuse an understanding of
what loyalty really means by hijacking the word and turning it into a synonym for what in reality is just a price promotion. There's nothing whatever wrong with price promotions – and they're all the more effective
and laudable when they are skilfully disguised – but that's what they are.

For the Case of the Golden Handcuffs, read the Case of the Green
Shield Stamps. The thinking behind trading stamps is precisely the same
as the thinking behind share options. They both exist to form a financial
disincentive to people to exercise free choice. They both seek to manacle
their recipients – not through affection but through money.

And so do, of course, what are called loyalty cards.

You'll remember that Sainsbury's got a very bad press for dismissing
the Tesco loyalty card as another version of Green Shield Stamps – and
they looked even more out-of-touch when the card soon proved to be a
huge success; but Sainsbury's was right. At root, in principle, with none
of the down-market overtones, the loyalty card is a close relation to the
trading stamp. And they're both Golden Handcuffs.

The equivalent in marketing of the husband's best friend is obviously
what has been called this morning brand affinity: a close, intense identification of person with brand that goes way, way beyond performance or
value.

I think I first became aware of it a great many years ago when sitting
in on group discussions and hearing women talk about Persil. Except
they didn't talk about Persil – they talked about *my* Persil. And you
realised that they were fiercely loyal to their Persil and would defend it
against all criticism and would deeply resent any attempts the makers

might make at radical change. And I have absolutely no doubt that this deep-seated, long-standing sense of affinity was what saved Persil from even greater trouble when it had problems with Persil Power just a few years ago. When people are truly loyal – truly affectionate – they can be almost limitlessly forgiving.

And anyone who still doubts the potential power and intensity of brand/consumer relationships should never forget the story of New Coke.

The Coca-Cola Company is no slouch at marketing. It had done more product research than any company ever – and had rock-solid evidence that a majority of its consumers preferred a slightly different flavour.

So, in 1986, at immense expense, New Coke was launched – and was instantly and comprehensively rejected by the American people. Within 77 days, Classic Coke – the original – was back on the market and being rapturously greeted by its adoring American public.

Sergio Zyman was the marketing mind behind this extraordinary event – and as he reveals in his new book, they'd asked all the right questions except one: they'd never tried to find out how people would feel if Coca-Cola – *their* Coca-Cola – was taken away from them. They'd never tried to quantify the loyalty factor – the irrational, affectionate, Husband's Best Friend factor.

It's not my intention this morning to praise one method of achieving brand loyalty at the expense of the other: simply to point out that they are very, very different, and that just about the only thing they have in common is a word.

Most good marketing demands both. If you rely totally on golden handcuffs – on loyalty cards and frequent flyer schemes – you run two risks.

First, that any such initiative, if successful, will very soon be leap-frogged by competitors. By the end of the trading stamp war, I remember being very disappointed to be offered less that quintuple stamps with every gallon of petrol. And second, they can breed a certain inner discontent. They can make people feel that they're captive – or *unhappy prisoners* in the language of this morning. It can make people wonder about their own motives – and whether they're not sacrificing something called quality in the interests of some not hugely significant savings.

Which is why the deliberate attempt to build and maintain the brand affinity type of loyalty – the Husband's Best Friend type of irrational loyalty – is such an important complementary activity.

It is of course very much harder to do and probably takes a good deal longer to prove its worth. But its worth, when achieved, is incalculable.

Unlike loyalty schemes, affinity loyalty cannot be leap-frogged. There is nothing very much your competitors can do about it. Because it's irrational and exists only in the heads of people, it cannot be challenged or copied or capped. Only a long period of inept brand management and inadequate brand investment will neutralise it.

The risks inherent in owning such loyalty are small – and the main one is the risk of management complacency. If you know you are loved and trusted by your consumers, you may be tempted to do nothing else but bask in the beam of their irrational affection. You may get away with it for a year or so – but not for much longer. Because consumers do not appreciate having their affection for a brand taken for granted. Affection and trust need to be continually earned. Activity, loyalty schemes, promotions (as long as they are in keeping with the brand personality) will all help to keep the brand vibrant and safe from self-satisfaction.

The distinction between the two kinds of loyalty is well illustrated by the tale of two airlines.

I have a British Airways posh card and I collect Air Miles and I fly British Airways whenever I can because I like my Air Miles and I like being able to be generous with my Air Miles to members of my family at absolutely no cost to myself. Technically, therefore, I am loyal to British Airways: a very high proportion of my discretionary flying is done with BA. But I have to tell you – I very slightly resent it. I am aware of the golden handcuffs. I know that I have been very slightly manacled. I have nothing but praise for British Airways – but I cannot find it in myself to be fond of them. That is why such loyalty as I have is technical, not emotional. My heart is not with them. I am always open to a better offer.

My feelings about Air Canada, however, are very different.

Many years ago, I was on an ordinary, everyday, Air Canada shuttle from Montreal to Toronto: quite short, utterly uneventful.

Uneventful, that is, until we came in to land. First we hit the concrete hard, but with the starboard wheels only. The plane bounced some 20 feet into the air and lurched to the left. Everything that was loose in the cabin went first to the roof of the cabin and then down again on to the passengers.

One or two of the passengers were loose themselves.

There were several screams, not all of them muffled.

Then we hit the ground again, this time with the other set of wheels, and bounced again and eventually settled. Reverse thrust was applied viciously, brakes screeched – and so, again, did a passenger or two. In almost complete silence, the plane came to a halt – and we heard the PA system come alive – with that little click. And I knew exactly what I was going to hear.

I was going to hear the captain explain that an unusual crosswind component over the threshold of Runway 27 Left had over-integrated with the jet vortex from a departing 747 thus precipitating acute wind-sheer.

But he didn't say that or anything like it. In a measured Canadian voice he said: 'Ladies and Gentleman, this is Captain Cooper speaking. I'd like you to know that I've been a qualified commercial pilot for over 15 years, 10 of them with Air Canada – and that's the worst fucking landing I've ever made. As soon as we arrive at the gate, I shall come through the cabin and apologise to you in person.'

We got to the gate...the plane came to a halt...Captain Cooper appeared through the curtains – and the entire cabin erupted with applause. As he walked down the aisle, we cheered and clapped – and blue-rinsed matrons, their eyes brimming with gratitude, stretched out their hands to touch the hem of his uniform.

He, who minutes earlier had very nearly killed us, was now our saviour. Air Canada became, for everyone on board, the world's favourite airline. Irrational, Husband's Best Friend loyalty had been established – in my case forever.

It did occur to me to wonder, on my way into Toronto, just how often Captain Cooper had used this approach – and indeed if he was now instructed to make such landings: perhaps as a routine part of Air Canada's Customer Loyalty and Retention Programme.

By trying to explore the anatomy of loyalty, I have hoped to underline its importance to brands and marketing. Anything that helps us understand the nature of loyalty – in its very different manifestations – will be of immediate interest and value.

Was it really more fun then?

*When people still working in advertising agencies realise that I first started
with an advertising agency over 40 years ago, they get a sort of wistful
gleam in their eye – and I know exactly what they're going to say. It is my
own most Frequently Asked Question: 'Was it really more fun then?'*

*Two things make an accurate answer difficult. The first is all to do with
growing up and being promoted and trying to become responsible and
having to hire and fire people and finding that other people are expecting
you to win business or keep business or restore morale or make budgets: and
that's certainly not as much fun as knocking out a couple of pretty good ads
in the morning and then playing snooker for the rest of the day.*

*I suppose there must be some people who get a great buzz from meeting
budgets and cutting costs and trying to hold on to flakey accounts and
smiling in the lift when they've just lost four new business pitches in a row –
but I wasn't one of them. There was a great deal of fun, all the way through:
but there was more at the beginning than at the end.*

*The other problem is memory. So in the hope of checking memory against
record, I've recently re-read two good advertising novels:* Murder Must
Advertise *by Dorothy L. Sayers, first published in 1933, and* The Agency
Game *by Bernard Gutteridge, first published in 1954.*

*To the modern eye, the Sayers agency seems quite formal. First names are
never used – everybody is either Mr Tallboy or Miss Rossiter – but they do
have fun. They make jokes, they gossip in the typing pool, they go out to
lunch, they have staff parties and they play cricket matches against their
clients. It's clear that the workers at Pym's Publicity were having a great
deal more fun than their equivalents in the City or in insurance.*

By the 1950s, to judge from The Agency Game, *advertising people were
having even more fun. The workers at Slender Oliphant & Queste scheme,*

lust and above all, drink. They drink Tio Pepe and beer and brandy and pink gin. The account man Shotover invariably starts his evening session at the Lion with a couple of double-double gins and tonic.

The two new products that occupy them most are a bra and a chocolate drink that turns out to be an aphrodisiac. They make a potent combination.

But I was pleased to note that both books confirmed my instinct. The people having the most fun were the juniors; and the people having the least fun were respectively Messrs Pym and Slender.

So I think the truthful answer to the 'Was it really more fun then?' question is:

> *Advertising has always been more fun than doing practically anything else and it probably still is. But if you want to go on having as much fun as you did at the beginning of your career, you must be careful never to get promoted.*

This means, of course, that before very long you won't have a career – but I'll leave you to sort that one out for yourself.

Part Five

Making advertising happen

Marketing 1948: how easy it was – just like Wembley

I haven't read them all, of course, so I may be wrong. But I believe it to be the case that every single marketing strategy written since 1955 contains the sentence: 'It is essential that we recognise the increasing sophistication of our consumers.' Every year, for at least 40 years, in compound leaps, consumers have been growing more and more sophisticated. Where, I sometimes wonder, will it all end?

The precise nature of this escalating sophistication is never specified, but day-to-day observation eliminates most alternatives. It can't mean better-mannered or more chicly dressed or more suavely articulate. So it can only mean smart. In other words, less gullible. In other words, less easy to sell things to.

And all at once, the reason for this annual sophistication warning becomes clear. What we're really saying is: hey, this is getting difficult. They're getting very stroppy out there. These days they're all marketing-literate and icon-saturated and can spot the flaws in the rural image through a one-way mirror. So don't be surprised if this relaunch bombs, know what I'm saying?

It's never actually said, but there's often a hint of regret about all this: an unspoken nostalgia for the good old days when all you had to do was tell the peasants to go out and buy something and, with a deferential touch to the flat cap or a bob of the bonnet, they would obediently do so. Consumers, in those days, knew their place. They'd been put on this earth to consume and that, with touching gratitude, is precisely what they did. How easy – how very, very easy – it must have been in marketing before all this sophistication set in.

I haven't read them all, of course, so I may be wrong. But I believe it to be the case that every single advertising brief written since 1955 contains the sentence: 'Given the intensified competition in the marketplace, we expect our advertising to work even harder for us in the coming fiscal.'

Every year, relentlessly, the job of the advertising agency gets more and more difficult. How easy it must have been – how very, very easy – when advertising briefs read: 'Given our product's significant price advantage and the buoyant state of the market as a whole, little if any contribution will be expected from our advertising in the coming fiscal.'

There are, I expect, athletes preparing for Atlanta who wish they were going to Wembley. How easy it must have been – how very, very easy – to win the 100 metres back in 1948.

It's a puzzling form of self-deception, this. Comparisons across time are meaningless. Winning things gets neither harder nor easier. The increased sophistication of your consumers, real or imagined, will affect your competitors no less than yourself. There has never been a time when advertising was expected to do anything other than work hard.

To the envious practitioners of 2040, marketing in the 1990s will presumably seem to have been a doddle. How easy, they will think, how very, very easy.

The reason it doesn't seem so now is because it isn't.

What Jim Young said. And what he didn't say

James Webb Young practised, taught and wrote about advertising for 50 years. For the whole of that time he either worked for, or was a consultant to, J. Walter Thompson. So much of what he taught and wrote had such a timeless sanity about it that I took to using his work – particularly *How To Become an Advertising Man* – as a basis for internal training. The following, edited piece started life in 1978 as a presentation, with a great many illustrative examples of advertising, to a meeting held in Majorca of J. Walter Thompson European managers. As in the title, the book employs the masculine throughout. This is not because Jim Young wrote it exclusively for men, or believed men more suited to advertising than women. Indeed, he worked closely for much of his life with Helen Resor, an outstanding copywriter and a great encourager of women in advertising. As was common at the time, he employed the masculine to represent both genders.

I'm taking as my text today Jim Young's book *How to Become an Advertising Man*. I suspect that most of you know it well and will have read it more than once. What I *don't* know is what proportion of all the people working in J. Walter Thompson offices around the world have read it – or even heard of it: but if the London office is any guide, I suspect the proportion is fairly small, such as one per cent.

I believe Jim Young was one of the more remarkable advertising men, and that this particular book is one of the best – and shortest and simplest – ever written on the subject by anyone, anywhere. What's more, he's *ours:* and arguably, second only to Stanley Resor, he was more responsible than anyone else for building the company and its reputation around the world.

It is *not* my intention to canonise Jim Young: to give him the kind of papal infallibility that some members of Ogilvy & Mather seem determined to confer on their remarkable but fallible founder. Nor is this talk more than a first attempt to see if, in Jim Young, we might not have an important and under-utilised resource that could help us professionally. We have often, as a company, been proud of the fact that we were once described as 'the university of advertising'. And I suspect, particularly over the last ten years or so, we have tried more systematically than most agencies to pass on knowledge, to think about theory and to generalise as well as practise – and to encourage those theories and generalisations to be questioned, modified, invalidated and improved.

Yet, unlike proper universities and more easily defined disciplines, there is a curious lack of agreed theory or accumulated knowledge on the subject of advertising. We often complain that everybody thinks they're an expert in advertising: whether they're consumerists, bureaucrats, people we meet at parties, consumers themselves or 23-year-old brand managers. But perhaps we make it all too easy for these varied groups to see themselves as experts – simply because we aren't expert ourselves. The mere fact that someone has worked in an advertising agency for a few years, with little or no formal training or education in the subject, does not, in my view, entitle that person to believe himself or herself to be an expert.

So my main objective, in redirecting our minds and attention to Jim Young's book, is not that we should stop thinking for ourselves and just accept without question or modification what the man said, but more to identify one of the rare pieces of clearly expressed advertising philosophy and use it as a kind of historical fix. What *was* he saying and doing and writing between 1912 and 1964? Are there any obvious truths and guidelines we've forgotten? Have we added anything since, and if so, what? And can a good, hard, respectful look back help us look forward – and be better at what we do than we currently are?

As Jim Young says in the Preface to his book: 'Becoming an Advertising Man is a life-long process. I have been engaged in it for over 50 years, and still see no end to the road.' And that wasn't just false modesty; he knew that to be true and of course it still is. He goes on to define, in Chapter 1, what he means by the term Advertising Man: 'The true Advertising Man, as the term is used in this book, is he who has the knowledge, skills, experience and insights to advise advertisers how best to use advertising to accomplish their objectives. *And* to execute the advertising to do this.'

Now, I've called this talk 'What Jim Young said. And what he didn't say' because I find that what he takes for granted, what is implicit – in other words, what he *doesn't* say – is at least as illuminating as what he *does*. And this definition is a good example. For as long as I can remember, we've put great emphasis in this company on the account group, or planning group, or project team. Certainly it has been agreed that the account man should ultimately be responsible for the output and the success of that group – but we never expect him to be good at everything. Jim Young makes no such assumptions. He talks about the Advertising Man as an *individual.*

In Chapter III, he picks up the word 'knowledge', that which he believes the advertising individual should try to acquire, and defines it as follows.

(1) Knowledge of propositions
(2) Knowledge of markets
(3) Knowledge of messages
(4) Knowledge of carriers of messages
(5) Knowledge of trade channels
(6) Knowledge of how advertising works
(7) Knowledge of the specific situation

He recounts how one young man responded to this list by saying 'Sounds to me as though only God Almighty could ever meet all the requirements.'

Young goes on to say: 'If you should have any such feeling, let me hasten to point out that in the practice of advertising today you will find yourself supported by specialists in many phases of these different categories, and will have at hand many tools in the way of reference books, and many developed techniques for acquiring current facts.'

So, while he is certainly conceding that help is, and should be, available to the Advertising Man, he is still not talking about a group or a team. He goes on to say: 'There is a very considerable range of knowledge in all these categories with which you must become familiar, and some of which you must master.'

So the first question I'd like to leave hanging in the air is this: 'Has the growth of the concept of the account group, composed of so-called specialists in media, creativity and planning, quite unintentionally made the existence of the complete Advertising Man less likely? What, today, is the role of the account executive? Does he know enough, *himself*, about advertising? And if he doesn't, does it matter?'

My own view is that it does matter. Clients today, no less than yesterday, are looking – at least at times – for a *man* (not a group) who has (to quote Jim Young) 'the knowledge, skills, experience and insights to advise advertisers on how to use advertising to accomplish their objectives'.

I'm not advocating the return of the one-man-band, nor the invariable use of the first person singular. I am suggesting that more of us ought to know more than we do; and that anyone entrusted with an account should be able to give, personally, expert advice to his client without having to say: 'I'll call a group meeting tomorrow morning and let you have our thoughts as soon as possible.' Could this just possibly be why more and more clients want to talk directly to the creative people?

So the first thing Jim Young didn't say was: 'Staff an account with an account group, which is a collection of specialists under the supervision of a man who isn't one himself.' If he had felt that, he wouldn't have given the book the title he did.

Many of you will know that Young, for years, used to write a series of book reviews for the New York office house magazine. And his constant sub-heading for these reviews was: 'The best books about advertising are not about advertising' – because Young believed that the really good Advertising Man should not only know a great deal about all aspects of advertising, but also a great deal about the real world outside. In his book he says this: 'No limits can be placed on the kinds of knowledge that are useful to the Advertising Man. Indeed, it can safely be said that the broader his education, and the better stocked his mental pantry, the better at his job he is likely to be.' And he goes on: 'Every really good creative person in advertising whom I have known has always had two noticeable characteristics. First, there was no subject under the sun in which he could not easily get interested. Second, he was an extensive browser in all sorts of fields.'

As I look at the advertising being produced at the moment, at least in Britain, it seems to me that much of it has been produced in total isolation from the real world. The prose style that's used in press copy owes nothing to any other prose style except that used in other advertisements. The makers of advertisements seem increasingly obsessed by only one subject: advertisements. If this is so, then two consequences will follow. First, since the receivers of advertisements are only too conscious of the rest of the world – socially, politically, culturally, economically – then the advertisement will fail adequately to connect the advertised brand or service to that bigger, truer world. And second, imitation and lack of originality become more likely. Advertising is feeding, I think, far too much on advertising, and not nearly enough on the wider, far more interesting world outside. We are becoming a bit like those economic forecasters who refuse to study, let alone build into their forecasts, social trends and human emotions.

Sometimes today we say about another: 'He's the complete advertising professional' – by which we mean he lives, eats and sleeps nothing but advertising and his clients' problems. He reads nothing but advertisements, talks nothing but advertising, plays nothing but golf with the advertising manager.

What Jim Young didn't say was that he would regard such a man not as a professional but as a narrow-minded amateur. *His* true professional was 'an extensive browser in all sorts of fields' – social, political and cultural. Movies, television, novels good and bad, biographies, specialist magazines in which he isn't personally interested, gossip, newspapers national and local: Jim Young's professional knows them all – and relates them all back to the job he does.

Isn't it just possible that we, today, tend to think of Young's professional as a dilettante? And isn't it just possible that our clients, obsessed as they have to be with labour relations, government intervention and the price and availability of cocoa beans and packaging material, might not welcome an advertising adviser with a wider knowledge and a wider view of the world than they themselves have the time or the inclination to acquire?

Let me turn now to Chapter IV, entitled 'Knowledge of Propositions'. Says Young:

> *Before you ever put pen to paper to prepare the advertisement, script or storyboard, you had better:*
>
> *(1) Be crystal clear in your own mind what the proposition is.*
> *(2) Have reason to believe that it is an appealing proposition to the particular group of people you are addressing.*

We all have some doubts today about the word 'proposition' because it seems to imply input rather than response. (See 'The consumer has a mind as well as a stomach', page 139.) I'm fairly certain, and this is a presumptuous statement, that Jim Young himself would happily agree that it is more useful, or less dangerous, to think in terms of consumer response, rather than messages or propositions; if only because there's a great deal of internal evidence in his book to suggest that's the way he instinctively thought. He took response theory so much for granted that he hardly bothers to stress its importance.

Just one example to justify this bold assertion. On the subject of messages he makes the point that simply gaining attention is not enough. What you must do, says Young, is 'say something which, in effect, makes him say: "Hello, what's this?" What you must say is something carefully calculated to touch an exposed nerve of your prospect's self-interest.' And he quotes two headlines which he once ran as a comparative test in mail-order bookselling: 'The Principles of Accounting by J.C. Bentley' and 'Are you an Accountant, or only a Bookkeeper?'.

He asks the reader which produced the more orders. He doesn't actually give the answer because he doesn't have to. The second headline is not, of course, a message or a proposition; it is a very simple stimulus that provoked a very powerful response. As Young again says, 'You must make so clear the relationship between what you have to offer and the prospect's wants, needs or existing desires that, hopefully, he will say: "That's for me!"' In other words, *response*.

Therefore, I think it fair to say that strongly implicit in Young's work is Response Theory – so let me go back to his propositions:

(1) 'Be crystal clear in your own mind what your proposition is.'
(2) 'Have reason to believe that it is an appealing proposition to the particular group of people you are addressing.'

Now – even accepting the implicit assumption of response rather than input here – I'm not sure that we would or should accept that completely today.

I'm reminded of the producer who is alleged to have said to a new-wave film director in some exasperation: 'You mean you don't accept that a good movie should have a beginning and a middle and an end?' To which, you may remember, the director replied: 'Oh I do, I do. But not necessarily in that order.'

Young's two points remain almost self-evidently valid: but not necessarily in that order. As we use qualitative interviews and group discussions more and more to get insights into the minds of our markets, we quite frequently discover what our proposition should be (Point 1) only *after* we've found out a great deal about the particular group of people we are addressing (Point 2).

In reality, the process is probably semi-circular anyway: you may start with Point 2, go back to Point 1 in order to form a hypothesis, return to Point 2 to validate or invalidate – and so on. Whatever the sequence, the objective must be right: as Young says later, 'I hope it will be clear to you how close is the relationship between the definition of your Proposition and the definition of your Market.'

Throughout the book, Young uses the word 'market' in a consistent and very specific sense. Not in the way that we talk about the beer market or the paper towel market or the wet soup market – but as a target group: a phrase I've never had much confidence in at the best of times.

Long before people became openly doubtful about the value of standard demographics and started talking about psychographics, Young had this to say: 'Often the key denominator of what constitutes a market is some *qualitative* factor of taste, interest or habit, not always indicated by the more measurable factors of income, age, education, home-ownership, etc. and not registered in available statistics.'

This seems to me just as true now as it ever was. The habit of defining a market, or a target group, as 'C1, C2 housewives, 25–34, with children' seems just as pointless and unhelpful. Unless you know why your market is your market, you won't find it easy either to understand them or to appeal to them.

It's often said of the J. Walter Thompson London office that the only time we show evidence of real imagination and originality is when we design leaving cards. According to the myth, this is because creativity is unshackled as the creative people are freed from the deadening effect of strategies, account planners, account executives and clients. If it *is* true, and if there *is* a reason, I suspect it's quite a different reason and almost the opposite of the myth. The writers and designers of the leaving card do not have unlimited freedom: they have very limited freedom indeed. They have to produce a leaving card that is precisely right for one particular individual. Their good fortune is that they know that one individual very well indeed. If you asked anyone to write and design a leaving card for an A/B 25–34 male living in the south-east of England, married with 2.4 children, I doubt you'd get the customary degree of relevance and originality.

Still on the subject of markets, Young has another point to make, one that I believe to be vastly more important today than ever.

We are all aware of the problem of what tends to be called 'advertising clutter'. We are bombarded with statistics that demonstrate that the average US housewife is subjected to 16.6 million commercial messages every day before lunch. We use phrases like 'share of mind' (which doesn't seem to me to mean anything very much). At least in part because of all this research, particularly in the United States at the moment, there is considerable dependence on a research system that Jim Young never heard about, called Day-After-Recall.

The day after a commercial has been screened, Mrs Burke's telephonists get to work and they phone around until they've talked to a given number of people who claim to have been watching the programme in which the commercial was placed. On the basis of these people's answers to certain questions, and for a considerable fee, Mrs Burke will then tell you whether your commercial beat, or did not beat, the 'norm' for that category. So if the norm is 24 and you get 29 you're still in business, but if you get 19 you're in trouble. One of the questions Mrs Burke and her competitors *don't* ask is whether the people answering the telephone were likely to be in the market (in Jim Young's sense) in the first place.

Yet, as Young has said, 'People select the advertisements they will give attention to just as they select the news items they will read in a newspaper. They can make an immediate classification of both as: "Of Interest" or "Not of Interest". They will classify your advertisement as "Of Interest" in proportion as they are "in the market" for what you have to offer them.'

The only way, now as then, to gain and *hold* attention is to evoke the response, 'That's for me.'

To quote Young: 'Few, if any, products or propositions have universal appeal at a given moment in time.'

So if our market is 10 per cent of the population, of which half isn't watching that particular television programme, Mrs Burke's telephonists are very expensively telling us whether or not our commercial was remembered by the 95 per cent of people we didn't want to influence in the first place.

And finally, another comment on what Jim Young *didn't* say. Not because he was ignorant or unenlightened but because in his time it didn't need to be said. Let me return to the word 'creativity'. It seems to me that today, in many countries, advertising agencies are evaluated primarily on what is called creativity – and such research as has been done bears out this view. There seems to be a single scale, a single dimension, like this:

Dull | Visible
Old-fashioned | Fashionable

No awards | Awards

The nearer you are to the left of this scale, the worse you are; and the nearer to the right, the better you are. And this perception of agencies – what might be termed the Clio Effect – seems to be held by clients, potential clients, trade press journalists, suppliers, and perhaps most strongly of all by the people who work in agencies.

What Jim Young didn't say – because he didn't have to – was that this was not his perception of agencies at all. He clearly had at the back – and the front – of his mind, a rather different dimension: a different scale altogether.

Two scales this time, with the upright line a dotted line: to suggest, as I believe, that it has lost its value. At the top: 'It works. Responsive. Advertis*ing*.' And at the bottom: 'Irresponsible. Self-indulgent. Advertise-*ments*.' (To which one might add: ignorant, amateur, thoughtless.)

Increasingly, advertising is talked about as though it had no function. We ourselves refer to our 'creative product' as though the advertisements we produce were ends in themselves, to be looked at and evaluated as if they were pictures in an art gallery. In Jim Young's book, the word 'creativity' is used very infrequently; and when he does use it, he uses it virtually as a synonym for effectiveness.

There are two ways of judging the Sydney Opera House. First: what does it *look* like? Is it aesthetically pleasing? Is it original and imaginative as a piece of design, as a piece of architecture? Second: does it *work*? Does it function as an opera house? Are the auditoriums the right size? Can you park? Is there enough height over the stage for storing scenery? Is it acoustically satisfactory?

More and more, when we look at our own work, we ask only the first set of questions. What does it look like on our showreel? Will it be a good advertisement for us? Will it make us seem 'creative'? When we should, of course, be asking: did it work? Did it make the client more successful? How did it do it?

I believe Jim Young would be, if not horrified, certainly bewildered.

I'm not suggesting that the horizontal line is unimportant nor that it will go away. I am suggesting that it is our job, as managers, to reinstate that vertical line in the minds of all those who evaluate advertising and advertising agencies.

'Did it work?' If it did, then it was – in the proper sense – creative. It created a desire in the mind of the market. It was money well spent. It is why advertising exists.

The horizontal line doesn't need to be argued: either an advertisement seems to be inventive and original or it doesn't. That's all you can say as a judge or a potential client viewing a showreel.

The vertical scale, effectiveness, is by contrast invisible. It's one of the biggest mistakes in the business to believe the old saying, 'Good advertising speaks for itself.' It doesn't. Somebody – us – has to speak for it. Somebody has to say: 'This was the problem, this was the budget, this was the competition, this is what the market thought, this is what they wanted to hear, this is how we thought of saying it, this is how we changed and improved it, this is the finished result – and this is what happened to sales.'

If you wanted to plot J. Walter Thompson on the map, I know where I'd like us to be – in the top, right-hand corner, as near to the top of the vertical scale as possible – and as near to the right of the horizontal scale as possible. But in that order.

Some of the accounts we handle, because of their nature and their consumers, allow us to develop – indeed, they demand – self-evidently 'creative' campaigns. Not one of those opportunities should be lost: our clients need them and so do we. But some of the accounts we handle do *not* necessarily require self-evidently creative treatment – and we're being irresponsible when we try to make them that way.

Every account ought to be high on the vertical scale. Every account should have a good story to tell, even if not an award-winning commercial to show.

I have been told on occasions that, in today's world, this approach sounds defensive and apologetic; that to talk about effectiveness sounds like an excuse for not being creative. I don't believe it. What, after all, are clients *paying for*?

We can't go on playing a game when we secretly disapprove of the rules.

Let's go back to James Webb Young: 'The true Advertising Man, as the term is used in this book, is he who has the knowledge, skills, experience and insights to advise advertisers how best to use advertising to accomplish their objectives.'

'*Accomplish* their *objectives*' – that is the key phrase.

It was suggested yesterday that agency people had to choose between being a creative person and being a businessman. The last thing Jim Young didn't say was that he would not have accepted the need to make such a distinction – and neither do I.

Training creative people
to carry newspapers

A long time ago, long before she became Maureen Lipman, Joyce Grenfell was half-way through her one-woman show to a packed and appreciative audience at the Fortune Theatre. The reviews had been excellent and, on her own admission, she was pretty pleased with herself. Then, in the middle of a dramatic silence she was rightly proud of being able to sustain, she heard a clear, ten-year-old voice from the stalls.

'Mummy,' it said. 'What is that lady for?'

As a question, it enjoys a certain healthy fundamentalism, which is why it's always a good one to ask: about governments, trade associations, laws, companies, conferences – and creative people in advertising agencies. What are they all *for*?

It should be very easy indeed to say what creative people are for – indeed, I think it is – but it seldom gets spelt out explicitly. I don't remember ever being told what my job really was: it was left to me to find out for myself. And while that kind of journey of self-discovery may be very good for the moral fibre, it can be a confusing and demoralising experience.

One obvious way of deducing what's expected of you is to work at it empirically. You register the times when you're praised and the times when you're shouted at; make a note of which caused what; and then attempt to incur more of the former and less of the latter. This is how dogs learn to carry newspapers.

So when your creative director goes out of his way to congratulate you on some new work, you know that the essence of your job is to earn the approval of your creative director. After all, he must know good advertising when he sees it: that's what he's paid all that money for.

Later that day, the same piece of work is rejected with contempt by the client. That in itself may not be too disconcerting; it's well known that clients are poor judges of advertising which is why they need agencies. It gets more perplexing when the client (who is a poor judge of advertising) embraces your campaign with enthusiasm while your creative director (who knows good advertising when he sees it) comes back from holiday and stamps all over it.

Then there is the client who awards the agency a huge new account entirely on the strength of your creative work. Is he still a poor judge of advertising? If so, is it ethical to accept the account? Or perhaps clients are poor judges of advertising only when they reject work? Perhaps a client who accepts your creative work is, by definition, a good judge of advertising; except, it would seem, on those occasions when your creative director doesn't agree with him?

Your account executive may not help. 'Thanks entirely to your creative work,' she says, 'that was a great meeting. Come and have a drink.' So you wonder if your reason for existence is to produce the kind of work which makes meetings good. People praise you a lot for that.

Ten days later, the same work is sunk irrecoverably by research. And while it's well known that had people listened to research, none of the world's ten greatest campaigns would ever have seen the light of day, this particular client is inclined to listen to research, and so, by coincidence, is the account director.

So perhaps what you're for is to produce campaigns that do well in research? I knew one very respected creative person in the States whose only skill lay in 'beating the norms', as he put it. Work that does well in research has a much better chance of being published than work that does not. But next time you go for a job interview, and you include on your reel a lot of work that has done very well in research, the creative director of the most exciting agency in town tells you that what you're doing is aesthetically and morally indefensible.

Nor does the confusion end there. A thoroughly crafted print campaign puts up sales by 12 per cent in a declining market and your creative director doesn't even shortlist it for his in-house awards. At the same time, several heavy golden objects are bestowed on a television campaign that is well known to have sold nothing to anybody and which will be withdrawn as soon as decency allows. The author of the television campaign receives a bigger merit bonus than the author of the thoroughly crafted print campaign. That year, not a single IPA Advertising Effectiveness Award goes to a piece of work that has also been recognised creatively. What on earth is going on here?

All this makes it very hard indeed for creative people to work out for themselves what they're for. So many conflicting and contradictory signals; so many different people making disconnected judgments; so many sets of rules and so many changes to each of them; the very same action incurring both gratitude and reproach – but not invariably so. If all this happened to dogs, they'd never learn to carry newspapers. As Pavlov's did, they'd go mad.

It seems to me, therefore, that much the most important first step in encouraging creative people to produce their best is to minimise confusion of purpose and inconsistency of judgment. We need to be a bit more explicit about what creative people are for and to make sure that the view is understood and shared.

We know what media buyers are for. Media buyers are for buying time and space. So are creative people for filling the time and space the media buyers have bought? Only up to a point; and the point in question is that absolutely anyone can fill time and space. What creative people are for is to fill any given item of time or space in such a manner that the client gets a better return on the investment in that time or space than he would have done had the time or space been filled by any old person. I apologise for such a clumsy and insultingly obvious definition but I don't remember having seen it anywhere before.

The calculation goes like this. Cost of time or space: 100 units of currency. Value to client of time or space left empty: minus 100. Value to client of time or space filled by any old person: anything from nought to, say, 110. Value to client of time or space filled by (good) creative person: say, 120 – and on occasions, of course, a good deal more.

Why creative persons deserve to be called creative is not just because they can think of things that the rest of us can't. It's because they can *make things happen* in a way that the rest of us can't: more quickly or more economically or more rewardingly or more lastingly.

They can help people understand complex arguments; they can bring freshness to old promises; they can engage people's minds and self-interest; they can develop a narrative; they can forge connections through visual and verbal metaphor. And they do all these things and many more not for the sake of it but as a calculated means to a clearly understood end. They use their skills and talents and imagination in order to make certain things happen.

But do they always know which precise things they're expected to make happen? Almost as bad as not knowing what you're for is not knowing what the advertising is for. The longest and apparently most comprehensive of briefs often fails to answer that most useful of all questions: what is the advertising expected to do?

To tell them portentously that the objective of the advertising is to increase sales doesn't help creative people at all. The brighter of them might even have guessed that for themselves. What they need to know, and agree with, is: which people might respond more favourably to the brand in the future if they felt or thought about it differently? Once that's understood and agreed, all subsequent discussion and debate has at least a chance of being constructive. Creative people understandably get demotivated very quickly if comment and criticism are presented in an erratic confusion of strategy and execution.

There are, in addition, a few other rules-of-thumb for managers that are worth at least thinking about.

In the development stage of advertising, very poor first thoughts often receive far more time and tender loving care than promising ones. This is almost always the wrong way round. A lot of time and care spent on a rotten idea can sometimes make it almost adequate. Exactly the same expenditure can turn a promising campaign into a brilliant one. Being told to start again is never enjoyable, but the pain doesn't last very long and vanishes completely as soon as the new idea materialises. Having a sub-standard idea nibbled to death by ducks goes on being unpleasant for months and leaves nothing to be proud of at the end of it.

Like any other currency, praise can get debased. You are not, therefore, demonstrating your creative management skills by describing everything you see as fantastic. By the time you see something good, your opinion will be worthless.

You hope your creative people will try to understand their audience; it's well worth your while trying to understand them. Knowing you've got to think of something can make you feel very lonely and vulnerable and bad-tempered – that's one of the reasons that working in pairs is so popular among creative people. It really is a different sort of job – or should be; but that doesn't mean you have to treat them with reverence.

Above all, remind your creative people what they're for, remind them what the advertising's for, and concentrate the praise on those who deliver. They're not always the most obvious candidates.

Irresponsibility at Princeton

> By 1970, I had been creative director of J. Walter Thompson London for six years. One of the continuing struggles in the creative department of an agency is between the apparently contradictory demands of responsible relevance and free-ranging originality. I say 'apparently' because there *is* no real conflict. What makes good advertising so hard to produce is the need to present the relevant in an arresting and rewarding manner. Neither alone is enough. Although I'd still not worked out what a creative director had to do (I never did) I had begun to understand that central to the job was the need to be as critical of irrelevance as of unoriginality. In August 1970, there was a J. Walter Thompson Worldwide creative directors' meeting in Princeton, New Jersey. It was, I think, the first such meeting; until then, only managers and senior account persons had been thought adult enough to exchange views across frontiers. The title I was given for my own contribution was 'Creative Responsibility'. The piece is edited.

Rather than talk to the title I was given, which sounds a little ponderous and depressing, I've elected to concentrate on creative *ir*responsibility.

In other words, by trying to illustrate some of the areas where creative people (not of course *us*) can occasionally be irresponsible, I hope to illuminate what the nature of creative responsibility should be.

All good creative people are, by definition, responsible to some degree. They may not get into the office until lunchtime; they may get drunk at lunchtime; they may wear sneakers, beads and waist-length hair (unless they're ladies); but that's not the sort of responsibility, or lack of it, I think we should be concerned with. It's *professional* responsibility rather than personal, social or sartorial that obviously matters more to us today.

I think that all good creative people are professionally responsible: if only out of sheer self-interest, self-absorption or self-esteem. Because, more than any other member of an agency, the creative person *is* what he *does*: and he knows it. He'll work all weekend or all night or both; not, if we're honest, because he's driven by an obsessive desire to put his client's sales up by two per cent (though he'll certainly be delighted if he does). He's driven more, I think, by the sheer satisfaction of laying an absolutely beautiful egg (in the English sense of that phrase).

But we're not perfect; and neither are the people we work with. So let me look at one or two examples of creative irresponsibility that have, I'm told, been known to happen, just occasionally, in other agencies, many years ago.

> *As long as it's not a washing-powder, packaged-food, pharmaceuticals, trade or corporate and spends at least two million, I'd be quite prepared to work on it.*

I suspect that in every agency there are accounts with a reputation for dreariness; so dreary people tend to be allocated to them. They proceed, predictably, to produce dreary advertising and this confirms us all in our belief that they were dreary accounts all along. I suspect that one of the most important differences between the talented amateur and the talented professional is the professional's genuine eagerness to work on anything – irrespective of product field, previous advertising or the size of the budget. *And to make something where nothing was before.*

It seems to me to be both irresponsible and unprofessional for a creative man to deign to work only on the 'easy' accounts. One of the greatest satisfactions available to a creative man is to take an allegedly 'difficult' account and make something of it. (And when that happens, it's surprising just how many other people are suddenly interested in working on it, too.)

> *Now at first sight, this might seem pretty ordinary. But if we shoot actually in Athens, with Mike Nichols directing, Twiggy as the housewife and music by McCartney, it could be sensational.*

Whenever you hear *that* from anyone (and whenever, indeed, you hear yourself saying it) you know that someone, somewhere has failed to have what you might call an *idea*. In more cases than not, I think, creative people get the reputation for irresponsibility because they try to use clients' money to add production values to a mediocre script or headline. We've all done it, and it's sad.

Many of the best commercials cost relatively little to make. The use of three helicopters and a transatlantic crane will never make a bad or nonexistent idea into an effective advertisement, but it may just lead younger creative people to believe that that's what's expected of them; so it becomes not only expensive but dangerous.

As everyone knows, much concern is currently being expressed about the soaring costs of commercial production. The production companies are blamed; the agency producers and art directors are blamed; and the unions are blamed. While none may be entirely blameless, it seems to me that there may be one person more responsible than any other, and that's the writer who taps out: 'We open on an aerial shot of Hong Kong at dawn' – without recognising that those 11 words may cost a few thousand dollars each. Are they worth it? They may be; they may not. If not, is there a more imaginative way of achieving the equivalent effect?

Don't confuse me with all that research. I'm creative.

I don't think there's much of this left but there is just a little, and by no means all of it is the creative man's fault. Some research people feel they have failed as professionals if anything they say is comprehensible. So if you're not careful, a situation develops in which two crucial members of the same group, each of whom needs the help of the other, are using two totally different vocabularies – almost two languages.

If, as creative people, we don't know what the hell the other man is talking about, it's our responsibility to say so. It will do him a lot of good to have to emerge from behind his comfortable smokescreen of jargon and it will make it possible for us to make use of what he has to offer. The more the research man and the creative man share a way of thinking and talking about advertising, the better for both of them and the better for the account. The introduction of account planning has done more than anything else to reduce our communications gap.

But over 84 per cent of women said they wanted *whiteness.*

It is just as irresponsible to lean on research as an excuse for predictable work as it is to ignore it altogether. Quantified research, basic market research, by definition deals with – at best – the very recent past. What we should be concerned with is the future. It is no good feeding basic marketing information into your personal computer and hoping you'll get a new campaign. All you'll do is invent yesterday. The other thing, of course, is that research of this kind, even at its best, probably tells you what people say they want from *all* washing powders, *all* breads, *all* razor blades. But we're not concerned with all; we're concerned with this particular one. So it seems to me that here the creative man's responsibility is to use research information as raw material from which to construct a relevant new idea for his brand – but rarely if ever to use it unprocessed.

Sure it's dull. But so's the product, for Chrissake.

To my mind, the man who performed one of the greatest disservices to the business is the man who invented the phrase 'low-interest product'. By inventing it, he provided the excuse for a lot of low-interest advertising. I don't, myself, know what a low-interest product is. If you've got piles, a new treatment for haemorrhoids may be the highest-interest product on the market. If you're a woman who has to buy bread for her family, and if you want good bread, then bread is a high-interest product. I suspect that, most of the time, low-interest means of low interest to the creative person. If a product seems dull, then it's more likely to seem dull because of the advertising than because of any intrinsic dullness it supposedly possesses.

If it is genuinely, intrinsically, universally, irretrievably dull, then it doesn't deserve to sell in the first place – and it almost certainly won't.

With a new name, new pack, new formulation, a lower price and a built-in virility agent, we could really do something with this one.

It's clearly the creative man's responsibility to think of, and recommend, product improvements whenever he can. But nothing, understandably, infuriates a client more than the suggestion that his agency is incapable of producing effective advertising for his product *as it stands*. For a creative man to adopt this attitude is, I believe, irresponsible – and a total abdication of his most important role.

Existing products, old-established products, universal products, over-familiar products; these can nearly always be revived and revitalised by imaginative advertising – with the obvious proviso that they haven't become genuinely and functionally obsolete.

I don't care how good the sales have been. Work like that could ruin my reputation.

There are some people whose first instinct on being appointed to an account is to want to change everything, absolutely. Now, if they've been assigned to that account because it has become quite clear that everything should be changed absolutely, that's fine. But there are some accounts where the sales are good, the campaign seems fine and what is required above all is continuity and extension rather than change. So the responsible creative man looks with respect at what has gone before (even though the work was not his) and simply tries to make it that little bit better. It may not be as satisfying to his ego and it may not look as good when he goes for his next job interview; but it's what the account ought to get.

If, *at the same time,* he chooses to take a completely fresh look; to develop an alternative approach that can be evaluated, preferably in the marketplace, against the original – so much the better. But to instigate change simply because you weren't around when what exists first took shape can't be responsible. And brand managers are no less culpable than agency people in this respect.

> *But I thought the client liked slice-of-life.*

Some creative people become so amazingly responsible that they become unfit for active service. It is the account man's job to know what the client likes, even if he chooses to ignore it. It is the creative man's job to know what the client should have. That may sound arrogant and unrealistic – but it's true.

The moment a creative group, at planning stage, allows itself consciously to take into account the known (or more often, supposed) prejudices and predilections of any given client, it will lose not only its own self-respect but also any value it might have had to that client.

> *What d'you mean, why? I tell you it's great, that's all.*

It is still a belief with some creative people that all they have to do is have a great idea. It is then up to other people to work out why it is great, and to persuade the client of this greatness. That would be lovely if it were realistic but it isn't. The creative man's responsibility is only half discharged when he's got an idea; he then has to spend at least as much time working out why it's good, why it's relevant – and preferably writing it all down. Certainly, he needs to tell his account man everything he knows about how he arrived at it, and why. The one thing that *isn't* irresponsible, whatever anyone may say, is to write your final strategy after you've done the advertising. Almost every modern writer on the workings of the mind and the process of creation recognises that any new idea is dependent, at some stage, on some sort of accident, on an intuitive leap, which can be rationalised and acknowledged as right only after the event. Edward de Bono says: 'It's sometimes necessary to get to the top of the mountain in order to discover the shortest way up.' I think the same is true for advertising; you may know how to do it only after you've done it. You must try not to cheat, of course – but there's no need to pretend that you wrote your strategy first if you didn't. It's becoming more and more respectable to admit to the truth.

But whether this is worked out before or after the event, it must remain the creative man's inescapable responsibility to know why as well as *what*; and to explain it, preferably in writing.

There are, I believe, only two important reasons for good work failing to be published.

The chief reason is that not nearly enough good work is done in the first place.

The next most important reason is that creative people don't spend nearly enough time helping others understand and imagine what they propose, and why they propose it.

There is, I believe, a final responsibility for the creative man; and that is, paradoxically, somehow to retain a degree of irresponsibility. He is, or should be, the leavening in the account group loaf. He should question accepted premises and turn the obvious upside-down. Most good creative work is done in an atmosphere of enjoyment and excitement. There are times when such an atmosphere ain't that easy to achieve; but it is the creative man's responsibility, I think, to try.

How do I know if I agree with what we think?

The client studies another incomprehensible script, the success of which hinges on a blind commitment to half a million pounds' worth of post-production ingenuity. The account executive tells the client for the third time that this is a mould-breaking idea.

'Tell me honestly, Simon,' says the client. 'What do you think?'

'We think it's an absolutely mould-breaking idea,' says the account executive.

'I mean *you*,' says the client. 'I mean *you Simon personally*. What do *you* think?'

Simon chuckles unconvincingly. 'I'm afraid I'm not allowed to tell you what *I* think. I'm only allowed to tell you what *we* think. And we think it's really ballsy, mould-breaking stuff.'

Sam Haskins has been taking excellent photographs for 40-something years. In a recent interview, he was asked his views on the old photography-as-art conundrum. He said, 'Stuff generated by advertising agencies usually dates within a year because most things conceived by a committee have in-built obsolescence.'

The quality that most agencies strive for in their work is distinctiveness. Yes, of course: it has to be relevant, it has to be 'on message' – but distinctiveness is what clients say they want and distinctiveness is what agencies honestly strive to provide. How curious, then, is this tendency to group-think; this addiction to the first-person plural; this clinging to the life-raft of the corporate we.

How would you feel about a director or a photographer or a Queen's Counsel or a neuro-surgeon who never told you what they, personally, thought? We go to them for singular, first-person views and talents; not to act as obedient representatives of some invisible cabinet. So why not to advertising agencies?

Because, I fear, today's account executive is only rarely respected as an advertising expert. And the decline in the standing of the agency account executive and the decline in the standing of the agency itself are closely related. How can a client trust his principal adviser when his adviser doesn't know what he thinks? Or does know what he thinks, but isn't allowed to say what he thinks? Or has to go back and consult his agency in order to find out what he is authorised to think?

How many times must a client suspect that, in his heart of hearts, Simon thinks this really ballsy, mould-breaking stuff is a steaming mound of self-indulgence?

Haskins is of course right: exceptional work is far more likely to emerge from individuals than from committees. But advertising is not art; ideas, once born, must always be constructively challenged. 'Trust me, I'm an art director' is an inadequate basis for the disposition of several million pounds of someone else's money.

The trouble with the corporate we is not that it exists, but that it's all too often used in the mindless defence of the mediocre, rather than in the convinced and exultant promotion of an outstanding idea, rigorously examined.

Thinking up things: the advertising creative process

There are a great many advertising and marketing case-histories in the public domain, most of them extremely comprehensive. Mainly, they follow a familiar pattern. There will be a detailed description of the nature and history of the market, the nature and history of the featured company and its competitors, the social and economic climate prevailing at the time and the strengths and weaknesses of the brand in question.

There will be well-documented detail about consumer beliefs and misconceptions and a painstaking description of the thought processes that led to a final advertising brief. That which the advertising is required to communicate, and to whom, is clinically identified and articulated.

And then, almost without exception, the case-history moves into fast-forward mode. We skip in less than a sentence from the Brief to the Idea: and then to the responses that the Idea achieved.

It is as if the case-history for the legendary 1950s Hathaway shirt campaign had identified the need for the shirts to be seen to be up-market, well made and masculine: to be followed immediately by an account of the success of the Man in the Hathaway Shirt advertisements.

What we most want to learn – so that we can do it, too, or do it more often – is how the idea happened. Yet how the idea happened is what we never get. It isn't quite *coitus interruptus*; it's more like the final chapter of a detective story in which the intuitive hero identifies the murderer as the bishop but declines to tell us how he worked it out.

We don't challenge his contention – any more than we challenge the success of the Man in the Hathaway Shirt campaign. But it leaves us

An adaptation of 'Archimedes and the efficacy of prayer', which appeared in the first two editions of *Behind the Scenes in Advertising*. This version was first published as 'The advertising creative process' in John Philip Jones (ed.), *The Advertising Business*, 1999. Reprinted by permission of Sage Publications, Inc.

unsatisfied and no better informed for the future.

So we are faced with a curious fact. That which clients find most valuable in advertising agencies is their ability to think of things: new products, brand personalities, brand extensions, advertising ideas, new ways to reach people, new strategies. Yet you can read a million words about advertising agencies without a single sentence being devoted to how they think of things.

You will learn about their processes and their proprietary methodologies and their systems for evaluation and their many successes. You will learn what they did *before* they'd had an idea; and you will learn what they did *after* they'd had an idea. But the one thing you'll never learn is *how* they had an idea.

It will probably never be possible to retrieve and record just what happened in one person's mind at one point in time when an idea occurred. Even the mind itself may not know; and by the time the idea has been relayed, challenged, modified and justified, the precise process of its generation will have gone forever. But this seems no reason to despair; to resign ourselves to an acceptance of magic moments, forever mysterious and never to be consciously replicated. There must be some value in the examination of the creative process; of the circumstances and contexts from which relevant ideas seem to emerge most frequently. There must be some help we can call upon from a world elsewhere.

The word 'creative' is a dodgy one. It deflects the mind dangerously towards the fine arts – and advertising has nothing to do with the fine arts. It is true that some advertisements may be pleasing enough to be appreciated as art is appreciated. But that is rare, almost certainly accidental, probably happens much later in the advertisement's life and has nothing to do with advertising's purpose.

It is the fact that advertising has a purpose in a way that art does not that makes references to the arts so foolish – and any expectation of relevant insight from them so futile.

A far more useful source of help is the study of scientific methodology – and the processes, deliberate or accidental, that have led to scientific discovery; and there are few more instructive starting points than the familiar but little understood story of Archimedes and his bath.

The story, accurate I believe in essential fact but told with a degree of poetic latitude, goes like this.

Two hundred and fifty years BC there lived a man called Hiero II who was Tyrant of Syracuse. His resident sage, problem-solver and creative consultant was called Archimedes.

One day, Hiero received an extravagant gift from a neighbouring tyrant, a man of whom Hiero had good reason to be suspicious. The gift in question was a crown of great and intricate beauty and was purportedly made of the finest, purest gold. Hiero, however, had his doubts.

So he called in his sage and he said to Archimedes: 'This crown may indeed be pure gold or there again it might be – as I strongly suspect – an alloy. You have until Wednesday week to tell me which.'

In the creation of a work of art, there is no problem to be solved (though it may be inspired by the existence of a problem). In scientific thought and in the creation of advertising, there always is: either a problem to be solved or a task to be undertaken. The brief that Archimedes took would be familiar enough to advertising agency people, as would the existence of a deadline.

To fulfil that brief, Archimedes needed two pieces of information: two numbers. He needed to know the weight of the crown and he needed to know its volume.

Establishing its weight presented no difficulty: the specific weight of pure gold was known fact. Establishing its volume was a different matter altogether.

The only objects whose volume could be accurately determined were those whose dimensions were strictly geometrical. Hiero's crown was complicated, asymmetrical and intricately wrought. It defied conventional measurement completely.

There was, of course, an obvious solution available to him. Had Archimedes simply melted down the crown in a crucible of measurable dimensions, the precise volume of metal could have been established as soon as it cooled. It is likely, however, that Archimedes was quick to spot the snag.

'Excuse me, Hiero. Good news, I'm happy to say. It *is* gold. Or to put it another way, it *was* gold. Had to boil it up, I'm afraid. Still, I cracked it…'.

He would have spent several sleepless nights. The problem never left him. It preoccupied him.

The days passed. Hiero would not have bothered to conceal his impatience. It is possible that Archimedes' contract was due for renewal. There was much talk of a new and younger sage in whom Hiero was rumoured to have expressed interest. The deadline loomed.

And then it was that Archimedes got into his bath.

Now, it is inconceivable that this was the first bath that Archimedes had ever taken. He must have taken many; perhaps one every day;

probably as many as thousands in the course of his lifetime. So he must have noticed many, many times that when he lowered himself into a bath, the water level rose; and that when he got out again, the water level sank.

But this time, he not only noticed this phenomenon: he made an instant connection between the behaviour of the water level and the problem that continued to occupy his mind. And that is when – and why – he cried 'Eureka!'

He'd made an instant, intuitive, hypothetical connection between the phenomenon of the bath water and the problem of the crown. And at once, he would have felt the need to test this instinct against hard logic.

I do not know how long this process took, but his sequence of thought must have gone something like this:

'My body, like Hiero's crown, is a complicated solid and I do not know its volume. But when I put it into water, the water level goes up and the more of it I put in, the higher the level goes. There must, therefore, be a relationship between the volume of my body and the amount of water it replaces. If I could measure the water levels both before and after my total immersion, I would have measured the precise equivalent of my own volume. But I can't because my bath is not geometrical in shape although there's no reason why it shouldn't be. So if I took a vessel of geometrical dimensions, half filled it with water, marked the level, totally submerged that bloody crown, marked the new level and then calculated the cubic difference – then I would have determined the volume of the crown itself. And kept both my job and my self-respect.'

No wonder he cried 'Eureka!' It must have been a wonderful moment.

With only a little licence, that is the true story of Archimedes: and, though the parallel is of course imperfect, it's instructive in a great many ways for those of us engaged in the rather more prosaic problem of trying to think up a new advertising campaign for, as it might be, canned pineapples.

Perhaps most importantly, it reminds us of the relationship of *problem* to *observation*. There was once a view that the purest form of observation was that conducted with an absolutely empty mind; one that was uncontaminated by prejudice or initial hypothesis. Indeed, there is the story of the well-educated person of the nineteenth century who recorded everything he observed, every day, during the full course of his adult life. And on his death, he left these observations to the British Museum, where they reside to this day: but of no value to anyone because they have no shape, were based on no hypotheses and so made no new connections.

Today, it is generally recognised that observation in the absence of hypothesis is likely to be valueless.

The hypothesis does not have to be sharply focused: it can exist in the form of a preoccupation or obsession. It means that all observation is coloured by the occupying belief that every thing observed, however randomly, is potentially relevant.

Preoccupation of this kind can come from many sources. There is a certain kind of driven, scientific mind that seems to provide its own obsessive stimulus. When Sir Isaac Newton was asked how he came upon his great discoveries, he replied: 'I keep the subject constantly before me, 'til the first dawnings open slowly, little by little, into the full and clear light.'

But most of us will be more like Archimedes: we need some external stimulus such as fear, greed, vanity or open competition to 'keep the subject constantly before' us. We need a client and a deadline.

From the moment that Hiero set his challenge and imposed his deadline, everything that Archimedes observed must have been considered at some level of consciousness for potential relevance. The phenomenon of the rising bathwater was not the only observation he made, nor was it a new one. It just happened to be the one that connected. Arthur Koestler calls this kind of collision 'bisociation'.

In essence, this process of invention is a kind of improvisation. If you want to feed birds in the winter, and keep them safe from predatory cats, you might look in your attic to see if you've got a bird-table. But if you set out to look for a bird-table, you will look narrowly, screening out everything that isn't a bird-table – and you may fail to find one.

Yet if you look not for a bird-table, but for something (or for some things) from which a bird-feeder could be improvised, you will see a dozen possibilities. Everything in your attic is seen and evaluated as you've never seen it before: not for what it is, but for what, quite specifically, it might be. That is how Archimedes saw his bathwater.

I do not know how David Ogilvy and his team settled on an elegant man in a black eye-patch for the Hathaway shirt campaign: but I would be prepared to bet that the process was not dissimilar from that of Archimedes.

They had, rationally and sequentially, decided on the desired positioning: up-market, male, well made. They then needed to find some (preferably non-verbal) stimulus that would evoke such responses in the minds of their audience. From that moment on, everything they saw – in life and in the media – would have been subconsciously assessed against this need. When they saw a man in an eye-patch, it would not have been the first man in an eye-patch they had ever seen: it was simply the first they had seen since they'd been preoccupied by the problem.

Creative people in advertising agencies sometimes yearn for greater freedom; for release from what they see as the tyranny of the brief. But it is, of course, precisely this tyranny that provides the stimulus for invention – painful as it may seem at the time. Ask a writer of fiction simply to write a story and he may not know how to begin. Ask the same writer to write a story about (at random) an international terrorist and a tube of toothpaste and he'll soon get started. (It may not be a very good story, but ideas do not have to be good to qualify as ideas.)

So the function of the brief is not just to ensure relevance; it is also to encourage original thinking. As Edward de Bono points out,[1] unfettered minds tend to drift into familar patterns of thought, as water will follow its own previous patterns through the sand. Only by building the equivalent of a dam will a new course be attempted. Indeed, one of the techniques for creative thinking that de Bono recommends is what he calls the Intermediate Impossible. For instance: you may be required to think of ways of maximising returns on expensive commercial aircraft; and the Intermediate Impossible is that the aircraft must never leave the ground. By consciously and artificially rejecting the obvious, at least initially, the mind is forced to explore original possibilities: the use of a Boeing 747 as an up-market restaurant or launch venue for a new product, for example.

The next critical lesson from the story of Archimedes is the importance of distinguishing between the act of discovery and the act of justification.

We still seem to believe that it is somehow unrespectable to admit that an idea may materialise apparently spontaneously, and can be seen to hold good, to withstand analytical challenge, only in retrospect. Disparagingly, this process is called post-rationalisation and we are taught that it's used only by people with little intellectual integrity.

But the truth of the matter is that the thought processes that lead to the first possibility of the discovery of an idea and the thought processes that then test its validity are almost totally different. The first is fast, intuitive, almost certainly in part subconscious. And the second is rational, rigorous, disciplined and may be extremely slow. Once an idea has materialised, by whatever means, we then have to ask ourselves: could I,

---

1. Edward de Bono, *The Use of Lateral Thinking*, Jonathan Cape, 1967

theoretically, have arrived at this answer logically and sequentially? In the words of Edward de Bono, 'It is sometimes necessary to get to the top of the mountain in order to discover the shortest way up.'

Arguments between those who claim that the creative process is all about intuition and those who claim that it's all about deduction and hard slog are barren arguments. The creative process demands both and we need to recognise and honour both.

But marketing case-histories, like scientific papers, seldom concede this truth. Because of the superstition that the only respectable scientific methodology is that which is relentlessly deductive and sequential, case-histories and scientific papers consistently cheat.

As the Nobel Prize winner Sir Peter Medawar has written: 'Scientific papers in the form in which they are communicated to learned journals are notorious for misrepresenting the processes of thought that led to whatever discoveries they describe.'

Advertising agencies and marketing directors should be just as notorious for exactly the same reason: the conclusions they reach may well be demonstrably valid, but they consistently misrepresent the processes of thought that led to them.

It is as if Archimedes, restored to favour by Hiero and with the threat of early retirement lifted, had chosen to write up his discovery in the following manner.

'The task of ascertaining the volume of complicated solids has perplexed scientists for centuries.

'We approached the problem logically, objectively and deductively. We reasoned that a solid object was no more nor less than the temporary formation of a liquid, as ice is to water. Thereoretically, therefore, all that was required was a methodology allowing a solid to become a notional liquid for the purposes of measurement. Since volume by definition implies space occupied, it followed that space occupied *within a liquid* allowed for the measurement of the volume of liquid both before and after the total immersion of the object in question. The difference between the two, which for the purposes of this paper we shall denominate 'displacement', therefore equalled the volume of the solid immersed. The only requirement thereafter was the choice of a vessel of the requisite size, and of a shape that was readily susceptible to conventional linear measurement.'

Here, as in so many papers and case-histories, the process of discovery has been totally falsified. In the interests of respectable rationality, the process of discovery has been tortured to match the process of justification.

There are those who think this doesn't matter. Why should it, as long as the discovery is valid, as long as the solution can be replicated and stands up to challenge?

But of course it matters a great deal; because, in advertising as in science, the ambition is to be more inventive more often. To believe that the processes of discovery and the processes of justification are identical is to approach your next problem in a manner that makes it less likely to be solved.

We need to remember all the time: that which leads us to form an opinion is only rarely that which justifies our holding it.

Within an advertising agency, the implications of all this for organisation and leadership should be fairly self-evident.

There is first the need to be clear about the precise function that the new advertising campaign is expected to perform, the equivalent of the need to measure the volume of a complicated solid. But by that I do not mean, 'This advertising campaign is expected to put up sales.' There should always be an intermediary stage, on which the strategy is based; and the intermediary stage will itself be a hypothesis.

'It is our belief that if more people knew that this product existed/felt that this product was modern/realised that you could use this product for making cakes/learnt that this airline went to Bali, then more people would buy or buy more often.' It is against this intermediary stage that the advertising will initially be judged. And it is this intermediary objective that must be clear and fixed in the minds of the creative group.

It is *not* the direct function of the advertising to increase sales. It is the direct function of the advertising to achieve changes in attitude or behaviour – *which, it is hypothesised, will then put up sales.*

The task of thinking of the idea – of creating the stimuli – to effect such changes is usually then allocated to the creative people: the writers, art directors and television specialists. And it is sometimes believed that the most efficient and thoughtful way of effecting the handover from strategy (what do we want to communicate) to execution (how are we going to communicate it) is the one-line brief. It is as if the creative mind is too tender and too intuitive to be burdened with information or engaged in deduction.

This is almost always a mistake. Even the best of briefs will be no more than an informed stab at something. It is often only in the search for a solution that the true nature of a problem will be revealed. And the chances of a brief being fully understood and accepted will be greatly enhanced if those left with the responsibility of meeting it have themselves been involved in its formulation.

Now is the time to go into non-rational mode. The objective is reasonably clear and has been accepted. The need has been articulated and transferred to the sub-conscious. Now add external stimuli, which must include a deadline. Because only when external stimuli are applied will the awareness of the need become so obsessive that everything the creative people observe or experience will be assessed against it. The process of improvisation has begun.

Random exercises should be encouraged; logic-based objections to putative ideas should not. There will be muddle and confusion and despair and absurdity – but everything will have become potentially relevant. And there will be many false starts, many nearly-Eureka moments.

Because at this stage in the process, an important difference from the scientific process becomes evident. While there may be more than one way to measure the volume of a complicated solid and there may be many non-toxic antibacterial agents to be discovered, in the search for a new advertising campaign, there is no limit at all to the number of potentially successful solutions. For this reason, Eureka moments in advertising will lack the instant sharp certainty that so delighted Archimedes.

Archimedes, having tested his hypothesis and found it solid, could be satisfied that his responsibilities had been discharged. In advertising, when an idea materialises and withstands the subsequent beady scrutiny (could we have arrived at this idea logically and sequentially?), the doubt remains: it may be a relevant idea; it may be a good idea; but is there a better idea?

In the assessment of an advertising idea, there can be no fine certainties.

But it must, of course, be tested: by which I do not mean subjected to some mechanical black-box procedure but that it should be probed and prodded. It is not a popular stage, this, with the idea's parents. They do not like to see their fragile, new-born concept being challenged so brutally. But an advertising idea is not a work of art; it should be as functional as a fork-lift truck and robust enough to survive the most exacting of interrogations.

And here it can be helpful to remember Sir Karl Popper's parable of the swans and why, even in science, it is seldom possible to validate a hypothesis completely.

Validation and invalidation, says Popper, are not symmetrical opposites: they are different in kind. For example, you may make an assumption that all swans are white. And you may spend the rest of your life observing swans, and every one of them is white: but you can never say that you have validated your hypothesis. The best you can say, with every white swan observed, is that you can entertain your hypothesis with a slightly higher level of confidence.

However, you have only to observe just one black swan – and your hypothesis is dead. Unlike validation, invalidation is cruel, clean, unarguable and immediate. There can be no argument about it.

So tempting though it undoubtedly is to persuade your client that your idea has been thoroughly validated, in truth it can't be. You can only say that the most conscientious attempts to invalidate it have so far failed and that he can therefore entertain its adoption with increasing confidence. And in answer to his question: 'Are you sure there isn't an even better idea?' you can only say no, you never can be.

This whole process is known as the hypothetico-deductive method of scientific thought; and in encapsulated form, what it says is this:

- We must make a clear distinction between *discovery* (or believed discovery) and *proof* or justification. The elementary act is having an idea, which must begin with a hypothesis. Techniques and pressures and preoccupation can help – but the process of having an idea is neither logical nor illogical; it is alogical; it is outside logic and cannot be made the subject of logical rules. For all that, the process is respectable, necessary and part of demonstrable scientific methodology.
- Having been generated, ideas must be criticised and tested: we now switch back to logical, deductive mode. If we can invalidate in the light of observable phenomena (a black swan), we feed back, modify or start again; but at the very least with a greater body of knowledge. The failure to invalidate does not imply validation.

In creating advertising, we need to be intuitive, instinctive, scared and lucky.

And we need to be rigorous, disciplined, logical and deductive.

Both kinds of mind and thought are required; the trick is to recognise which kind we need and when we need it.

Wanted: a new kind of incubator for hatching Harry Potters

In the days when sixth forms had debating societies, this is the motion they mostly debated: 'In the Opinion of this House, the Artist is Superior to the Scientist'.

The most telling argument from the earnest young proposers was invariably the comparison they made between Einstein and Shakespeare. Even if Einstein had never been born, they pointed out, sooner or later someone else would have stumbled on the General Theory of Relativity. Just as, sooner or later, someone would have invented the wheel and the telephone and the electric light bulb and the microprocessor. That is the nature of scientific discovery.

By contrast, said the William Hague wannabes, had Shakespeare never been born, no one would ever have written *Hamlet*. Only Picasso can invent Picasso. That is the nature of creative art; that is the fundamental difference between the two; and that is why the Artist is the superior person. The motion is carried.

On the evidence of the past 50 years or so, marketing directors and venture capitalists don't seem to have been very active members of sixth-form debating societies. Why, otherwise, are they so slow to recognise that there are two categories of invention that are of value to competitive business; that both should be pursued; but whereas inventions belonging to the first category will inevitably be gazumped by a competitor within a matter of months, those belonging to the second category remain priceless and impregnable until the end of time?

Between the wars, Walt Disney perfected and patented a great many ingenious new techniques to make the production of animated films more efficient. He also invented Mickey Mouse.

Some 70 years on, which of those inventions would you rather own?

His new techniques were scientific inventions. They were hugely valuable and they served him well. But had Disney not developed them, then sooner or later, someone else would have done. Most, of course, were obsolescent within a matter of years and all are now dead: long since spreadeagled in the slow lane by faster, cheaper, more effective methods. That is the predetermined fate of all scientific inventions.

But Mickey Mouse is alive and well and living in France and Florida and just about everywhere else in the world. Mickey Mouse has made more money for Walt Disney than every one of his scientific inventions put together. Mickey Mouse is the kind of invention that makes competitors jump up and down on their spreadsheets in despair: he is unique, timeless and unchallengeable.

When your competitor comes up with a miracle new ingredient, you know immediately what to do: you bark crisp orders at your lab technicians. 'Interrogate that formula until it begs for mercy,' you snarl. 'And don't come back to me until you've gone one better.'

But you can't do that with Mickey Mouse. Mickey's secret is wholly mysterious. You can't deconstruct Mickey Mouse, analyse each component part, and then add 15 per cent more all-family empathy

For as long as I can remember, marketing directors have been bemoaning the fact that lead-times are getting ever shorter. Functional advantages, hard to achieve at the best of times, evaporate almost overnight. Yet the search for the new, scientific breakthrough still seems to take precedence over the search for your very own Mickey Mouse.

The very word invention carries functional overtones. (But not, oddly, the word inventive.) Ask a few hundred marketing people or financial analysts to name some inventors and you'll probably get Sinclair and Dyson and Gates...and then a very long pause.

Here are some names I guarantee you won't get. A.A. Milne, Ian Fleming, J.M. Barrie, the Rev. W. Awdry, Bram Stoker, Charles Schulz, J.K. Rowling.

Winnie-the-Pooh, James Bond, Peter Pan, Thomas the Tank Engine, Dracula, Charlie Brown and Harry Potter are all inventions – just as Hamlet is an invention. Because this is a column in a marketing magazine, and therefore concerned only with crass commercial matters, I make no quality distinctions between them. They all belong to that category of unchallengeable, timeless inventions. And they are all beyond price.

What, I often wonder, has been the aggregated value to the Minnesota Valley Canning Company of the Jolly Green Giant? He was invented by Leo Burnett in about 1936 – he's a year or two younger than Mickey Mouse – and has been bestowing added value on sweetcorn ever since.

Kimberly-Clark found competing with the Andrex puppy so exhausting that they finally moved into the same kennel.

Nobody has ever met Mr Kipling; no one has ever seen him and no one has even heard him speak. Yet his cakes are known to be so exceedingly good that his company keeps getting bought for millions of pounds.

In spite of their spectacular success, inventions such as these still seem to happen both infrequently and by chance.

But no company would rely on chance in its search for scientific discoveries. There will be teams of highly qualified people, a huge research and development budget, regular progress reviews, and a main board director to be held finally accountable.

I know of no company that undertakes any such systematic programme designed to create, identify and evaluate the next Andrex puppy or the next Mickey Mouse.

It cannot be cost that holds them back. In the right hands, and inspired by the right minds, the raw materials required to invent the next Mickey Mouse (or Dracula or Harry Potter) can be found in the corporate stationery cupboard.

It can only, I think, be a kind of embarrassment.

Serious corporate persons can, with self-respect intact, confidently put a case to their board for sponsoring experimental laboratories, investing in a lot more more R&D and hiring another six postgraduate chemists. They feel a great deal less manly when asking their boards to contemplate the astonishing commercial potential of an untried animated vampire duck.

Yet according to Charles Handy and Charles Leadbeater and others who've given it a great deal of thought, the new economy will be all about alchemy: the creation of wealth not from land, labour and machinery, but from thin air; from the fertile minds of creative artists, armed at most with an Apple Mac or a magic marker.

Marketing companies with a will to win could do a great deal worse than start their own form of incubator. Eggs would be welcomed from all sources and introduced to a controlled and conducive atmosphere. Some would prove infertile. Others would hatch but fail to achieve healthy growth. And a few would burst from their shells, captivate millions and bestow on their sponsors that most prized of all marketing possessions: the brand differentiator that's yours for ever.

What are account planners for, Daddy?

Account planning, in both name and function, came into being in a few London advertising agencies in the 1960s. The two individuals most properly credited with its introduction are the late, great Stanley Pollitt of Boase Massimi Pollitt, and Stephen King of J. Walter Thompson, by far the best planner I ever worked with. By 1978, the date of this piece, there were enough account planners in London agencies to justify the formation of a society – the Account Planning Group. Although never a planner myself (other than by instinct) I was invited to address their inaugural meeting. Doubts and self-doubts continue to surround planning and planners. Some agencies have never adopted it as a discrete discipline. A few have abandoned it. American agencies, in the main, have found no compelling reasons for introducing it. Twenty-five years on, I don't think there's a lot I would either change or add. There is still, to my knowledge, no commonly agreed and commonly used job definition. I note, but without apology, that I've again used James Webb Young's definition of an Advertising Man. See 'What Jim Young said. And what he didn't say' (page 191).

It was kind of you to invite me to give you my personal view of account planning. I have found it a useful exercise. I have now worked with account planners for ten years less one day and I've never – until this evening – been forced to work out in my own mind exactly what my personal opinion of account planning is. I very much agree with A.J.P. Taylor when he says that the only reason he writes is to discover what he thinks.

I suppose the greatest difficulty I've encountered over these ten years is the problem of explaining, first to the creative department and later to clients and potential clients, exactly what an account planner *does*.

The potential client, being a canny fellow and deeply scarred from previous experiences, demands to see the actual, real-life team who would be working on his account. You introduce them.

'This is the director-in-charge,' you say. They nod. They know.

'This is the creative chappie,' you say. They nod. They know.

'And this,' you say, 'is the account planner.' And nobody nods.

At this point you've got two choices. Keep talking or try to explain. I've tried both and neither works.

Keep talking, and the client will say: 'Excuse me, but that's the *who*?' So you end up having to explain anyway.

'I'm glad you asked,' you lie. 'We consider the account planner to be one of the most valuable members of the account group.'

'In what respect?' says the client.

'That's a very good question,' you stall. 'You see, we believe there has to be one member of the account group who knows very precisely, very sensitively, what's going on in the world, in the marketplace, in the consumer's mind.'

'Ah,' says the client, deeply relieved. 'Research person.'

'Well, up to a point and in a manner of speaking, yes. But as such, actually not.'

'In what way not?'

'Well – we were hoping to find time to show you some case histories,' you say, 'and perhaps when you hear the account planner *talk* you'll get a rather clearer idea…'.

But the client insists. Entirely reasonably, he wants to know what the account planner does, why we've got one, how he or she works with the rest of the account group and why the account executive doesn't do the job himself because surely that's part of his job or is he too stupid?

And I have to tell you that, ten years on, having tried several hundred definitions, job descriptions, anecdotes and analogies, I've still not succeeded in explaining, satisfactorily, what the account planner is *for*. Without, that is, simultaneously conveying serious doubts about the adequacy of the rest of the agency and – worse still – the client's own highly trained and expensive marketing department.

There is more than one possible explanation for this dismal record of failure. The first – which I reject out of hand – is my own incompetence. The second is that there *is* no real role for the account planner: an explanation still favoured by some and occasionally, I have to say, when faced with the question, even by me. The third is that – at least until this evening – account planners have themselves failed to define what they are for and what they do.

Which, when you consider what account planners are *supposed* to do, must rank as one of life's richer ironies.

Yet, 12 years ago, there were no account planners. Today, looking around, there are certainly more than that. Could it be that the account planners' greatest achievement to date is – on the basis of there being no satisfactory explanation for their existence – to have lowered by as much as a hundred the unemployment figures in this country?

I must therefore ask two questions. If account planners hadn't been invented, what would you all be doing for a living?

Second: if you *weren't* all account planners, who, if anyone, would be doing what you may or may not have convinced your employers you do all day?

And if, as account planners, you can't provide satisfactory answers to both those questions, you have – in my personal view – totally failed to justify your own existence. So it could well be that the first, the inaugural, meeting of the Account Planning Group will – to nobody's great surprise – turn out also to be the last.

However, it would I think be churlish and ungrateful of me not to hold out some small flickering hope for your survival, even if I think that in a different sort of world, a simpler and more sensible world, there would indeed be no good reason for your existence.

If you've read the few good books about advertising – and I hope you have, particularly since you have so little else to do all day – you will know that in the 1920s and the 1930s and the 1940s and the 1950s, particularly in America, there was really only one kind of person of value in an agency. This same character emerges clearly from the work of Claude Hopkins, Albert Lasker, David Ogilvy, Rosser Reeves, James Webb Young and a handful of others.

He or she was not a media man, not an account man, not a creative man and certainly, it goes without saying, not an account planner. He was, quite simply, an Advertising Man. In his book, *How To Become An Advertising Man,* James Webb Young has this to say: 'The true Advertising Man, as the term is used in this book, is he who has the knowledge, the skills, experience and insights to advise advertisers how best to use advertising to accomplish their objectives. *And* to execute the advertising to do this.'

Notice that Jim Young is referring to an individual – not a group. He expected the Advertising Man, like himself, to be capable of market analysis, competitive analysis, definition of role – *and* creative execution.

Further, he expected this singular individual to acquire seven different categories of knowledge. I quote: 'Knowledge of Propositions, Knowledge of Markets (by which he meant people, not Nielsen),

Knowledge of Messages, Knowledge of Carriers of Messages (which means more to me at least than media), Knowledge of Trade Channels, Knowledge of How Advertising Works and, finally, Knowledge of the Specific Situation'.

And that's quite a lot of knowledge for one individual to acquire and apply – even before the days of television rating points, cluster analysis, day-after-recall, the Kelley Repertory Grid and burst-versus-drip.

But even that wasn't enough for Young. He goes on to say: 'No limits can be placed on the kinds of knowledge that are useful to the Advertising Man. Indeed, it can safely be said that the broader his education, and the better stocked his mental pantry, the better at his job he is likely to be. Every really good person in advertising whom I have known has always had two noticeable characteristics. First, there was no subject under the sun in which he could not easily get interested. Second, he was an extensive browser in all sorts of fields.'

Now, as I look, from my personal view, at much of the advertising that's produced in both the States and Britain at the moment, it seems to me to have been produced in total isolation from, and total ignorance of, the real world outside. The prose style used in print copy owes nothing to any other prose style except that used in other print advertisements.

The makers of advertisements appear increasingly to be obsessed by only one subject: their own and other people's advertisements. Increasingly, there is a preoccupation with *advertisements* at the expense of *advertising*.

If true, why has this happened? In all honesty I don't know. The glib and obvious answer may be the right one. The business has become so complicated, so competitive, so specialised, that Jim Young's ideal Advertising Man can no longer realistically be expected to exist.

The account man is obsessed not with the world outside, but with the complexities and language of the grocery market or the electricity supply industry. He has become a surrogate client. The creative man is obsessed not with real people and their wants and desires, but with creativity as an end in itself. And since nobody can tell him what creativity *is*, he is forced to conclude that it is anything that wins the Grand Prix de L'Arc de Triomphe at the Wexford Film Festival.

So, for whatever reason, or set of reasons, the real world outside has become forgotten.

And since one of the prime functions – if not the only function – of most advertising is to build an understanding and sympathetic bridge between the potential supplier and the real world outside, this is a very serious omission indeed. The implications are very clear and very serious: advertising money is likely to be less well spent and the return on the investment of that advertising money will be much reduced. Advertisers will notice, will value advertising less, will divert their limited resources elsewhere – and all of us, of whatever discipline, will quite deservedly suffer.

If I am right in this analysis, then the reason for your existence, and the justification of your pay cheques, begins to become clear.

The account planner – if he does nothing else – must be obsessed with the real world outside; must have a well-stocked mental pantry. There should be no subject under the sun in which he cannot easily become interested.

Then – and this may be more easily said than done – he must represent and illuminate that world outside to the myopic specialists with whom he works. You must be interpreters – but you must interpret in a vivid, evocative, imaginative, allegorical way. Do not give us computer printouts or documents that are appreciated by you on weight and density alone.

At your most valuable, you can illuminate and inspire; you can simplify the complicated; you can provide insights and intuitive hypotheses; and you can clarify and crystallise. You can make sure that your agency remains an *advertising* agency, and does not degenerate into a contracted supplier of commissionable advertisements.

At your least valuable, you can do the reverse. You can complicate the simple, obfuscate the obvious, invent your own language, your own religion, your own self-congratulatory, inward-looking, impenetrable jargon.

So a word of warning if I may, however patronising and unnecessary, about the formation of this group. As members of this group, talking only to each other, you have no value whatsoever. Your *entire* value resides in continuing to be members of working account groups – uncontaminated by too much knowledge of each other.

As people who should be better able than most to imagine what it's like to be *other* people – don't forget what it's like to be an account man or a creative man. Don't forget the *exposure* of the client meeting, the *tyranny* of the blank sheet of paper.

Feel as vulnerable, as committed, as excited, as frightened as the people who've got to produce the ads. Don't sit back smugly after you've written your brief and leave the office at 5:29. Recognise that – however helpful you've been, however useful the insights you've provided – somebody still has to have what is called an Idea.

Please: never forget that knowing you've got to give birth to an idea – however trivial, however small, however unimportant in the greater scheme of things – is very personal and very scary. Never forget that having given birth to one idea and having had it rejected, there is the double fear of not being able to give birth to another.

Please: behave like any understanding, compassionate husband. Hold the hand of your creative partners – and breathe and grunt in rhythm and sympathy.

Share the fright, and share the personal vulnerability. If you don't, you'll soon lose friends and the opportunity and right to influence people.

And then comes evaluation. It may well lie with you, as interpreter again, to report on how the real world accepted, understood and appreciated that small, frail idea that almost certainly wasn't yours in the first place.

To your writer and art director, this can be the equivalent of reading the first edition reviews of a play it's taken two years to write.

Certainly, if the notices are bad, don't lie. But look at them and interpret them with responsible optimism. If there's a genuine flicker of hope, breathe on it gently: don't bash it into extinction with self-satisfied pleasure.

Above all, don't be seen to *disown* an idea just because it becomes apparent it's a rotten idea. Observe carefully your own use of the possessive pronoun. If you talk about 'our' campaign when the results are good, and 'your' campaign when the results are rotten: then you've opted out.

Finally, never forget that advertising and agencies existed without you for over a hundred years and could well exist without you again. Sooner or later, somebody's got to write the words – so, competent or incompetent, there will always be a job for a writer. But if you don't continue to demonstrate your usefulness, your ability to help other people be better at what they do – then, quite simply and quite quickly, you will find yourself unused, unconsulted, unrespected and unhired.

That, in my personal view, is *your* particular discipline's discipline – your vulnerability. You need to be wanted – and that, even more than for most of us, depends on performance.

I believe that you will, and even more fervently, I *hope* that you will. Which is why, almost for the first time in my life, I can say without hypocrisy that I was touched and pleased to be invited to speak at your meeting today.

Account planning and account planners have helped me, educated me, guided me a very great deal. They've continued to remind me that advertising is about effectiveness and results: and that's where our objectives should be, and where our satisfactions should come from.

So may I thank you for having asked me today; may I thank the account planner who provided the imaginative, intuitive, evocative brief on which this speech was based; and may I ask you to let me know, with some urgency, just as soon as you've agreed a comprehensible definition of what an account planner actually *does*?

Why giraffes are luckier than ad agencies

Here are a few of the things whose imminent end has been authoritatively predicted.

History, newspapers, Noddy, shoe-laces, live beer, motor-cycles, paper documents, cross-channel ferries, trams, offices, democracy, cash, corsets, pubs, milk-bars, advertising agencies, cinemas, network television, spam, marriage, books, the House of Lords and the hand-held countersink drill.

After the Black & Decker revolution, few saw a future for the hand-held countersink drill; but they were wrong. 'Tired of Changing Bits?' said the card on the hardware stall. 'You need a hand-held countersink drill!' And I did. Television did not kill regional newspapers. They're different now and many of them are free. But they survive and prosper and they tell you what's on television tonight. The pub is going through an extraordinary change: I saw a sign last week that said Smoking Area Available On Request. The pub won't die.

But the fact that most things that are confidently predicted to die don't, leads other threatened species to conclude that they don't have to change; and that's a different matter altogether.

Nature can mostly rely on Darwin. Over a few thousand years or so, giraffes' necks get longer so they can still eat. Competitive commerce enjoys no such luxury. When threatened by events, businesses can't hang around waiting for Darwin: they have to do a little urgent planning of their own.

And that, of course, is what thoughtful advertising agencies are trying to do at the moment. With the de-coupling of media, the significant presence of free-standing brand strategists, the growing attraction of non-conventional communications and the wide availability of freelance creative talent, traditional advertising agencies have no self-evident future function.

It will be fascinating to see if agencies, faced with the need to do a rigorous professional audit on themselves, have the detachment to do it; and what they will then conclude is their most valuable future role.

I hope they will identify not a product but a process. It has no name (though planning is close) and it is seen not as an end in itself but as an irksome but necessary means to an end: which is why it is never charged for. It is the advertising development process.

As countless IPA Advertising Effectiveness papers testify, the development process can be creative, inspirationally practical and of priceless value to the client company. No other form of consultant gets close – because no other form of consultant starts and finishes with the ultimate consumer.

The development process stimulates and records real people's reactions to real communications about real brands and real companies. It illuminates the links, weak and strong, between companies and consumers. It combines the creative generation of hypotheses with ruthless discipline. It recognises both fact and feeling. And it helps you understand what you need to do next.

From being an optional extra, planning – repositioned, proudly presented, professionally staffed and decently paid for – could become the central, profit-earning, respect-enhancing function of the new creative agency.

Anti-clockwise starting from the middle

As a novice copywriter, I wrote strip cartoons for Horlicks. Each story plotted the roller-coaster career of a different protagonist. 1: drama – narrowly averted disaster. 2: diagnosis – Night Starvation. 3: prescription – Horlicks. 4: outcome – a good night's sleep followed immediately by promotion to works manager or twins, according to context.

I would send my copy by messenger to a distant art director – who in due course would return it, now attached to a hand-lettered layout.

One tense story about a school bus driver was headlined: I WAS A PUBLIC DANGER. It came back as: I WAS A PUBIC DANCER. That was the first time I realised that art directors can't read.

For contemporary evidence, look no further than the three words I fear more than any others: *clockwise from top*.

All art directors hate all words; but the words they hate most are captions.

It's understandable, I suppose: if you can't read, captions must seem a bit pointless; all captions do is bugger up layouts.

There you are, ace art director, with 14 photographs of the first-night party to accommodate on a single page – and after three high-adrenaline hours, you've done it. It's an aesthetic triumph: elegant, disciplined yet deceptively free.

And then some subeditor or creative director – some *wordperson* – says: 'Where are you going to put the captions?'

Well, naturally, you throw your crayons on the floor, invoke Michelangelo, accuse the wordperson of moral bankruptcy, hand in your resignation; and then remember that there is, after all, a way out: a way that will not only preserve your artistic integrity but also infuriate any idiot readers hoping to find out who all those people in the photographs actually are. (*Readers!* – the very word is an affront! Why isn't there a word for people who just like pictures?)

So what you do is leave all 14 photographs exactly as they are and you add one small block of lemon yellow. And in this block you reverse out in white: *clockwise from top*. Then you list, with no numbers and certainly no visual key, 23 names in random order. (There will be 23 rather than 14 because some of the photographs are of two or more people.)

Naturally enough, the reader's eye goes first to the top – and here you've planted your first surprise. There is no top. There are two photographs quite close to the top, either of which might be where to start. The first caption is Amanda Vanderbilt – so which one looks like her? They both look like her.

Well done: the reader is already out of sync. The second name is Miranda Moss-Wilkinson and the picture is of two men in Highland evening dress.

As a direction, clockwise is fine for clocks, which have no numbers in the middle; 14 photographs artistically arranged do have a middle. By the time the reader has gone round the outside, there are still 9 names left over.

The last picture shows seven members of the Redgrave family and the nearest available caption reads Zoë Ball.

Final score: Reader – 0; Art director – 26. And another resounding blow for artistic integrity.

The consumer is not your enemy so hold your fire

Scan down the index of almost any book on military strategy and the index of almost any book on marketing and the overlap in vocabulary is remarkable. Strategy itself, tactics, targeting, weapons, armoury, campaign, aggressiveness, operation, concentration of forces: you'll find them all in both. Sir Basil H. Liddell Hart could as well be a Visiting Professor of Marketing.

It's not, of course, surprising. Marketing is a fiercely competitive business; there's nothing more competitive than war; and wars have been at it a lot longer. But wars are never confused about the identity of their enemies; and marketing, it seems, sometimes is.

I'm not quite sure when I first heard the phrase about 'getting in under the radar' but it's round quite a lot at the moment.

If this metaphor means anything, it must mean that marketing professionals see their job a bit like this. There are regiments of people out there with just one thing in common: they are not buying the product and are therefore the enemy. They are being bombarded (note 'bombarded') by tens of thousands of commercial messages every day before breakfast and have learned how to dodge them. They have become increasingly media-savvy and icon-literate and can therefore spot our post-modern ironies at a hundred paces and will dismiss our new compassionate positioning with a toss of the pony-tail.

So the only way to win, the argument goes, is to devise new and devilishly cunning weaponry that will outwit the target group's defensive mechanism by coming in under the radar. (It's not entirely clear what this means – but it sounds immensely skilful.)

If all this were true, we'd have to leave the business; but luckily, of course, it isn't. Because what this imagery does is to confuse the cause with the enemy.

Wars are fought *against* enemies *for* causes. In the same way, marketing wars are fought *against* competitive companies *for* consumer approval.

But much macho marketing sees not the competition but the consumer as the enemy. The cause becomes the object of attack, in the way that Vietnamese villages had first to be destroyed before they could be liberated.

I don't know whether marketing companies and their agencies in truth see their potential users in this way or if they just talk like this to make themselves feel manly. Identify your target; invest in an arsenal; concentrate your fire-power; and nuke them into submission.

> *All warfare is based on deception. Hence, when able to attack, we must seem unable; when using our forces, we must seem inactive; when we are near, we must make the enemy believe that we are away; when far away, we must make him believe we are near. Feign disorder, and crush him.*

First articulated by Sun Tzu 2,500 years ago, this remains pretty good advice for Avis vs. Hertz, Sainsbury vs. Tesco, Reebok vs. Nike.

But it's a rotten way to schmooze a punter.

Poor old Abraham Lincoln: not a single bullet point in his armoury

If I am to conform to the Columnists' Code of Practice, some reference to the millennium is apparently mandatory: so here it is. It is my contention that the language of marketing has become increasingly sterile and formulaic; and that, over the last thousand years, the most pernicious contribution to the dumbing down of marketing language has been the bullet point.

To be valuable, marketing documents need to be works of advocacy: combining hard fact and evocative persuasion in equal measure. Any document with even half an eye on the future needs to speculate, and speculation without imagery, metaphor or allegory is inert. The bullet point emasculates language. With its attendant vocabulary, it anaesthetises the reader's imagination.

Luckily for him, Abraham Lincoln was dead by the time the bullet point was invented; so there he was, standing in the cemetery at Gettysburg, with not a single bullet point to help him. You may remember how he began:

> *Four score and seven years ago our Fathers brought forth on this continent, a new nation, conceived in Liberty, and dedicated to the proposition that all men are created equal.*

> *Now we are engaged in a great civil war, testing whether that nation, or any nation so conceived and so dedicated, can long endure.*

How different it would be today. Today's Abraham Lincoln doesn't bother to think of the words before he utters them; makes no attempt at originality, colour, or memorability. He just bangs out a few bullet points on his Powerpoint – and then adlibs ponderously around them. His favourite phrase is 'in terms of ...', which he uses remorselessly as a link. And when it comes to the document (or 'leave-behind' as we must now call it) he simply prints out hard copies of his bullet points and has them spiral-bound. This is how today's Abraham Lincoln would hold the attention of his nation.

- *US of A – SWOT analysis*

- *Launch date 1776*

- *Social context – The New Egalitarianism. (See Henley Centre)*

- *Initial proposition – global consumer homogeneity in terms of per capita significance. Zero weightings re. net worth, demographics, geographics, psychographics etc.* (Much more authoritative than 'all men are created equal', don't you agree?)

- *From fiscal 1861, new external context, fragmentation of customer base, significant attitudinal deviations on regional basis* (Or 'Civil War', as it used to be known.)

- *Bottom line: can initial proposition hold good or is there case for major re-think?*

My most fervent wish for the next thousand years is for marketing language to recover some of its passion and flavour. I do not believe we are short of good new ideas; just that many new ideas remain unrecognised because they are so lamely advocated. If new ideas are to be championed, they need to appeal to both sides of the brain; they need irrational commitment; they need to ignite the imagination; they need to defuse pessimism and inspire hope.

Today's dead language of marketing confines them forever to the pending file.

Old consumers never die: they just get richer and start surfing the internet

The older I get, the more joy I derive from marketing's mounting perplexity with what to do about the old.

Once upon a time, and not so very long ago at that, we knew perfectly well what to do about the old. You ignored them. Old people had no job, no money, no influence, no car, no investment portfolio, no holiday plans and no future. Except for the occasional COI campaign addressed to unheated pensioners, the top-whack target group was 55–65. After 65, oblivion. It was an irresponsible waste of a marketing budget to address tempting messages to anyone older; and perhaps even morally reprehensible, too, since it would only excite the poor old things to yet more unsatiable desires. To marketing people, everyone over 65 was already dead.

I haven't forgotten Saga. It is certainly true that, as middle-class persons began to retire early, with paid-up mortgages, handsome occupational pensions, freehold properties increasing in value by 15 per cent a year and above all, *time*, marketing began to see them as a market. But Saga people have never been *old*. Older, yes; but absolutely never old. Saga qualification begins at 50.

Look at the advertisements. Saga people are young people with tanned faces. Are those lines around the eyes? I believe they are: but they're laughter lines, surely, not crow's feet? Saga people are slim and fit and still movingly in love. Only their abundant white hair, elegant, slightly dated clothes and those two enchanting grandchildren (one, meltingly, with missing front teeth) tip us off: these are not people in the springtime of their lives. But neither are they old: all they are is older.

For the past year or two, however, we've been flooded with astonishing statistics and informed of a great new ordnance depot of demographic time-bombs. You know the data better than I do, but what they amount to is roughly this.

Not only is just about everybody in the country already old, but they are all going to go on living for a long while yet and – deeply disconcertingly – quite a lot of them are rich.

It's this last fact that causes the greatest consternation. People have only two levers of influence: their money and their vote. As the government has recently, if belatedly, recognised, old people, however poor, are still voters and can wield power. Marketing, however, ruthless as ever, is perfectly entitled to ignore poor people of whatever age; so when you could safely assume that everyone over 65 was by definition penniless, that was one whole sub-sector you could cheerfully forget about. But not any longer. You absolutely cannot turn your back on several million people with no responsibilities, great white spaces of discretionary time and a lot of disposable cash. You've got to face reality. You've got to talk to these people. But what are you going to call them, for heaven's sake? And what do they look like?

When all people over the age of 65 were dead, it stood to reason that they didn't need a name. For social purposes, Senior Citizen served well enough; but note the choice of noun. No one spoke of the Senior Consumer, since they were widely acknowledged not to.

But now that many of the old are rich, they have become, in marketing terms, alive again; and being alive, demand a name. And they haven't got one.

Euphemisms proliferate. Colours provide usefully imprecise allusions: you don't need to specify precisely when grey becomes silver. And evergreen is wonderfully sycophantic – if not hugely helpful when drawing up a media schedule. The search continues. Marketing badly needs an answer. But whatever the old finally come to be known as, you may be sure it won't be old.

Then what do they look like? Are they just like Saga people with a few more wrinkles? Or are they more accurately represented by that roadsign that warns us of Elderly People crossing? (I have to say, if elderly is younger than old, which it should be, it's hard to imagine anyone being older than the elderly two on the crossing. The word may have been chosen to protect their sensibilities but the picture is a piece of raw brutality.) Just who, the marketing men ask themselves fretfully, just who will the old identify with? Surely not with the old?

Forrester Research has recently lit another fuse. It's long been unchallenged fact that age and comfort with technology are incompatible: that while any six-year-old can set the VCR and send an e-mail simultaneously, no one over 50 can adjust the clock on the microwave. This has always seemed to me a suspect theory since it presupposes that age groups are static: that, mysteriously, as people progress from teens to twenties to over-forties, they quite forget how to use a keyboard. Today's children grow up with computers. In 60 years' time, to their intense astonishment, today's children will be old. And they'll still be as happy as they ever have been – and perhaps even happier – to have tomorrow's computers on their laps (or in their palms or behind their ears or invisibly embedded in an upper arm). Indeed, as Forrester Research unnervingly reveals, the old – or certainly the older – are already some of the most knowledgeable and demanding of internet enthusiasts.

They are called, as you would expect, silver surfers. Their numbers are increasing more rapidly than that of any other group of net users. Many spend more time on-line than they do watching television. And they've got money to spend.

No wonder the marketing world is bemused. Just what is going on here? The celebration of youth continues unabated: if you haven't made your million by the time you're 29, then hop off the bus, baby, and take up topiary. And all the while, those cunning, stealthy and untrustworthy *oldies* have been husbanding money and skill and influence – and we've now got to take them seriously.

It will be fascinating to see how it all works out. It's just such a shame that I'm far too old to expect to witness it.

The focus group: its use and abuse

Politics, not content with giving politics a bad name, is now well on its way to giving marketing a bad name.

The President-elect of the United States of America will owe his eventual election not to the compelling coherence of his programme but to the level and skill of his promotional campaign. And the same will be true if it turns out to be the other one.

Every word that either candidate uttered was first checked out by countless telephone interviews and focus groups. As opinion polls gave first one and then the other a wafer-thin lead, the penalties attached to the most modest of gaffes became disproportionate. Policies and programmes were hedged and fudged: far better to say nothing comprehensible than risk offending a single voter.

This is not marketing. Marketing starts with an original hypothesis.

And before we Brits get too smug about all this, it wasn't much better for us in 1997 and it'll be even worse in 2001.[1]

To start with, most marketing people seemed quite chuffed that, however belatedly, politics was beginning to adopt professional marketing techniques. We saw it as something of an endorsement of our trade – providing not only a degree of social respectability (how low can you go?) but maybe even some slight protection against future legislation. (Do not forget that a tax on advertising has been in more than one draft manifesto over the last 40 years.)

What we mostly failed to spot, however – and the omission continues – was that the political process and the marketing process have little in common.

Marketing, November 2000

1   *2003 note*: It was

Political marketing is almost exclusively confined to campaigning; and campaigning is totally dominated by election day. Win on that day – pick up the gold – and you've got a four-year guaranteed leasehold on power, with every chance of a shoo-in renewal. But lose on that day, and you don't get silver. No second prizes, no sharing of power, no consolations of any kind. Just a few hundred votes short out of 100 million cast; and you're nowhere and nothing and the world will do its best to consign you to some unrevered oblivion.

But in the marketing of goods and services, there is no equivalent of election day. Elections are taking place, choices are being made, every day of every year, in a sort of rolling referendum.

We both use focus groups and we're both right to do so. But we use them for very different reasons.

Marketing people use focus groups to find out what's in people's heads; what hopes and prejudices are lurking there; how they say they might respond to new ideas or propositions. But marketers do not (or should not) use focus groups to tell them what to do – or even what to say.

Politicians use focus groups to construct their product; to shape their manifesto; to avoid raising fears or disturbing loyalties. It is an abdication of leadership of which the feeblest of marketing directors would feel deeply ashamed: yet the tyranny of election day makes it inevitable. While elections are run as elections are run; while winner, by however slender a margin, continues to take all: then that's the way it will continue to be.

But it has nothing whatever to do with marketing – and marketing would be wise to blazon the distinction.

Ten tried and trusted ways of getting the least from your advertising agency

Agencies find their clients invaluable as scapegoats for undistinguished advertising. Clients are accused of over-reliance on research, of cowardice, of demanding original ideas that have already been proved effective in the marketplace. Agencies that lack confidence blame their clients far too much: it is, after all, the agency's job not only to invent the right campaign in the first place but also to persuade its client to run it. But, as all clients should agree, the primary responsibility for a healthy and productive agency relationship must lie with the principal, the client himself. Clients (and individuals within client companies) differ widely in their appreciation of this fact and in their ability to do anything about it. The following piece started life as a presentation to a Johnson Wax marketing seminar on Rhodes in June 1978. Thirteen years later, when the speech was being prepared for the first edition of this book, it was observed that there were actually 11 tried and trusted ways, not ten. I had put in two number tens and nobody had noticed. In the interests of historical accuracy, we have kept it that way. I'm still, in 2003, invited to give this presentation. So things can't have changed a lot.

You have asked me to speak on the subject of client/agency relationships. I was initially tempted to talk at very great length about mother-love and mutual trust and partnerships and shared goals – but before I had time to get down to the clichés, I read a piece in *Campaign* by Tom Rayfield who is one of our creative supervisors at J. Walter Thompson, London. His article was called 'How to make the least of your advertising agency', which struck me as an altogether more promising approach. So what I've done, with his permission, is adapt his title. The content that follows is mine; so I wouldn't want you to take it out on Tom afterwards.

I shall take you through, one by one, my ten tried and trusted ways of getting the least from your advertising agency – every one of which I've personally experienced and can therefore warmly recommend. I have to admit that few clients, however dedicated, have mastered all ten – though the simultaneous use of five or six is not unusual. But if you listen carefully, and take notes, you could be the first client in the world to bring your agency to a hysterical, bankrupt standstill.

Method No 1: Keep them feeling insecure

Advertising agencies, even big ones, are very small businesses. If they're any good, they'll have on their payroll an unusually large number of sensitive, talented, fallible, competitive and insecure people.

If there are 50 people working on your account, perhaps three will be motivated by the amount of money you spend with them and the amount of profit they make. (That would be the managing director, the financial director and, only to a limited extent, the person in charge of your account.)

The other 47 will be motivated by an interest in producing good advertising that helps you to be more successful, and by the sheer, fascinating difficulty of doing the job.

By not trusting your agency you can – instantly – *demotivate* all those 47 people whose help (presumably) you need.

An elementary but nonetheless effective stratagem is to let it be known that you are visiting other agencies. Not seriously, of course: you're just doing your job by keeping in touch with the marketplace. Ideally, the news of your visits should first reach your agency through the pages of the trade press.

This course of action will have the immediate effect of making your agency devote all its efforts to pleasing you, rather than trying to produce the right answers to your marketing and advertising problems.

All agencies are insecure – and if they aren't, they ought to be. The loss of an account is a serious matter and the agency, quite properly, will usually accept more than 70 per cent of the blame. Any signs of complacency in your agency can quickly be corrected by a short, sharp telephone call and a follow-up letter. But that's sensible. Far more enjoyable to increase their sense of insecurity to the level of mindless dither.

Method No 2: Keep them in the dark

Tell your agency that you have a fully staffed, highly professional marketing department and that all you need from them is some advertisements.

This technique means that you can legitimately keep from your agency such irrelevant information as sales figures, research data, competitive activity and any other knowledge you may have about the nature of your market.

However big or small your agency, this kind of relationship can be guaranteed to encourage irrelevant advertising.

It will deny you access to anyone in the agency who might just be able to help you with your marketing planning, and will encourage the agency to assess its own work on some vacuous scale of creativity. Thus at one stroke you screw up the relationship and fail to get the best value for the fees or commissions you pay. Very quickly you will begin to wonder if the agency isn't making more money than you are.

Method No 3: Employ at least one incompetent, underworked junior

These words are carefully chosen. He or she must be incompetent, underworked *and* junior – otherwise this method has been known to fail.

His job (or to be more accurate, his non-job) is to waste your agency's time. He is *always* in the agency – because in the agency he feels important whereas back in his own office he feels little more than an incompetent, underworked junior.

Ideally, he or she should have a slightly ridiculous Christian name, such as Beverley, so that the agency group can say, 'Oh, Christ. Beverley's in again and wants lunch.' If he's really incompetent, he can not only waste the agency's time but mislead them. He will gossip continually – about his superiors, their personal habits, their rivalries, what they really think of the agency; and what they thought of the other agencies they've been seeing secretly.

Naturally, any agency with courage, principles and a sound relationship with a more senior client will soon make it clear that Beverley is doing far more harm than good. Equally naturally, the senior client, who has been to management school and knows the importance of being seen to back your own people, will be embarrassed. Also, that week, by sheer chance, the agency will have sent in its first inaccurate invoice for two years.

The courageous, principled agency will therefore find itself immediately on the defensive; the senior client will question Beverley closely about his (or her) views of the agency; Beverley will claim single-handed credit for keeping them on their toes (why else would he need to spend so much time in the agency?); and another close and fruitful partnership will begin to disintegrate. No client with serious ambitions to be bad can afford to be without a Beverley.

Method No 4: Tell different people different things

You have plenty of scope for doing this if you have a highly structured and graded marketing department, the value of which I shall return to later. It also helps if you are part of a multinational marketing company. This gives you the opportunity to tell the *management* of your agency that the sort of advertising you really want is the sort that Chuck Rebozo will understand back in Akron, Ohio. Meanwhile, your advertising manager is telling the *account executive*, the hell with Chuck Rebozo – what *he* wants is advertising that will shift product in the Philippines.

By the time the agency management and the account executive have exchanged notes, it will be impossible for them to formulate a brief or motivate the creative group.

Another small tip, here. Tell your agency that you are deeply suspicious of any advertising that wins prizes, while simultaneously expressing mild disappointment that the work they do for you never does.

Method No 5: Never put the truth in writing

A simple technique – and one that seems to come quite naturally to many clients. Write a letter after the first presentation of the creative material congratulating the agency on its fresh and stimulating approach and encouraging them to develop it. *At the same time* instigate a series of internal discussions designed to spread unease and uncertainty among your own people. I strongly recommend phrases such as 'Creativity for its own sake…', 'Certainly all in favour of originality, but…' and 'I can't help wondering what Chuck Rebozo will make of it.'

At all these meetings, make absolutely certain that Beverley is present. You may safely rely on him to do the rest.

When asked at the annual agency/client review your opinion of the account group, reply, in writing, 'Absolutely first-class.' Within a month, ask the managing director of your agency if you could have a word with him sometime on the subject of staffing…

Method No 6: Never admit to a mistake

This technique has two advantages. First, it keeps your own record clean: important if you are at all ambitious. Even more valuably, it means that your agency will soon adopt the same practice and never admit to a mistake either.

As we all know, the best advertising emerges from a totally open and honest assessment of a brand's strengths and weaknesses, and general agreement on past errors and omissions. With neither side ever admitting to a mistake, this kind of discussion becomes immediately impossible. Mistakes, instead of being swiftly rectified, are perpetuated; and you should be able to look forward quite confidently to inferior and irrelevant work.

Method No 7: Change your main contact with the agency at least once a year

This can often be achieved without even trying, but check that you aren't inadvertently allowing any really fruitful professional relationships to take root.

Simultaneously, insist that your agency maintains complete stability at their end. This will ensure that only stale minds are brought to bear on your problems.

After three years, and three quite different advertising managers from your side, you should be able to review the work on your brands and demonstrate a sad lack of consistency. And that, of course, is the time to suggest an entirely new agency group – which in turn will guarantee a fourth new campaign in as many years.

Any successful brand must retain some elements of consistency in its advertising. Somebody must, through sheer experience and sensitivity, be the guardian, the custodian, of that brand's essential values. By switching your agency contact frequently, you hand over that responsibility to your agency – which in turn allows you, quite justly, to accuse them of reluctance to change and a paucity of original thought.

This technique, when mastered, can destroy not only your agency but also your most profitable brands.

Method No 8: Demonstrate a complete absence of concern about agency profitability

I have said that very few people in an agency are motivated by the amount of money your account makes: and that's true.

However, the really shrewd bad client recognises that the reverse does not necessarily apply.

If everyone in the agency knows that: a) you've asked for four different creative groups to work on your Christmas promotion; b) you plan to spend virtually nothing on that promotion; c) your account has been a financial haemorrhage for five years; and d) you don't care – then you've pulled off a neat trick. You've turned people who only care about standards into people who only care about money.

And while on this subject, asking for four separate creative groups to work on your account is worth bearing in mind even if – despite your best efforts – the account remains profitable. There's a simple law called the Law of Diminishing Responsibility. The more people you ask to think about a problem, the less time and thought and commitment each will feel required to apply. You therefore get four superficial solutions at four times the expense of one excellent solution. You will find Beverley particularly valuable at moments like this, since he will have the time to mislead even more people than usual.

Method No 9: Never say thank you

As I'm sure you know, good agency people are fuelled and refuelled mainly by gratitude, encouragement and appreciation.

A word of advice: *starve them of it.*

It should always be too early to say thank you – or too late. Your campaign may not work; or it was done so long ago that by now you've changed your agency contact.

One handwritten letter thanking your account executive or creative director could bring you enough enthusiasm and commitment to keep up a flow of good advertising for another year – and what really bad client wants *that,* for God's sake?

Method No 10: Never pay for a drink

This is far more important that it may seem at first glance. It doesn't just confirm your agency's view of your essential mean-spiritedness – though that in itself shouldn't be under-estimated.

By never buying a drink, you establish beyond doubt your fundamental view of the client/agency relationship. None of this partnership rubbish we hear so much about. The relationship is one of principal and supplier, master and servant. The function of a supplier, it stands to reason, is to supply: ideas, advertising, specially designed birthday cards for your chairman's wife. And drinks.

A supplier is by definition inferior to a principal, and why should you waste your company's money buying drinks for inferiors?

And if you *did* buy them a drink, they might think you quite liked them or appreciated them or something – and we all know what that could lead to. The same old trap: good work.

And finally…

Second Method No 10: Install a highly complex, hierarchical approval system

Naturally, you can only be certain of what sort of system to adopt if you first understand how good advertising can sometimes slip through by mistake.

As I think we've recognised before at these seminars, good advertising is most likely to be produced by a combination of disciplined and shared thinking about strategy, and the undisciplined, unfettered, uninhibited search for ideas. It may well be – indeed, it often is – the case that only in the search for the solution will the true problem be fully recognised and understood. In other words, in the creative process, an element of muddle, of experiment, of feedback, of modification, of trial and error, and of mutual trust and a shared excitement in discovery are all essential if problem and solution are to be elegantly and successfully resolved.

Your approval system, therefore, must ensure that none of this, under any circumstances, is possible.

I have two suggestions which I hope you find helpful. Neither is original, I'm afraid – but I've never been too proud to steal other people's ideas as long as they're bad ones.

First: insist not only that a communications strategy is written down and agreed – that's reasonable. Go further: make it clear that any deviation from that strategy, particularly in the event of new insights and understanding emerging, is at all times prohibited.

Second: in your hierarchy of approval, have as many different levels as you can reasonably afford and *always start at the bottom*.

Naturally enough, Beverley comes in handy here. Because he or she is only 23 and knows nothing about advertising, he must see all the agency's work first. Vest in him the right to say 'no'. (For most Beverleys this is unnecessary: they appropriate such power anyway.) Do not, of course, allow him to say 'yes'.

After he's sent the work back three times for revision, he should allow it to be seen by his two superiors. It's always more effective if they can see the work at different times, and when one of them is going to be out of the country for the next ten days, so they can't consult. They can then put their conflicting views in writing for the agency to consider.

Then I recommend a committee: as large as possible and preferably chaired by the managing director who has to keep leaving the room to talk to major retailers and trades union leaders. The client's people should be on one side of the table, agency people on the other. (A detail, I agree, but these things are important.)

Even more crucial: no one from the client side should admit to having already seen the work, let alone to supporting it.

The agency presents. There is a pause. The managing director (if he's in the room) says, 'Very interesting. What's your view, Beverley?' From that moment on, everything should flow smoothly. No one is going to say anything that means anything until they know what the managing director thinks. And the managing director isn't going to know what he thinks until he's heard all the others not saying what they think.

The changes insisted on by Beverley are challenged by the marketing director. Beverley invites the agency to defend these changes.

The managing director calls on the sales director who says he's not really qualified to speak on behalf of the consumer but he doesn't think it would go down very well with his sales force who prefer cartoons.

Eventually the managing director sums up. 'It would seem,' he says, 'that there's not total unanimity about these proposals' – and then goes on to suggest that, while the recommendation is by no means dead, there does seem to be a case for the agency asking a second group to work to the same brief so that the committee would be in a position to consider two or more alternatives.

And at that stage, if there is still no sign of general agreement being reached, perhaps some method of formal pre-testing technique should be considered…?

So those are my ten tried and trusted ways of getting the least from your advertising agency. In all fairness, I think you should be given equal time to make a presentation to me: which you might like to call 'ten tried and trusted ways of infuriating your client'.[1]

---

1   *2003 note*: This last challenge was accepted – and very funny and chastening it was, too

Astonish your clients – listen to them

As Peter Ustinov once observed, Chekhov's dialogue is not strictly dialogue at all: it is more a series of interrupted monologues.

Exactly the same is true for client/agency meetings. Nothing more clearly demonstrates the yawning gulf that exists between the average marketing manager and the average account executive than the nature of their conversations. Here is the unedited transcript of part of one recent client/agency encounter.

Marketing manager: I'm not at all happy about cycle 12 it looks as if all the multiples are cutting inventory Heinz have just bulked-up on their 350-gramme can and the pipeline's clogged so just when seasonal pull ought to be coming through strong the only shot we've got in the locker is a three-for-two in independents ...

Account executive: ... and we're pretty pissed off too I can tell you I don't know if you've seen it but our new Burgrips commercial is all hand-held and very very vérité and the people there really love it and it was all set to get a Lion at Cannes but in the end missed out by one vote apparently simply because some dickhead Chilean didn't get the irony ...

Here are two people with almost nothing in common. They have different interests, different priorities and different vocabularies; but both see business meetings as a ballgame. Before you can score, you must first gain possession. Blunt interruption is sometimes employed but is generally frowned upon. In the example above, possession was gained through *interception* – rather as a flyhalf might gain possession at Twickenham.

(You may have failed to spot the opportunity yourself – you've got to be quite quick and extremely imaginative – so would you like a slo-mo replay? Yes: you're right. The trigger word was *'can'*. To the marketing manager, 350 grammes of competitive product; to the agency executive,

a shrine to creativity. And neither remotely interested in the disappointments of the other.)

In the good old days, speeding express trains would snatch a bag of
mail from a well-placed hook at the rail side. In much the same way,
young advertising executives, keen to demonstrate enthusiasm and creativity, and obsessed by the goings-on in their own tiny village, will
attempt to snatch the initiative in client meetings.

It can surely be no accident that the word *converse* (vb) means 'to
engage in conversation with', while the word *converse* (adj) means 'opposite' or 'contrary'. Client/agency conversations are frequently highly
competitive engagements, with participants vying for occupancy rather
than cogency or value.

What all this has done, of course, is to bring about the end of what
used to be called *listening*. Listening no longer plays any part at all in
business meetings. Listening is dead, extinct, defunct. Listening has been
gathered to its fathers.

To listen is to concede the possibility that that which the other person
is already saying may be of greater interest than that which we ourselves
are about to say; and we know this to be unlikely.

It is true that even the most enthusiastic of account executives occasionally falls silent and you may be tempted to interpret this as evidence
of listening – but you would be wrong. Listening and remaining silent,
like marketing managers and account executives, have almost nothing in
common.

Practised conversational contestants use periods of self-silence not to
absorb the views or arguments of their opponent but to prepare and polish their own next missile – to be launched just as soon as repossession
has been achieved. You can test this contention by a further study of
transcripts.

Speaker A loses possession while protesting passionately about the
cost of commercial airtime. Speaker B hijacks the exchange and speaks
with equal vehemence about the editorial bias exhibited weekly by
Campaign magazine. Speaker A re-enters the joust quite seamlessly with
a sentence ending '…at the very least on BBC2.'

Neither speaker informs or affects the other in the very slightest.

Interrupted monologues may be fine for reflective Russian drama but
they are rotten for business. Objectives are never fully shared, briefs
remain misunderstood and legitimate anxieties go unrecognised. And all
this leads to error: invariably expensive, with both sides feeling bewildered, hard-done-by and grievously misunderstood.

In the febrile, high-energy, tautly competitive territory occupied by advertising agencies, one key acre of brand-positioning lies vacant: the agency that listens. And having listened, absorbs, considers, challenges, contributes – and returns constructively.

The riches, the fame and the professional supremacy that await such an occupant defy calculation. But no such move will of course be made. Because nobody's listening.

The case of the missing policeman

After-dinner speech to the Solus Club (an advertising club) at the Hyde Park Hotel in London on 16 November 1989. Edited. Not to be trusted on facts and dates.

I thought what I would do this evening, if that's all right with you, is deliver myself of a bit of a history lesson.

As a matter of fact, even if it's not all right with you, that's what I'm going to do. I thought I would have a look at how the advertising trade has changed – and how attitudes to the advertising trade have changed – over the last 35 years.

I pick 35 years because it is 35 years and one month since I first got paid for being in the advertising trade, and it's also how long that man whose name I forget ran Bulgaria, and only stopped running it six days ago. Isn't that a coincidence?

Thirty-five years and one month is really quite a long period, and I obviously can't do justice to all of it in the time at my disposal this evening. In fact, you'll realise just how sketchy my treatment is going to be when I tell you that I can't really devote much more than a couple of minutes to each year. That is, if we're to have questions. I'm also comforted by the knowledge that most of this splendid audience has been working in advertising far longer than I have. Please feel free therefore to interrupt throughout and correct me on any points of detail, particularly if they are trivial.

In 1954, advertising was still – just – respectable. It was even quite smart. The heroes of short stories in women's magazines quite often worked in advertising agencies, and you couldn't get much smarter than that.

My final interview at J. Walter Thompson was with the chairman. It was the first time I'd ever been inside an office. I'd been summoned from Dunstable Downs where I'd been on a gliding course, and I was feeling very nervous indeed. I can only remember one question the chairman asked me – and for all I know, it was the only question he did ask me. 'Tell me,

Bullmore,' he said, 'how much money of your own do you have?' You must admit, that's classy. You don't get a chairman these days asking that question – not on the milk round you don't. It's true, as I later discovered, that J. Walter Thompson was a particularly classy agency, but I still think that gives you a bit of the flavour of the 1950s. A youngish BBC producer said to me earlier this year: 'You know – I think that the sixties were more influenced by the fifties than they were by the seventies.' I agreed with him. Furthermore, the fifties were more influenced by the thirties and the forties than they were by the sixties which, you may remember, hadn't yet happened. In many ways, the first half of the fifties was still pre-war.

The chairman's question was certainly a pre-war question, but I thought I should nevertheless answer it truthfully. Until a month before I'd been absolutely broke but then I'd sold a one-hour drama script to BBC radio. In 1954, the BBC paid radio writers a guinea a minute – so a one-hour Wednesday matinee play earned £63. This practice of paying for length rather than quality had – as you might expect – a fundamental effect on playwriting technique. Whenever you wrote: 'There is a long pause' you knew you'd earned half-a-crown. Even better: 'For some 30 seconds we hear nothing but the shrill call of seagulls' was worth ten bob.

Quite long books have been written by scholars of the theatre trying to identify the cultural precedents that most influenced Harold Pinter. All they really needed to know was that in the 1950s long silences paid good money.

So I said to the chairman (who, you may remember, had asked me this question) '43 pounds'. Because that was how much I had left. He slapped his leather-topped desk in delight at my inventiveness and hired me immediately.

Well, very nearly immediately, anyway. It was such a gentlemanly place that they offered me a choice of remuneration: would I prefer £500 a year or £10 a week? In those days, annual pay was salary and went to gentlemen, and weekly pay was wages and went to – well, all the other people. Quick as always with the mental arithmetic, I went for the wages.

As it happens, 1954 was the last pre-war year because the next year, you may remember, was 1955 – and things were never the same again.

It was because of the imminence of commercial television that I had been hired in the first place. I'd written some undergraduate review material which had been produced first at Oxford, then on the Edinburgh fringe and later still in a small, underground club theatre in London. There were some songs and some humorous sketches. You may judge for yourself just how humorous the humorous sketches were because I shall now describe one to you.

In this particular humorous sketch, the object of my satirical attention was the then advertising campaign for Horlicks malted milk. You will remember that it took the form of stories told in strip continuity style. A person was failing in his job; he would go to the doctor who told him that there was nothing organically wrong with him, it was just that he was suffering from what we doctors call Night Starvation. The patient should drink a cup of hot Horlicks every night at bedtime starting forthwith. Quite soon afterwards, the hero became managing director and/or won a Nobel Peace Prize.

My first breakthrough was to realise just how very humorous it would be if a person whose job demanded that he remain awake at night should start to drink Horlicks and as a direct consequence get fired. My second breakthrough was to realise that the first breakthrough would have an even greater comic effect if the sketch were to be written in rhyming couplets. Oh, my. I was hot in those days.

So I made my hero a fireman, who said things like:

Though I get all the sleep that is required
I always seem to wake up feeling tired.
I really cannot think why this should be
I think there must be something wrong with me.

With his wife, he goes to see the doctor. The wife says:

Though he gets all the sleep that is required
He always seems to wake up feeling tired.

It's not widely known that these were among the first words uttered on the London stage by Maggie Smith. Within a few years, she was playing Desdemona opposite Olivier. It's extraordinary what good writing can do for otherwise quite workaday actors.

The revue was produced by Ned Sherrin and bits of it, including this richly comic sketch, were picked up by the BBC and turned into a 40-minute television programme – which must have reached an audience of well over several hundred people. One of these people, as it turned out, was the then head of the art department of J. Walter Thompson who was extremely anxious to outflank the then head of the copy department in gaining control of the vibrant new forthcoming medium. Since this revue had appeared on television, it seemed logical to the head of the art department that those of us who had written and produced it must know all about television. In fact, of course, we knew absolutely nothing about television. He was also much taken by the comic fireman sketch since J. Walter Thompson was the agency that had invented the Night Starvation campaign. So a letter went off inviting us to come in and have a chat, which both Ned and I duly did, and the unanimous view in 40 Berkeley Square was that Ned had little to offer the television medium whereas I did.

Four years later, I was the writer/producer on the Horlicks account. I'm a great admirer of the Almighty – I'd like Him to know that – but I particularly admire his sense of plot, shape and irony. Getting me to become the writer/producer on the Horlicks account must have given him quite a few private chuckles I should imagine.

In 1958, Horlicks was still a private, family company. The board was made up of the Horlick family itself, one or two hired managers of a lower social status altogether, and a number of delightful non-executive directors.

They were all getting on a bit and they were mostly Earls and Duchesses and Baronets and they all lived in places like Ross & Cromarty and Rutland. Their great treat came once a year when they set out for London in their Lagondas and sedan chairs to take up residence in, as I remember, this very hotel. Here they had an absolutely spiffing dinner and then met again the following morning to approve the year's advertising. And for something like 20 years, the advertising they'd been asked to approve had all been strip continuities about Night Starvation appearing in the newspapers, and they knew all about it and knew that it was good.

But 1958 was three years after 1955 and everything had changed. In 1958, for the very first time, Horlicks was going to be advertised on television – and it was to be my proud privilege to present the work.

A week beforehand, I met the managing director – a commoner, as I recall – and he gave me a very thorough briefing. The main point he made was that I would be unwise to assume that the members of the board would be at all familiar with the nature of the television medium itself. Some of them might well have heard of it, he told me, but none would have been actually exposed to it as such.

The day arrived and so did the board, seething and chuntering away with suppressed excitement. One of them, I remember, handed round a bag of humbugs.

I began. I explained that there had recently been a most interesting development in communications. It was, I said, a form of wireless set – but a wireless set combined with moving pictures not unlike a bioscope. It had come to be called 'television'. Many ordinary people, I explained – servants and that sort of person – now had television sets in their drawing rooms on which they would watch news programmes and musical comedies and other popular attractions. Furthermore, I told them, it was now possible to place advertisements on this television in much the same way as it had always been possible to place advertisements in newspapers, and, this year, that was precisely what their company proposed to do. There were going to be moving advertisements, with sound, for Horlicks, on television sets in millions of ordinary people's homes. They looked at each other in excited disbelief.

The commercials had already been made, and the agency had recently installed an extremely expensive closed-circuit system so that the films could be shown on television monitors. I pointed to these monitors, telling the board that these were not dissimilar to the kind of apparatus now to be found in ordinary people's homes – but that usually there was only one. I then phoned through to the boys in the back room and asked them to run the films.

In total silence, the films were shown. The silence held.

'Is that all?' said one peer. So, naturally, we showed them again.

And again there was silence.

'Just one thing,' said another. 'Just wonder, Chairman, if I might, through you…wasn't absolutely certain what the policeman was doin'.' And the chairman nodded and looked to me for a comment.

Now I'd written and produced those commercials and I must have seen them 50 times. Even so, I had to check my memory to be absolutely sure. Not only was there no policeman in any of them but there wasn't even anyone who might remotely have been mistaken for a policeman. So I said, forced by desperation to resort to veracity: 'As a matter of fact, sir, there wasn't a policeman.'

And with absolutely no hesitation the peer said: 'In that case, I think they're absolutely first-class.'

And so the half-million-pound budget was enthusiastically approved – the equivalent of five million or more today. And they had a terrific lunch and home they went to Rutland. That was in 1958, and it was probably the last pre-war advertising meeting ever to be held in this country.

The coming of commercial television remains by far the biggest single change to our trade over the whole of that 35 years.

It was at about this time that I was privileged to witness the birth of corporate advertising as we now know it. This story has never before been told in public.

The agency had recently been appointed by Cyril Lord. Cyril Lord, you will remember, sold carpets – and he claimed to sell them very cheaply because he'd cut out the middleman. There were no shops, you understand – Cyril Lord sold his carpets straight off the page. If the ad didn't generate sales, there were no sales.

J. Walter Thompson studied his previous campaign and concluded that it was very vulgar indeed. Instead of the eight-inch doubles – remember them? – we prepared an elegant and extremely expensive double-page spread for the Sunday Express. Just acres of carpet and a few bits of Chippendale to give it a homey look. At the very last minute, the art director was persuaded to include a small coupon.

The first ad ran – and after ten days, seven people had responded. We knew from an analysis of previous advertising that we could expect some 15 per cent of generated leads to be converted to sales. We could therefore confidently look forward, having used no more than 20 per cent of that year's total advertising budget, to making one sale.

Cyril Lord – in person – telephoned several times a day. It hardly helped at all when an eighth coupon arrived. The agency called a crisis meeting of very senior people to see what could be done – but there were few useful ideas.

Then one of our directors spoke. 'Just an idea,' he said, taking off his glasses and polishing them for emphasis. 'May be nothing in it, of course. But one thing we could do is take out the coupon altogether and call it a corporate ad.'

Nearly 30 years later, this test still works. Look at any corporate advertisement running today and ask yourself how many people would respond if it carried a coupon. If you can confidently say none, then it deserves the very highest praise and a D&AD gold pencil.

To nobody's surprise, Cyril Lord took his account away and gave it to a provincial upstart called Peter Marsh, who produced some extremely vulgar television advertising which sold many square miles of luxury carpet you can afford and made Mr Lord – for a little while at least – very rich. It also, rather later, made Mr Marsh very poor indeed   but luckily that didn't last long either.

It was exactly this kind of advertising – or to be fair, television advertising in general – that began to have an extremely adverse effect on the reputation of advertising as a trade – at any rate among the chattering classes.

Television advertising possessed two characteristics which the middle classes found intolerable. First, it was intrusive – which is to say that it was noticed. And second, it worked. Here was clear evidence that vulnerable and unsophisticated people – in other words, the sort of people who would watch television – were being manipulated, almost certainly subliminally, by sociology graduates who had been brainwashed by capitalism. It wasn't, of course, necessary to have read The Hidden Persuaders *to know precisely what was going on. As long as all advertising had remained as inoffensive and invisible as corporate advertising, we'd never have had any of that trouble – but trouble we got all right and it was all television's fault. Before the explosion came, the fuse burned slowly for nearly 20 years – but I'm getting ahead of myself again.*

1969 is memorable for having been the year in which the least memorable advertising event of the last 35 years took place.

For months and months, agencies and production companies gave presentations, conference companies laid on conferences, advertisers sent delegates on expensive training courses and the trade papers did their best to sustain a ferment of speculation. It was the biggest thing to happen to commercial television since commercial television, and you've all forgotten. It was of course colour.

When I was asked for the tenth time by the trade press how quickly colour television was going to take off, I said I thought the official industry forecast was probably right, but of course if it so happened that the Queen was assassinated and the country was given nine months to prepare for the coronation of King Charles, then the penetration of colour television sets might well take place with somewhat greater speed. Two weeks later the New Statesman *ran a small piece in 'This England': 'How to boost colour TV sales? Adman Jeremy Bullimore advocates killing Queen.'*

Like most of my recommendations, this was ignored. Colour came and stayed and nobody's mentioned it for 20 years until this evening and that will certainly do for another 20 years.

Meanwhile the fuse was still burning and the bang nearly happened in 1974.

1974, you may remember, was not a good year for Ted Heath.

Come to think of it, he hasn't had many good years since. He lost two elections, and at the Advertising Association conference that year Shirley Williams and the first Director General of Fair Trading, John Methven, told us what they thought of the advertising business and its voluntary controls.

Threats of statutory controls of a quite unworkable kind were really not very far away. At that same conference, Ronnie Kirkwood and I attempted to put another point of view – which was more or less encapsulated in a short duologue. It went like this:

Good morning.

Good *morning? Good in relation to what? Do you mean in the sense of having desirable qualities?*

I mean hullo.

Then why didn't you say so? I might have been misled.

But you weren't.

I wasn't misled – but many people less perceptive and less well educated than I might have been misled.

Don't you think that everyone knows that 'good morning' is simply a greeting?

Are you saying that the word good has become so debased by people like you that it no longer carries its true meaning?

The phrase has been around for a long time.

So have prostitution, poverty, corruption, white slavery and child-beating. Are you saying that anything's defensible if it's been around long enough?

Almost everyone says 'good morning'.

And almost everyone exceeds the speed limit.

I can't help feeling this conversation is getting out of proportion.

Are you suggesting that deliberate attempts to mislead, the debasement of language, white slavery, child-beating and the mowing down at speed of defenceless pedestrians are matters of minor concern?

No – I was suggesting that saying 'good morning' wasn't quite the same as white slavery.

And white slavery isn't the same as child-beating, I suppose. Can't you appreciate that degree is no defence?

I don't think saying 'good morning' is anything to be ashamed of.

*Which is precisely what concerns me. You say 'good morning',
admit that you didn't mean to suggest that the morning was good,
become defensive in the extreme, retreat behind endless excuses of
precedent and common practice and then say you've nothing to be
ashamed of.*

Most people become defensive when they're attacked.

*But why? Why can't they admit the attack is justified and mend
their ways?*

All right then. I concede. Goodbye.

Why are you saying 'goodbye'?

Because I'm going away now.

*Are you suggesting that your going will have certain desirable
qualities?*

Yes.

*Debates about advertising control had sunk to about that level. The risk of
statutory control was real and imminent. To its immense and lasting credit,
the trade acted very quickly and very well. The Advertising Standards
Board of Finance was formed (ASBOF, now of course more widely known as
the acronym for the Amalgamated Society of Boring Old Farts), the levy was
invented and the Advertising Standards Authority was strengthened – and a
great many people these days don't even know what happened and how
lucky they still are.*

*Four years later, Roy Hattersley – as he then was – told a conference in
Bournemouth that he was opposed to excessive statutory control. It was
interesting to learn that Mr Hattersley was opposed to excess, but it didn't
win many votes and the subject went quiet. It will not, however, remain quiet
for all time.*

*Meanwhile, the advertising trade was suffering from an acute loss of self-
confidence. The agency business has always been pretty insecure, of course.
Take 1927, for example (you thought I was making progress, didn't you?),
only a deeply insecure bunch of people would choose to call themselves, as far
back as 1927, the Institute of Practitioners in Advertising.*

They were of course what they are now – advertisement agents; but desperately searching for respectability. That's why they invented exams for themselves. I expect some of you even took the IPA exams. There was one question – a real one – which asked candidates to draw up a marketing plan for a new range of knee-high fashion boots for men. I often wondered who scored well on that one.

Imprudently – and impertinently – I suggested that the questions were nothing to do with how to be a good agency person: they were all to do with irrelevant matters such as knowledge and experience. So I made so bold as to draft some better questions which I put to the IPA, and I can still remember three of them:

(1) *You are an account executive. You arrive late for a meeting in Carlisle, at which you are to show your client next year's television planning for a range of aerosol pudding-tops. On opening your chart-case, you discover that you've brought with you three press layouts for earth-moving equipment. In five minutes, relevantly, relate the latter to the former.*

(2) *You are the chairman of a middle-sized agency. You read in* Campaign *that your managing director and three of your other directors have resigned, taking with them your one profitable account and both your top creative men. Draft a letter to your remaining clients explaining how these changes will dramatically improve the quality of your service.*

(3) *One of your older clients has just appointed a new marketing director fresh from Procter & Gamble. In the course of your first meeting, he turns to you and says: 'But surely you have to agree that the frequency distribution of dosage-weighted opportunities to see can only be related to average issue readership of press media by application of response functions derived from single-source data?' By means of a diagram or a rough sketch, illustrate the most responsible facial expression with which this remark should be greeted.*

I argued that those were real *questions, designed to identify real talent for the real agency world. The IPA disagreed – and not long afterwards abandoned examinations altogether. And not long after that, the reputation of advertising again began to burgeon.*

From 1979 onwards, advertising became a thoroughly good thing for *anything, in anything, however much – and the government joined in enthusiastically. Junior ministers in the Thatcher administration began to*

ask for Tim Bell's autograph. Lord Young should certainly have received the
Mackintosh Medal for services to advertising.

These days, of course, I rely on the newspapers and very old friends to
keep me in touch with the challenging, dynamic, fast-moving world I still
fondly if dimly remember. I was therefore grateful to the Observer
Magazine *of some 12 days ago for bringing me absolutely up to date in time*
for this important engagement with you this evening. The creative director of
a London agency is quoted. He says: 'I wear a suit once a week. I adjust
what I wear depending on which clients I'm meeting. The myth of
advertising has been blown out of all proportion. Basically, to succeed one
has to be professional, have charisma and be able to produce a great
commercial for half the price that another agency could.' That is all he says.

I'm afraid I didn't know any of that. How easy it is to get out of touch.

Part Six
Beyond advertising

How to postpone the beginning of the next recession

There was the one that started in 1974 and there was the one that started in 1981 and there was the one that started in 1990 and there's been quite a lot of talk recently about the one that may or may not start in 1998.

What I thought you might find valuable is some actionable advice on how to keep this next recession at bay for a bit.

Like all good economic theories, this one is based on an analytical understanding of human absurdity.

In all communities – in all villages, in all families and certainly in all companies – there are two quite distinct groups of people. The first are called Go-For-Its and the second are called Toothsuckers. These names are self-explanatory so let me explain them to you.

Go-For-Its are genetically, thoughtlessly optimistic. They worship action and despise thought. When faced with a predicament, a crossroads or a choice of any kind, their immediate instinct is to say, 'Let's go for it!' They will expand, acquire, invest, gamble, proliferate, launch 17 brand variants and confidently set out to take the American retail market by storm.

All communities, particularly commercial communities, need Go-For-Its. Without Go-For-Its, little if anything would ever happen.

Toothsuckers are different. When faced with a predicament, a crossroads or a choice of any kind, their immediate instinct is to suck their teeth. 'Oh dear, oh dear, oh dear, oh dear, I can't say I like the look of this one, Chairman.' Irrespective of the intrinsic merits of the circumstance, they will argue for caution, dilution, circumspection and a ten-year test market.

All communities, particularly commercial communities, need Toothsuckers. Without Toothsuckers, companies would go bust even more frequently than they do.

These two groups are in constant conflict. And the critical factor that determines expansion or recession is the prevailing balance of power between them.

A brief historical review.

The Thatcher years did not favour the Toothsuckers. For the best part of a decade, doubt was not only unfashionable but unconstitutional. And so it was that the Toothsuckers were made to feel lowly people: derided, despised, ignored. For nearly nine years, not a single Toothsucker's name appeared on the Honours List.

With only the most muted of challenges, the Go-For-Its held the rampant stage. All over the country you could hear their cries: 'Let's go for it! Let's go for it!' While almost inaudibly, in the background, you might just pick up a weak and plaintive: 'Oh dear oh dear oh dear...'.

And then came 1990 – and the Toothsuckers were back in business.

It is wrong to believe that everybody hates recessions. Toothsuckers love them.

Toothsuckers have their own vocabulary – and within days of the downturn, it was joyously taken out of mothballs and returned to front-line use: 'inappropriate'; 'imprudent'; 'precipitate'; 'not altogether timely, Chairman'.

So, after ten years in opposition, the Toothsuckers, in a landslide result, not only re-acquired power but became doggedly determined to retain it. Throughout the land, unreported, Toothsuckers moved stealthily into top management positions.

The recession continued. Economic commentators expressed surprise that consumer confidence was so slow to return. Those of us in marketing didn't. Marketing people know a great deal more about human nature than economists do. Marketing people (although they don't like to acknowledge it) have every reason to be grateful for the existence of reluctant consumers: if it weren't for them, we wouldn't have jobs. Can you imagine if all consumers were Go-For-Its? Marketing departments and advertising agencies would become obsolete overnight. (Unless, of course, their talents were re-employed in a mammoth state-funded campaign in favour of consumer restraint.)

Luckily for us, a great many consumers have a natural aversion to consumption. They are some of Nature's most stubborn Toothsuckers. Often, they seem to be in the majority – and they are not stupid.

Toothsucking consumers are the only ones who've rumbled what consumer confidence really means; it means re-acquiring enough confidence to get back into debt. No wonder the length of the recession continued to baffle the economists.

Because what a rattling good recession does is give congenital Toothsuckers the confidence *not* to consume. It legitimises caution and sanctifies parsimony. Visit any furniture showroom and look and listen. A slow shake of the head. 'I only wish we could, my love' – said with lingering enjoyment.

The reason that the 1990 bust hasn't yet turned into another boom that is about to bust is that at least some top executive Toothsuckers are still hanging on in there. But if they came to power in the early 1990s, then most of them will soon be slipping into their Home Counties cardigans to be replaced by a new, eager generation of managers; a generation who didn't (as managers) live through the pain of 1990; so a generation, as likely as not, containing an unusual number of Go-For-Its.

Maintaining the balance of power between Toothsuckers and Go-For-Its cannot be left to market forces alone: that's what induces cyclical economic turbulence. This is a job for a small, low-profile group called the 'Head-Scratchers'. Head-Scratchers honour both Go-For-Its and Toothsuckers but value balance more.

There is bound to be another recession, I suppose. But if every company listens very carefully to its resident Head-Scratcher, it needn't come just yet.

2003 note: Indeed, there has been another recession and it's still with us. That its start was delayed until the year 2000 cannot, I suppose, be attributed entirely to the influence of this essay; but there again, I don't see why not

Marks & Spencer: once the Citizen Kane of the High Street

In many ways, potential clients visiting an advertising agency resemble patients visiting a Harley Street consultant. They're fairly sure there's something wrong with them but they're not sure what; they hope that the consultant will recognise their symptoms; but at the same time, they know themselves to be different from the rest of humanity, so will be deeply suspicious of instant, all-purpose nostrums.

There is one common disease from which clients suffer and I'm pretty confident that I was the first to identify it. It's called Reputational Deficiency and it means that the client's product is a great deal better than its reputation. Clients are always pleased to be told this because it means they won't have to do anything radical and expensive such as respecify the product; they just need a better advertising campaign.

Less well recognised, however, is an even more serious condition – where the reputation is a great deal better than the product. To my knowledge, it has no name – but it might be called the *Citizen Kane* syndrome, since it is universally agreed that *Citizen Kane* is the only perfect film ever made. To question this judgment is to brand oneself a fool and a philistine.

This is OK for a film; but when living, changing, competitive enterprises acquire *Citizen Kane* status, disaster looms. The glory may be wonderful but it cannot blaze forever. And when the glory does go, it will go with savage suddenness.

For a great many years, Marks & Spencer was the *Citizen Kane* of the High Street. Those who held doubts about M&S kept prudently silent, for to be critical of M&S was to betray oneself as envious and mean-spirited.

After all: this was the highly profitable operation that provided free chiropody for its staff; that attracted more graduate applicants every year than Unilever; that was equally, effortlessly expert in sandwiches and halter-necks, boxer shorts and avocado dip, pashminas and personal pension plans. Its reluctance to advertise was further confirmation of its intrinsic merit. When it provided no loos and no changing-rooms and declined to accept other people's credit cards, it was fondly indulged: how confident, we thought; how principled. And management basked in the glow of its own reputation and knew itself to be good.

But a business that is never exposed to the cold, fresh winds of dissenting comment is living in a barometric dangerland. When the weather finally breaks, the storm will be of biblical severity. And so it has come to be.

Suddenly, Marks & Spencer is fallible; and suddenly, we have all been introduced to a kind of *glasnost*. For the very first time, free speech has been granted to us. And it is as though the captive doubts of a hundred years have been simultaneously unleashed, bringing havoc and devastation in their wake.

The question is put in every business column: will Marks & Spencer ever be the same? The answer is no. Once this kind of critical immunity has been breached, it can never be fully restored.

But this, of course, is excellent news for customers. And after a nightmare year or two, it will be welcomed by staff, shareholders and even management.

2003 note: It's never much fun kicking a man when he's down and it's good news all round that M&S seems well on the way to a full recovery. But it will never again, I trust, believe itself to possess Citizen Kane status

What we need is millions more peers, peeresses, poodles and placemen

I suppose it's quite gratifying that the Prime Minister has finally come round to my way of thinking. The trouble is, he still hasn't come far enough.

I'm talking, of course, about the House of Lords.

I've long been convinced that, before any sensible reform of our second chamber can take place, the existing model must first be drained of dignity. The Prime Minister seems to agree.

If you had bet me, in 1996, that it was possible, in the name of reform, to make the House of Lords an even less defensible legislative body, I would have confidently offered to double your money. And I would have lost.

The new rules for elevation to the House of Lords are ingenious. We now know that anyone prepared to accept a life peerage is by definition unfit to serve. This, surely, must be seen as progress? The beginning of the end of that empty authority the Lords traditionally enjoys?

But I bet not. I bet that peers and peeresses, placemen and poodles continue to be granted immunity from healthy sceptical scrutiny. I bet they go on getting the best tables. The House of Lords is a far more resilient brand than Mr Blair has recognised. The time has come for desperate measures.

And luckily, I have a desperate measure to hand.

It is, though I say so myself, quite brilliant. It will simultaneously bring the House of Lords into terminal disrepute while making a fortune for the Treasury. It is not often that a piece of radical constitutional reform can also make a significant contribution to our balance of payments – but then it is not often that an idea emerges of the purity of Nobility Bonds.

Thriftily using the same Electronic Random Number generator that selects Premium Bonds, Nobility Bonds confer not money on the lucky winners but titles.

Nobility Bonds can be bought by anyone. Foreign investment is particularly encouraged. There is no maximum holding. Neither age nor criminal record forms a barrier to entry: six-year-olds and convicted bigamists would be equally welcome and dodgy off-shore billionaires singled out for platinum promotion.

Every month, ERNIE would choose 5,000 knights (the general debasement of titles is an important strategic element) and 500 life peers. And every month, just one fortunate investor would become either a Duke or a Duchess.

Demand for Nobility Bonds would be worldwide, clamorous and unstoppable. Donald Trump and Chris Evans would compete recklessly for early ennoblement. Overseas monies would flow into the nation's coffers. And within one year, the House of Lords would contain another 6,000 members: no less worthy and chosen no less democratically than the few hundred they joined.

Such rampant inflation would have its customary effect. Just as we lose respect for banknotes, so we would lose respect for titles. It could surely be only a matter of months before the vainer peers offered good money to be allowed out. Reform, at last, becomes possible.

There is, it is true, a snag. The Nobility Bond Bill would have to seek approval from the House of Lords – and they might just be smart enough to realise its implications. But there again, they might not.

At last a vote, at last a voice – the Royal Family of your choice!

It seems to be agreed that, since 2 June 1953, the monarchy's lost a bit of its oomph. Diana cheered things up for a while, but well before her melodramatic end she'd become decidedly counter-productive.

Today, the polls continue to show declining enthusiasm for this mysterious institution. Inevitably, the call goes out for better marketing – and that's where it gets interesting.

All the best books tell us that proper marketing starts with the identification of the wants and needs of the consuming public. Marketing gurus and practitioners are as one: long before promotion begins, product design must match identified market need. Proper marketing is not just a bolt-on technique for flogging more of what already exists: it's a continuous management process, embracing everything from research and development, through publicity, delivery and after-sales service and back again to product improvement. So goes the chunter. And Hear! Hear! we all cry.

It's therefore a nonsense (with one exception to which I shall return) to say that the monarchy needs marketing. A product that cannot be modified to suit changing public taste cannot, in any full sense, be marketed.

As consumer services (which is what they are) our Kings and Queens are in a category of their own: they are delivered to us without choice or consultation. Our votes, our views, our spending power, directly or indirectly, have absolutely no effect on outcome. Once they've made it, our monarchs have security of tenure until they abdicate or die. That is a non-judgmental fact – and almost certainly a central part of their remaining fascination.

Time-and-Motion Man and the Mad Inventor

All evidence suggests that successful companies become and remain successful by adopting two apparently irreconcilable policies. They then insist that these two policies co-habit in conditions of mutual respect and are meticulous in never consistently favouring one at the expense of the other.

They have no commonly accepted names, but one of the best and earliest descriptions of them comes from E.F. Schumacher's 1973 classic, *Small Is Beautiful*. In a passage about corporate organisation (quoted approvingly in 1997 by Niall FitzGerald, Chairman of Unilever) Schumacher writes:

> *Without order, planning, predictability, central control, accountancy, instructions to the underlings, obedience, discipline – without these nothing fruitful can happen, because everything disintegrates. And yet – without the magnanimity of disorder, the happy abandon, the entrepreneurship venturing into the unknown and incalculable, without the risk and the gamble, the creative imagination rushing in where bureaucratic angels fear to tread – without this, life is a mockery and a disgrace.*

Here, wonderfully well evoked, are the two nameless and apparently contradictory policies. In honour of Schumacher, they might be known simply as Order and Disorder but that hardly does them just justice. I like to think of them as Time-and-Motion Man and the Mad Inventor.

An essay from the WPP Group plc Annual Report and Accounts published in 1999

But for the past 50 years, as British citizens have been gradually shedding their deference, so we've been growing in confidence. We now know that we can not only bring down governments, but supermarkets as well. We can cause great airlines to stumble and drive once-impregnable corporations to seek executive saviours from foreign parts.

We can even change government policy between elections. For all the criticism of policy-making by focus group, it is at least evidence that government is listening; and having listened, is prepared to act accordingly. We may think it timid and evidence of a woeful lack of leadership: but marketing people should concede that government is not just promoting its product but, in the hopes of meeting market sentiment, is willing to modify it, too.

But with the monarchy, it's take it or leave it. No classic British fudge on hand here to save jobs and faces. No chance of doing a House of Lords on the House of Windsor. The product is immutable. And that's why the monarchy debate will prove particularly interesting. Will the British people continue to tolerate this one exception to their sovereignty?

There is, of course, a solution now in sight. Only just in sight, I grant you, and still some way away. But within a generation or so – just a tick of the clock in the life of the monarchy – it will be possible to offer the people of this country not just the Royal Family you happen to get lumbered with, but the Royal Family Of Your Choice: genetically modified to meet consumer-generated specifications. Now, that would be marketing.

For myself, I'd rather go on taking pot-luck.

We know them both well, of course. But because the human mind finds paradox uncomfortable, we feel we need to side with one of them at the expense of the other: we cannot, we believe, be best friends with both. And we find it quite impossible to imagine that they could ever be partners – as indeed, it has to be said, do they. It is Time-and-Motion's conviction that Mad Inventors have no place whatsoever in well-ordered corporate affairs; and every Mad Inventor knows that Time-and-Motion means the death of creativity and enterprise.

It was Schumacher's great contribution to point out that much of good management consists in the reconciling and balancing of conflicting demands – while still retaining the ability to function; in much the same way, he said, as the successful management of societies consists in reconciling and balancing the conflicting demands of individual liberty and social cohesiveness. In theory, it seems impossible. In practice, we manage it every day.

The importance of Time-and-Motion Man to competitive business hardly needs rehearsing: and recessions and rumours of recessions remind us of it all the time. To achieve and maintain a low-cost base; to buy efficiently; to concentrate your points of manufacture; to manage money; to look always for less labour-intensive ways of doing things: to become leaner and meaner. No manager can doubt that, to have even a chance of sustained success, today's competitive companies must be constant in their employment of the Time-and-Motion Man: 'Planning, central control, accountancy, discipline – without these, everything disintegrates.' Without these, you're dead.

And so the legitimate demands of Time-and-Motion Man have influenced company structures, company cultures – and company policies on recruitment and reward. Efficiency is honoured, waste is deplored; and quite right, too.

The mistake, of course, without budging for a moment from one's total commitment to Time-and-Motion Man, is to believe that he is the only employee we need. And there are good reasons to believe that, in 1999, this could be a bigger mistake than at any time in commercial history.

Commentators are surprisingly agreed. Business – and businesses – are changing fast. There is a new alchemy around. Two 20-year-olds in a garage, without access to capital or raw materials or plant, can found a company that within 25 years will become the world's biggest.

Where once there was an industrial age, and then an information age, we're now well into the age of the imagination: an age where the price and availability of knowledge and technology may favour the small over the large; the innocent over the experienced; the bold over the cautious; the inventive (and frequently wrong) over percentage-playing consolidators. An age where something called intellectual capital can make a nonsense of conventional balance sheets.

The nature of risk has changed, too. Because new thoughts can be test-flown so quickly, it may be a great deal more risky to do nothing than to do something. Too many management careers are still driven by the need to circumnavigate failure. In Silicon Valley, early failure is seen as evidence of enterprise and a necessary qualification for future support.

What all these changes are doing is to put an even greater premium on the value of ideas: product ideas, process ideas, distribution ideas, positioning ideas, brand extension ideas, communications ideas. So increasingly, companies must look to their cultures and structures; because the structures and cultures that were installed at the insistence of Time-and-Motion Man are often hostile to challenge and unorthodoxy; to the free-thinking generation of new hypotheses; to the kind of habitat in which the Mad Inventor will flourish most productively.

The Mad Inventor invents indiscriminately; and will promote his bad ideas as relentlessly as his good ones. He has only to hear of an accepted practice to know that it needs to be overthrown. He is vain, unreliable, and whimsical in his judgments. He despises timesheets. But the Mad Inventor – at least some of the time – is challenging the conventional, teasing out hypotheses, forging new connections, making new analogies – and haphazardly scattering seeds; some of which, in a few years' time, will become the harvest on which the whole of his organisation lives.

The happier he is in his habitat, the more fertile he will be. He does not respond gracefully to insistent micro-management by Time-and-Motion Man. If he feels the constraints of the corporate straitjacket, he will not succumb meekly and catch his usual 6.14 home. He will leave; even if he has nowhere else to go.

In his 1996 book *The Hungry Spirit*, Charles Handy echoes Schumacher:

> *Creativity needs a bit of untidiness. Make everything too neat*
> *and tidy and there is no room for experiment. Keep a tight rein on*
> *costs and there is no cash available to try new things or new*
> *ways. Cram your days too full and it's hard to find time to think.*
> *We all need a bit of slack to give us the space to experiment.*

All good marketing case-histories celebrate the contribution of a great idea. But you can read a thousand and still be left wondering how great ideas happen. You will read about the market analysis that was done, the conclusions that were drawn, the strategy that was adopted. And then it says something like: 'And so the Giant Platypus was born.' Two thousand words later we will have learned how the Giant Platypus has increased brand share by 10 percentage points and profits by several million – but the one thing we will not have learned is how the Giant Platypus came into being in the first place.

The idea may be a product idea, a positioning idea, a communications idea. You may be certain of only one thing: the precise circumstance of its emergence will remain forever unknown and unchronicled. And so it is always bound to be.

It is no good instructing Time-and-Motion Man to instal procedures designed to optimise idea production on schedule and within budget. As Schumacher, Handy and the chief executives of marketing communications companies know only too well, that is not the way that ideas happen. Increasing the quantity and quality of ideas is partly about recruiting a Mad Inventor or two – and at least as much about creating an environment in which Mad Inventors are honoured.

Commercial communications companies – advertising, design, public relations – are unusual. Their only raw material is information and their only manufacturing facility is the human brain. Data is delivered to the back door; is subjected to analysis, experience and interpretation; and is then transformed, after intense exposure to the imagination, into An Idea. These are companies who for all their lives have recognised the claims of both Time-and-Motion Man and the Mad Inventor; and have enjoyed some modest success in learning how to manage them.

The trick, of course, is to know when in the creative process to give precedence to each. There are times for rigour and there are times to fly.

And it is this experience, surely, that could be of far greater value to client companies in the future. If a conscious application of the imagination is to be extended into the corporate whole, if company strategy is to be as creative as corporate communications strive to be, then it would seem to make sense to adopt similar planning procedures.

The first stage is the selection and analysis of all relevant information. What is our current situation? How do we seem to our customers? How do we stand competitively? Do we see trends – and if so, in which direction? No room for whimsy, here. No room for guesswork or flair or approximations, just hard, rigorous, clinical interrogation. For outside

advisers, the client company may well look to the management consultant. Time-and-Motion Man is in his element.

Then: what is possible for the future? What is our most desirable
(practical) destination? Subtly, the rules of engagement change –
because there's now a need for speculation. The Mad Inventor, until now
on the benches, is called on to the field.

If invited to speculate, Time-and-Motion man becomes unhappy. He
is interested in a destination only if he can see immediately how to get
there. By contrast, the Mad Inventor finds speculation irresistible – and
can become irrationally committed to a destination whether or not there
is discernible access to it. Between them, skilfully managed, a hypothesis
is formed. Given the technology, given our knowledge and our foresight;
this is where we could be.

And then finally: how do we get there? What actions, deeds, changes,
inventions, investments do we need to make our arrival at that destination most probable?

This, with a small roll of drums, is the Mad Inventor's big moment.
Because it is now that we need 'the magnanimity of disorder, the happy
abandon, the *entrepreneurship* venturing into the unknown and the incalculable…'. It is at this moment (for the moment) that Time-and-Motion
Man should be gagged and bound and left in the locker-room. And
where the advertising agency, the design consultant or the public relations counsel could be involved and motivated and encouraged to think
irresponsible thoughts; to supplement internal corporate resource; to
augment 'the creative imagination rushing in where bureaucratic angels
fear to tread'.

Ideas do not have to be good ideas to be useful. Thinking impossible
thoughts has a value. The deliberate suspension of censorious judgment
may be the only way to liberate minds from the deeply rutted convictions
of earlier times. The imagination flies free.

And then, of course, comes the final stage. The flying is over and
rigour returns. Time-and-Motion Man is released from his bonds.
Assessment begins.

But the scope of the opportunities and the richness of the landscape
ahead will far exceed anything that a more responsible, methodical,
deductive approach might have generated. And more efficiently, too; and
a great deal more enjoyably.

As business learns to compete in the new creative age, the efficient
exploitation of the imagination will be as critical to success as the
exploitation of coal once was. And it would be good to think that some

of the management skills and tricks that its communications advisers have painfully accumulated over the years could be brought more usefully and centrally to bear.

There are two final points to be made about Time-and Motion Man and the Mad Inventor.

They do not, of course, have to be men. And even more importantly, they do not even have to be two people.

In most of us, there are traces of both Time-and-Motion Man and Mad Inventor; though some of us may have a great deal more of one than the other. If the phrase 'managing the imagination' means any one thing, it is the ability to value both; to honour both; and to know when, as ringmaster, to give each of these star performers top billing.

Free with this issue! How to write your own best-selling business book kit!

Business books were once a well-intentioned branch of publishing, designed to make their readers rich. Today, of course, the sole purpose of business books is to make their writers rich.

It's not at all difficult to write a best-selling business book. If I were not already rich, I might well have written one myself. Instead, in an unprecedented display of altruism, I'm about to tell you how you can write one yourself. And not just the theory of it, you understand. Read on and you will find a complete kit, including all working parts, title and assembly instructions – in fact, everything you need to make your very own business book, guaranteed to sell five million copies in English-speaking countries and another three million in Japan as long as you don't translate it. It may never, of course, be read: but that needn't trouble you.

Your opening need is to find the title most likely to attract your target market, so first you need to understand them. To save you time, here, as part of your kit, is a brief description of those most likely to buy multiple copies of new business books.

Multinational senior executives, aged 35–57. They are in what used to be called secure positions but these days feel threatened: there are too many things going on that they don't understand. They are both vain and lazy. They will be anxious to improve their company's performance – the talk is all about shareholder value – but are deeply averse to both change and investment. They've had the consultants in twice now, and never again.

This is the group for whom the title of your book must have immediate appeal. Now, I know that, in higher forms of literature, it is fashionable to denigrate alliteration, but in the construction of titles for best-selling business books it is essential. So the title I offer you, absolutely free, with my flat-pack, DIY, Build-A-Better-Business-Book Kit is *Dynamic Delegation.*

Though I say it myself, this is an outstandingly good title. It appeals to both the idle and the assiduous. It suggests, simultaneously, iron executive control yet plenty of time for the golf-course. And when subjected to close scrutiny, it reveals absolutely nothing that you could be judged against.

Next you must tackle the section on Change. If it weren't for lawyers, you would be well advised to lift this section unedited from any of the Henley Centre's excellent publications on the subject; many of your fellow authors have clearly chosen this course. You should cover, at some length, the following: convergence, disintermediation, trust, open source communications and the gift economy, a wide selection of demographic time-bombs, the death of deference, the empowerment of the consumer, new challenges to capitalism, the globalisation of intellectual property, the implications of over-production and the long-term consequences of HIV.

As you can see, there will be nothing new in this section but it is nonetheless essential. Without it, you would never reach that key, pivotal, apocalyptic moment in the book where you get to write:

> *And so it can be seen that the old order can no longer be trusted to serve these new paradigms. To confront the future armed only with the faded nostrums of the last century is for today's embattled chief executive to enter the post-nuclear age armed only with crossbow and flintlock. What is needed – and needed with a compelling urgency – is nothing less than a revolution in the way we think about people.*

(I'm fairly certain that I've stolen this vile paragraph word-for-word from some other best-selling business book – but feel safe in the knowledge that nobody of right mind would want to claim original authorship.)

Luckily, of course, the revolutionary thought has already been hatched. It has been derived from in-depth studies of 25 of the world's most admired companies. Astoundingly, when subjected to analysis, it emerges that every single one of them shares a common approach to management. They all employ a managerial version of subsidiarity: they ask no executive to undertake a task that could be as well despatched by an executive of a lower rank. In short, these visionary managers, many, of course, without realising it, are all convinced exponents of *Dynamic Delegation*. Eerie, isn't it?

But you may now be worried. These in-depth case-studies, 25 of them from around the world: they sound a bit like hard work, don't they? Oh dear, reader, how little you trust me. These studies, forming as they do the bulk of the book, require no effort on your part whatsoever.

Well, just a very little effort. Because what you do is write a letter to each of those 25 global chief executives, expressing awed admiration for the way in which they have elevated their corporations to unprecedented heights of commercial triumph, ethical governance and market capitalisation. The world would be a better place, you grovel, were they able to open a window or two, say 2,000 words – their own words – on the secrets of their astonishing success. And you should prompt them to this degree: you should say that, to the awestruck outsider – observing as you have the executive's ability to govern one of the world's greatest commercial enterprises while all the while finding effortless time for family, friends and deserving causes – it would seem, however instinctively, that he or she must have mastered the art of what is becoming ever more widely recognised as *Dynamic Delegation*.

Everything now falls into place; 25 chief executives immediately employ their instinctive talent for dynamic delegation by instructing their corporate affairs officers to write 2,000 words of totally objective corporate hagiography. Within weeks, at zero cost, 50,000 words of text will be in your hands.

Furthermore, when the book is published (and publishers will fight for the right to publish it) 25 global chief executive officers will each order many thousands of copies for distribution to staff, financial analysts and other members of the golf club. Best-seller status is guaranteed.

And if you are feeling mischievous, you may like to include a tailpiece that reads: *'The alert reader will have noted that much of this book has been assembled according to the principle it espouses.'*

Wanted: a snappy soundbite or two in favour of profound complexity

It was Roy Hattersley, I think, who first identified the damage inflicted on understanding by the interviewing techniques of the more belligerent media interrogators.

By asking questions on immensely complex topics, and then insisting on a 20-second answer, they force their respondents, in Hattersley's words, 'to choose between the simple lie and the complicated truth'. (I quote from suspect memory.)

> *Now tell me, in a sentence, as a committed europhile: why should we surrender our national sovereignty to a bunch of unelected bureaucrats in Brussels?*

I have just read, with much pleasure, a book called *Democracy in Europe* by Larry Siedentop. It is written with great lucidity and there is little spare fat in its 270 pages. It has not, in itself, strengthened my existing preference for greater integration with Europe but it has provided me with some much needed additional scaffolding of understanding and argument. As a result, of course, I would be even less able than before to support that preference in a single sentence: the subject is far too multi-layered, too shrouded in a deadly and ambiguous vocabulary; and I am now far too encumbered with fact.

Anyone who did attempt to answer that question with the complicated truth would live to regret it; 20 seconds into an absolutely necessary preamble, time would be up. *'And there, I'm afraid, we must leave it.'* Next time, the experienced, battle-scarred interviewee will have learnt to say:

'There's an express train about to leave from platform 1. We either jump on board now – or find ourselves hoping to hitch a lift on the roadsides of Europe.'

This is an acceptable answer. Never mind that its grotesque compression constitutes a lie. Never mind that no opportunity has been granted to challenge the premise of the question. Misleading simplicity is much to be preferred to well-intentioned complexity – to hell with understanding.

It sometimes seems as if, over-excited by the digital age, we need to reduce all debate to the binary principle. Everything must be either a zero or a 1; heads or tails; black or white; in or out; Brussels or Britain.

Do you believe in

a) individual freedom   ☐
or b) social order?   ☐

Check one box only.

The basis for this unhealthy trend would seem to be what might grandly be called the Presumption of Mutual Exclusivity. You admit to liking American musicals and are thereby assumed to dislike Shakespeare. To enjoy *Hello!* is to brand yourself a philistine. You voice a fondness for roast beef and are known at once to dislike garlic. Show enthusiasm for Europe and your patriotism is suspect. Preach the value of decentralisation in a company and you are held to believe that the centre has no value.

The Presumption of Mutual Exclusivity makes no allowances for muddle, subtlety, tolerance, ambiguity or people's astonishing ability to manage conflict.

The great E.F. Schumacher (writing 40 years ago and long overdue for rediscovery and renaissance) had this to say: 'Once a large organisation has come into being, it normally goes into alternating phases of *centralising* and *decentralising*, like swings of a pendulum. Whenever one encounters such *opposites*, each of them with persuasive arguments in its favour, it is worth looking into the depth of the problem for something more than compromise, more than a half-and-half solution. Maybe what we really need is not *either-or* but *the-one-and-the-other-at-the-same-time.*' And in another part of the same book: '…people find it most difficult to keep two seemingly opposite necessities of truth in their minds at the same time. They always tend to clamour for a final solution, as if in actual life there could ever be a final solution other than death. For constructive work, the principal task is always the restoration of some kind of balance.'

Try synthesising that in a 20-second answer on the *Today* programme. Try bringing your *Any Questions?* audience to rapturous life with a thoughtful plea for balance; for the-one-and-the-other-at-the-same-time. Audiences crave either-ors. The starker they are, the louder they clap.

It is, of course, a profound irony that Schumacher's book is called *Small is Beautiful*. Because of the Presumption of Mutual Exclusivity, it is instantly assumed by all those familiar only with his title that Schumacher must therefore be totally opposed to size – but of course he's not. Of the 'almost universal idolatry of giantism,' he writes, 'If there were a prevailing idolatry of smallness, irrespective of subject or purpose, one would have to try and exercise influence in the other direction.'

So he probably wanted to call his book something like: *The Need to Ascertain the Optimum Scale for a Varied Range of Functions and Activities* but his publisher thought *Small is Beautiful* would sell more and of course he was right. It is not, however, what the book is about. Its title is a simple lie while the book is about a complicated truth.

For myself, I plan to offer a small prize for the best advertising campaign on behalf of balance, compromise, coping, tolerance, ambiguity, and the moral need to elucidate complexity. Contestants will be required to communicate the virtues of all the above using eight words or less.

Saving on the chardonnay: your very own conference theme while-u-wait

An edited version of a speech given at a Marketing Society pre-conference dinner, 1995. The annual Marketing Society conference is held in London in November and is preceded by a dinner on the night before in the Great Room of the Grosvenor House Hotel. The speaker is expected to say something relevant about marketing while keeping 1,200 marketing persons from going to sleep or throwing bread rolls.

It is my reluctant duty this evening to do two things.

First, according to my brief from the Society, I am to introduce and explain the conference theme to you. And second, I am to draw some lofty lessons from the past which might still be of value to us as we trundle off down the superhighway.

So that, dutifully, having made it quite clear to you that it wasn't my idea, is what I shall – at quite astonishing length – attempt to do.

I am bound to say that I find it a great deal easier to introduce the conference theme than to explain it to you. It has, as I'm sure you know, just three words: future; marketing; the. (Though not in that order.)

When I was first told about it, the conference committee had already gone firm on the words but was still apparently locked in dispute over the punctuation.

Was it to be: 'Marketing – The Future?'? Or without the question mark since the future could reasonably be expected to arrive? Or was it to be 'Marketing the Future'? (An ambitious project, certainly, but surely not beyond the combined talents of the Society.)

Conscious, perhaps, of some lingering ambiguity, the conference literature later added what was presumably meant to be an explanatory thought. It said: *'If you're not part of the future, you're part of the past.'*

I'll just pause here for moment so that you can take that in.

Right, now let me take you through it slowly. On second thoughts, why do I need to? Let me just call it profoundly simplistic, transparently opaque, self-evidently enigmatic. And so on.

I've always been fond of slogans that play about with time. One, which gives me great comfort even as I speak, is: Remember that tomorrow, today will be yesterday. I once invented an all-purpose slogan for an all-purpose corporate campaign for an all-purpose company. It said: Anglo-Galvanized (put your company name here): *Where Past and Future Meet.*

All corporate affairs directors love that slogan. The earnest ones love it because they say it sums up the very drive and spirit of their company and the bright ones love it because it's got something for both the retiring chairman and the new young chief executive – while on examination meaning absolutely nothing. Unlike, naturally, this year's conference theme.

If you're not part of the future, you're part of the past. So if you *are* part of the future, you aren't part of the past. Or rather, you weren't. And if you're only *part* of the past, what else were you doing?

I will, I promise – well, threaten, I suppose – return to the conference theme – all conference themes, as a matter of fact – in due course. But not until I've done my second duty – the lofty lesson from the past bit.

If you ask a lot of bright young graduates what they want to do with their lives, quite a lot of them these days say they want to go into marketing. Very gratifying – until you come to think about it. Thousands of very bright graduates out there, all wanting to do your jobs. (And *they* aren't part of the past, I can tell you.)

And then you ask them what exactly they'd like to market and they look confused. They've never thought about that. They just want to go into marketing; to market anything: personal pensions, package holidays, potato chips or charities. Because they've read that marketing is now a discrete and recognised skill in its own right and they want to practise it.

Then, have you noticed those little items in the trade press: barely rewritten press releases, most of them: 'Anglo-Galvanized announces the appointment of Clive Thrust as marketing manager, Aggregates. He has previously held similar positions with Scottish Widows, Pedigree Petfoods, Rentokil and the Bristol Zoo.'

Is there no limit to Clive's abilities? (I've always thought that almost everybody in marketing was called Clive. As a matter of interest, how many Clives are there here tonight?) [*A show of hands revealed a great many.*]

Now compare that fictional press release with another fictional press release. 'Anglo-Galvanized announce the appointment of Geoffrey Turner as production director, Aggregates. He has previously held similar positions with Häagen-Dazs, Vodafone, Mothercare and the Royal Bank of Scotland.'

You just wouldn't believe it about Geoff, would you? But you would about Clive. Production needs expert knowledge of the specific product. Marketing – apparently – doesn't.

It made a lot of sense, all those years ago, when marketing began to emerge as an identified skill. And it was also good news when people said that proper marketing was not just a skill, but a management process that should be the focal point for a company's total activity. (If you find these phrases a touch on the portentous side, it's because they've been lifted straight from your Society's literature.)

But then, I think, something else began to happen. Marketing is supposed to begin, metaphorically speaking, inside the factory and extend all the way to the final satisfied or dissastisfied user. But as marketing began to be more of a job than a process, its starting point began to move, very, very slowly and again very metaphorically, from inside the factory to outside the factory gates.

As the discrete skill of something called marketing has become more and more free-standing, more and more portable, more and more applicable to Scottish Widows, Pedigree Petfoods, Rentokil and the Bristol Zoo – so, unsurprisingly, it's become increasingly detached from design and production. As marketing persons go from pizzas to pension-schemes to OTC medicines, they've neither the time nor the inclination to learn much about the creation and manufacture of any of those items. They simply apply their all-purpose skills to selling more and more of what already exists.

All the best books on marketing tell us that this shouldn't be the case: that proper marketing starts with the wants and needs of the consuming public; that long before promotion begins, product design should match identified market.

But in real life, it doesn't always happen. In real life, marketing all too often begins outside the factory gates. All too often, marketing has come to mean getting rid of more of what you already make.

And while Colin Thrust goes from job to job and becomes the role model for thousands of ambitious graduates – God help them – who gets increasingly neglected?

The inventor, that's who: the product designer, the engineer, the thinker-up of things, the chemist, the brewer, the boffin. The people who are obsessed by the product itself; who willingly accept that the sizzle's important, but who get their personal kicks from trying to make an ever better steak. Or, as it might be, a better personal pension, a better ice-cream or a better inclusive holiday.

Car companies used to be run by people who loved cars. They knew how to make cars themselves and were always trying to make them better. Retail companies used to be run by people who loved shops, and a hundred and something years ago, George Safford Parker was nutty about fountain pens. As businesses got bigger and more complex, these obsessive, impractical, product-driven enthusiasts couldn't cope any longer. They had to be helped: by money-men and lawyers and marketing persons and advertisement agents. Now they've been helped so much, they hardly exist any more.

You may remember the story of one of our greatest ever national makers, Isambard Kingdom Brunel. He was so ashamed of his socially inferior trade that he decided to give his two sons a better start in life by sending them to Harrow – where they were able to learn several dead languages and were never heard of again.

From that moment on, the status of the maker in this country has been in steady decline. Engineers are men in dungarees. Inventors, at best, are like Sir Clive Sinclair, slightly batty figures from an early Ealing comedy. And the rise and rise of marketing persons, through no fault of theirs, has done nothing to help.

There's almost a case for saying that this country is already too good at marketing: at least in its partial sense. Skilful marketing can patch things up – just as floundering governments try to patch things up through what they like to call presentation.

Skilful marketing can disguise – at least for long enough to be dangerous – the absence of research and development and innovation and invention. The marketing leg is over-used and grows stronger. And so, as is the way with these things, the invention and production leg withers through lack of exercise.

Now a little more research. I've mentioned inventors and product designers and production directors and chemists and engineers and brewers and thinkers-up of things: all key people, as we must surely agree, in a proper marketing process. And since this is the Marketing Society – just how many here tonight, as a full-time job, do any of those things? [*Another show of hands; except that very few were raised.*]

It's all a bit like the old light bulb jokes, really. How many marketing men does it take? I've always been intrigued by things called gift shops. 'Good morning sir, can I help you?' 'Thank you. It's my wife's birthday next week and I was thinking of giving her a parcel.' 'Well, you've certainly come to the right place, sir. Did you have anything particular in mind?' 'Yes – I rather thought something quite heavy but small enough to go in my briefcase.'

Gift shops exist to sell things to put into parcels – nobody much minds what. I would hate to see marketing going any further in that direction but I fear it might.

As the means of communication available to us become ever more distractingly fascinating, rightly and irresistibly so, there's a very real risk that we'll think even more about the how, and even less about the what; that the sizzle will continue to be valued more than the steak; that the parcel will become even more important than the object inside.

It might even be, I think, that the erosion of our manufacturing sector, and the rise and rise of our service sector, is in part connected with the decoupling of making things from marketing things.

So if this is a drift – and if it's a drift with unhelpful future consequences – who should we look to to correct it?

My own view is that we should look no further (and again I quote from the literature) than to *the* professional body for senior practising marketing people.

And that's my lofty lesson from the past, for the future. (And perhaps I should remind you at this point, that if you're not part of the past, you can't have had enough experience to be here tonight.)

And now, as I threatened, to the theme of your conference – Marketing the Future – or words to that effect.

Thinking up themes for conferences must be one of life's least rewarding occupations. Sales conferences are worst, though it'll be easy enough next year of course – it always is in Olympics year. They'll all be called *Going for Gold.* I've often thought that it would be somehow more British to call a conference *Settling for Silver.* I mean, I'd settle for silver, any time. Not at all bad, coming second. And a great deal more realistic. But I could never find a sales director to agree with me. Funny lot, sales directors.

Anyway, you all know how marketing conference themes are produced. First, the Society appoints a committee, then the full committee appoints a conference sub-committee. Then the conference sub-committee subpoenas five of its most inventive members to become the conference theme sub-sub-committee. And they meet. And they meet. Creatively drained, they open a bottle or two of chardonnay. And they meet again. And after five months, they've cracked it. The breakthrough. Eureka! Marketing the Future. (Punctuation yet to be determined, but one thing at a time chaps.)

It's my pleasure this evening to tell you how it should be done.

Earlier this year, I commissioned some research into all the marketing conferences that have ever been held since marketing was invented and submitted their themes to rigorous linguistic analysis. A fascinating fact emerged. In the phrasing of the 3,412 themes analysed, a total of no more than 30 different words was used.

Words, for example, to pick a couple at random, such as Marketing and Future. Now clearly, once this fact is known, planning becomes a great deal easier. We can, as we say in our business, eliminate the variables. Conference theme planning becomes a matter not of months, but of minutes. I now plan to demonstrate this with your help. As a gift from us all to your new director general, we shall shortly present him with next year's conference theme.

I have brought with me tonight five wooden cubes. On each side of each cube is written one of the 30 recognised marketing conference words. (Such as 'future' and 'marketing'.) Please note that I call them cubes. It would be quite wrong to associate a discipline as rigorous as marketing with anything as irresponsible as dice. They are *cubes*; or to give them their full, registered descriptor, *Conference Planning Cubes*.

They are, you should know, the world's first Conference Planning Cubes.

Let me explain first the procedure and then the rules.

My independent assistant Melvyn Simpson, starting now, will hand one cube to each of the five tables in front of me.

I will then ask the first table to roll a cube and call out the word on the upward-facing surface; then the second – and so on.

Within one minute we will have five words.

Now here are the rules. Of the five words available, at least three must be used in the composition of next year's conference theme. No significant extra words may be added. Singulars may become plurals, and articles, prepositions, conjunctions and punctuation may be freely sprinkled, like salt and vinegar, at the customer's discretion. A re-roll is permissible under only two circumstances. First, if – as is only too likely – we end up with *this* year's theme. And second, if the result looks as if it's going to be deeply embarrassing for me.

These rules have been internationally recognised.

[*The five tables rolled the five dice and the following words were revealed in this order: Adding; Multinational; World; Dynamic; Future.*]

So, Nick – you'll be pleased to learn that your conference theme for next year will be: *The Future of Multinationals in a Dynamic World.* Which makes a great deal more sense than...well, many others, if you ask me.

All in two minutes. Not only democratic, but interactive. And what a saving on the chardonnay.

Would you like us to do 1997 as well while we're about it?

These planning cubes will soon be on sale throughout the developed world – and I'm in the process of designing other sets for other purposes. There's to be one set for *political party* conferences for example: where, interestingly, I've found a need for only *two* cubes. And another set for executive titles in advertisement agencies: strategic, deputy, managing, vice, international, senior, worldwide, associate, president, chairman, senior associate, global, multi-disciplinary – that sort of thing. (Rather more cubes needed there.)

But before too long, there's one modification I'd like to make to this original set. Of the 30 words I found in my research, not one was directly related to *making*. No invention, no production, no product design. What I'd like to do – when the Marketing Society has flexed its muscles and rehabilitated the great makers and reintroduced making into marketing – is introduce a sixth cube, with all those solid, unfashionable product and manufacturing words on it. And then we can have another roll and see what comes up. George Safford Parker, he who was nutty about fountain pens, once said: '*Make something better and people will buy it.*'

As a conference theme, it has much to be said for it: though not nearly as much, naturally, as the theme for this year's conference; which, as instructed, I shall now explain to you.

Tomorrow's conference will concern itself with the future of marketing.

I hope that's cleared things up.

I was going to wish you all a useful and inspiring conference; but I understand that some of you, at least, *do* think it's possible to be part of this evening without being part of tomorrow.

I suppose you know what you're doing. You can hardly claim you weren't warned. Just watch out for those graduates, that's all.

It now gives me great pleasure to ask Melvyn to present the world's first complete set of Marketing Conference Planning Cubes to your new director-general, Nick Turnbull – and through him, in perpetuity, to the Marketing Society; to thank you for your attention; and to hope that – most of you at least – will find some sort of future to be a part of.

Farewell, Berkeley Square

On Friday 13th August 1954, I put on my blue suit for the third time and presented myself at No. 40 Berkeley Square for my final interview with J. Walter Thompson Company Limited. I had been summoned to it by reply-paid telegram (3 shillings) and it was to be with the chairman. I can't remember if I found it surprising at the time that the chairman of the country's largest advertising agency should find the time to interview a totally inexperienced would-be copywriter of 24, but I certainly find it surprising now.

Douglas Saunders, MC, was a chairman from central casting: tanned, handsome, deep-voiced, beautifully tailored and beautifully mannered. I instinctively addressed him as Sir, which he clearly found appropriate.

And it was he, (as recounted in 'The case of the missing policeman' p. 267), who asked me how much money of my own I had.

I misunderstood him. It wasn't until much later that I learnt that JWT was widely believed to be staffed exclusively by Etonians of independent means and that the current witticism held that it was an excellent agency to join if your parents could afford to put you down for it.

I was never told that I'd been accepted. As I left the chairman's office, he shook my hand and said he hoped that I'd enjoy my time with the agency. Neither of us can have known quite how long that time was going to be, or quite how much I would enjoy most of it.

I spent 33 years and two months at No. 40 Berkeley Square. Though some of that time I was in Berger House next door and some of that time I was in Hill Street round the corner, for over 33 years my business address was No. 40 Berkeley Square.

When I retired from JWT at the end of 1987, Martin Sorrell offered me an office in 27 Farm Street, once the home of JWT's European operation and then as now the headquarters of WPP Group plc. The front door of

No. 27 Farm Street is exactly 79 paces from the back door of No. 40 Berkeley Square.

That was 15 years ago. As I write this, at the end of 2002, I have trotted off to an untidy office on a small island of Mayfair most working days for 48 years and two months.

If I'd read this of another person, I would be appalled. I am even appalled when I think of it in relation to myself; but it's a little bit late to decide on a more adventurous business life.

But if I'm still here, No. 40 Berkeley Square is not. J. Walter Thompson moved out in early 2002 – plummeting downmarket to No. 1 Knightsbridge Green – and within days the demolition teams arrived.

Up went the boards and down came the building. Soon, a huge, mud-filled cavity was all there was to show for London advertising's most famous address; and I knew I should find in this fact a deep and potent symbolism.

I failed, I'm afraid. JWT sails on serenely in its elegant new headquarters. Advertising itself has changed a bit – but in some ways the changes have been a return to former days.

In November 2002, the Design & Art Direction association published a massive 40-year retrospective of creative work called Rewind. *I was invited to contribute an essay. It's called 'Last word on the future' and it ends like this:*

> *'Over the next 40 years, as always, there'll be winners and losers. The winners will be those –* from whatever discipline *– that continue to combine an informed and intuitive sense of business with an alchemist's ability to turn strategy into enviable execution. These are the companies that will make their clients successful, earn themselves authority and thereby fully justify their premium price. The losers will be those who turn their backs on the business of business in the pursuit some unanchored concept called creativity.'*

It could have been written on Friday 13th August 1954.

Bibliography

Aranguren, J.L. *Human Communication*, McGraw-Hill (1967)

Beckham, V. *Learning to Fly, The Autobiography*, Michael Joseph (2001)

Bernstein, D. *Creative Advertising: For This You Went To Oxford?*, Longman Group (1976)

Boyle, D. *The Tyranny of Numbers*, HarperCollins (2000)

Carey, J. *The Intellectuals and the Masses*, Faber & Faber (1992)

de Bono, E. *The Use of Lateral Thinking*, Jonathan Cape (1967)

Fletcher, W. *Advertising Advertising*, Profile Books (1999)

Fletcher, W. *Teach Yourself Advertising*, Hodder & Stoughton (1978)

Gardner, B.B. & Levy, S.J. 'The product and the brand', *Harvard Business Review*, March/April (1955)

Heath, R. *The Hidden Power of Advertising*, World Adverising Research Center (2001)

Hopkins, C. *My Life in Advertising/Scientific Advertising*, Advertising Publications Inc (1966)

King, S. *Developing New Brands*, Pitman (1973), JWT (1984)

Klein, N. *No Logo*, Flamingo (2000)

Koestler, A. *The Act of Creation*, Hutchinson (1964), Penguin (1975)

Locke, C., Levine, R., Searls, D. & Weinberger, D. *The Cluetrain Manifesto*, Perseus Publishing (2000)

Magee, B. *Popper*, Fontana Modern Masters (1985)

Medawar, P.B *Induction and Intuition in Scientific Thought*, Methuen (University Paperbacks) (1969)

Medawar, P.B. *The Art of the Soluble*, Methuen (1967), Pelican Books (1969)

Medawar, P.B. *Pluto's Republic*, Oxford University Press (1982)

Medawar, P.B. Review of *The Act of Creation*, *New Statesman*, July (1964)

Ogilvy, D. *Confessions of an Advertising Man*, Atheneum (1962)

Ogilvy, D. *Ogilvy on Advertising*, Crown Publishers Inc (1983)
Packard, V. *The Hidden Persuaders*, D. Mackay & Co (1957)
Peters, T. & Waterman, R. *In Search of Excellence*, Harper & Row (1982)
Reeves, R. *Reality in Advertising*, Alfred Knopf (1961)
Schumacher, E.F. *Small Is Beautiful*, Blond and Briggs (1973)
Upshaw, L. & Taylor, E. *The Masterbrand Mandate*, John Wiley (2000)
Young, J.W. *How to Become an Advertising Man*, Advertising
    Publications Inc (1963)
Young, J.W. *A Technique for Producing Ideas*, Crain Books (1975), NTC
    Business Book (1989)
Williamson, J. *Decoding Advertisements: Ideology and Meaning in
    Advertising*, Open Forum, Marion Boyers (1978)

Index